Challenges
to Consensual Politics

Democracy, Identity, and Populist Protest
in the Alpine Region

P.I.E.-Peter Lang

Bruxelles · Bern · Berlin · Frankfurt am Main · New York · Oxford · Wien

Daniele CARAMANI & Yves MÉNY (eds.)

Challenges
to Consensual Politics

Democracy, Identity, and Populist Protest in the Alpine Region

"Regionalism & Federalism"
No.6

© P.I.E.-Peter Lang S.A.
PRESSES INTERUNIVERSITAIRES EUROPÉENNES
Brussels, 2005
1 avenue Maurice, 1050 Brussels, Belgium
info@peterlang.com; www.peterlang.net

ISSN 1379-4507
ISBN 90-5201-250-4
US ISBN 0-8204-6642-5
D/2005/5678/15
Printed in Germany

Bibliographic information published by "Die Deutsche Bibliothek"

"Die Deutsche Bibliothek" lists this publication in the "Deutsche Nationalbibliografie"; detailed bibliographic data is avalaible in the Internet at <http://dnb.ddb.de>.

CIP available from the British Library, GB
and the Library of Congress, USA.

Contents

Preface and Acknowledgements

This book originates from the wish to link distinct but related problems within a theoretical framework based on the historical comparative sociology tradition which allows to analyse the emergence of new political cleavages in the forming Europeanwide party system: (1) the emergence of a transnational and supranational region in the Alps; (2) the concentration in this region of strong and persistent populist/regionalist parties which have reacted to consociational and corporatist interest intermediation; and (3) the specific (critical and sceptical) attitude of these parties, and the Alpine political culture more generally, toward European integration.

To discuss these issues two conferences were organised in October 2003 and March 2004 at the European University Institute (jointly promoted by the EUI and the Mannheim Centre for European Social Research) on *The Heart of Europe: The Alpine Political Culture and Its Relationship to European Integration* with specifically and carefully selected international experts on regionalism, populism, European integration, and on the various cases which have been analysed.

This book is the result of those two highly stimulating meetings. The various chapters analyse populist and regionalist political parties which are either exclusively located in the Alpine region or use typical Alpine themes in their political discourse. The book is interdisciplinary, touching upon several themes and approaches to comparative politics: (1) the regionalist phenomenon to which increasing attention is devoted in a sub-national, transnational, and supranational perspective; (2) party politics – and, more specifically, the populist protest right-wing parties – in a historical comparative sociology perspective; (3) political cultures and attitudes as well as consociational and federal traditions of policy-making processes; (4) the process of European integration.

We believe that the volume makes two main contributions. First, it analyses new dimensions of the process of European integration, in particular of the formation of a Europeanwide cleavage constellation. These new dimensions are *the regional and territorial centre–periphery dimension* which results from the specificity of the Alpine regions and the *critical attitude* of the several regional-populist parties with regard to the current type of consensual democracy, assimilationist identity, and European integration. This dimension is closely related to factors of ethno-linguistic and religious distinctiveness which have been neglected by the previous literature which has focussed mainly on the left–right and pro/anti-integration dimensions.

Second, the volume adds an empirical contribution to the various theoretical debates around the analysis of regional and territorial cleavages in Europe. For the first time, an empirical case-study which allows us to complement and refine through an empirical analysis the theoretical perspectives based on Albert Hirschman's "exit–voice" and Stein Rokkan's "political structuring" models applied to the process of European integration is presented. The book shows that the political, social, and geo-economic specificities of the Alpine transnational region determine an alternative conception of identity, democracy, and European integration – expressed in strong and persistent populist protest parties – which have led to a new dimension within the emerging Europeanwide cleavage constellation.

For their contribution to the discussions during the two meetings we are grateful to Stefano Bartolini and Yves Surel. For comments on earlier versions of the single chapters we would like to thank Domenico Comino, Chris Engert, Monika de Frantz, Alberto Sciandrafor, and Jonathan Wheatley. Finally, for her friendly and efficient logistic support we are deeply thankful to Alexandra Howarth.

Daniele Caramani and Yves Mény
Florence, November 2004

Tables and Figures

Abbreviations

AN	*Alleanza Nazionale*
CDU	*Christlich-Demokratische Union* (Christian Democratic Union, German Christian Democrats)
CSU	*Christlich-Soziale Union* (Christian Social Union, Bavarian Christian Democrats)
DC	*Democrazia Cristiana* (Italian Christian Democracy)
FDP	*Freie Demokratische Partei* (Free Democratic Party, German liberals)
FPÖ	*Freiheitliche Partei Österreichs* (Austrian Freedom Party)
EDD	Europe of Democracy and Diversity
ELDR	European Liberal, Democratic, and Reformist Group
EMU	European Monetary Union
EP	European Parliament
EEP	European People's Party
EU	European Union
LS	*Ligue Savoisienne*
MRS	*Mouvement Région Savoie*
ÖVP	*Österreichische Volkspartei* (Austrian People's Party)
PCI	*Partito Comunista Italiano* (Italian Communist Party)
PES	Party of European Socialists
SPÖ	*Sozialistische Partei Österreichs* (Austrian Socialist Party)
SVP	*Schweizerische Volkspartei* (Swiss People's Party; also *Union Démocratique du Centre*)
UV	*Union Valdôtaine*

Abstracts

INTRODUCTION
The Alpine Challenge to Identity, Consensus, and European Integration

Daniele CARAMANI and Yves MÉNY

This chapter stresses the relevance of the empirical case study of the Alpine space, and presents its political, geo-economic, and cultural specificities, from the distinctive patterns of state formation to the economic, de-centralised, and morphological configurations to political culture. The typical consociational or negotiation type of democracy in the Alpine area and multi-layered forms of governance determined by regionalised political-administrative structures has led to the emergence of a strong populist protest. The alternative view of identity, representation, and European integration that emerges from the political discourse of the parties analysed in the book is described, together with the strong challenge that they represent both at national level and at the level of the supranational EU political system. In this regard, the chapter finally discusses the impact of this challenge on the Europeanwide cleavage constellation and its relationship to other alignments.

CHAPTER 1
Regionalism in the Alps: Subnational, Supranational, and Transnational

Michael KEATING

This chapter analyses regionalism, an important theme in European politics, in three forms which are particularly relevant for the Alpine space. First, sub-state regionalism is producing a new balance between centre and periphery, and various types of institutional reform. This comes in both conservative/defensive and modernising forms. Second, supranational regionalism refers to a grouping of states themselves, such as the European Union. Third, transnational regionalism occurs when regional movements of the first type seek to extend their sphere of action beyond state borders, through co-operation with other regions, cross-border co-operation or by acting within the European institutional structures. Within the Alpine area, sub-state regionalism of a conservative type has been strong, combined with a certain resistance to supra-national regionalism, but this is most characteristic of the German and Italian speaking areas. Transnational regionalism has been weakened by national and ethnic divisions, although, in recent years, some signs have appeared.

CHAPTER 2
Populism as the Other Side of Consociational Multi-Level Democracies

Yannis PAPADOPOULOS

Historical conditions have determined a concentration of consociational or negotiation democracies in the Alpine space, a characteristic which in many cases is strengthened by complex and intermingled structures of multi-level governance. In this chapter, it is argued that such characteristics of a political system strongly contribute to the generation and success of anti-establishment populist parties. First, negotiation democracies display fragmented decisional structures, and their political systems are deliberately designed so as to raise obstacles to (abuses of) popular sovereignty, by checking majoritarian influence through several veto points. Second, consociationalism awards more autonomy to the political élites, and, at the same time, reduces the degree of competition between them. Third, the multi-level governance structures necessitate élite co-operation often in informal, opaque, and selective decisional circuits where visibility and accountability of public action is reduced. Finally, the chapter discusses the capacity of consociational systems to integrate protest parties.

CHAPTER 3
Natural Cultures: The Alpine Political Culture and Its Relationship to the Nation-State and European Integration

Daniele CARAMANI

This chapter deals with the political culture of the Alpine region and its expression in the strategies of regionalist-populist parties. This culture is described as a set of attitudes and values which overlap with the religious, rural–urban, and ethno-linguistic dimensions which emerged from the specific patterns of state formation, nation-building, and economic modernisation in this region. Three dimensions are considered: orientations, identity, and evaluation of the political system. It is shown that the Alpine culture incorporates anti-modern, religious, and traditional attitudes, by emphasising themes of nature, work ethics, and communitarian identity in the political discourse. The chapter argues that the Alpine political culture perceives itself as being under the threat of changing lifestyles, artificial identities, and processes of economic and political globalisation which lead to a defensive response. This type of political culture is particularly relevant as it may represent a crucial dimension in the emerging Europeanwide cleavage constellation, thus presenting an alternative "image" of European integration.

CHAPTER 4
Leadership, Ideology, and Anti-European Politics in the Italian *Lega Nord*
Patricia CHIANTERA-STUTTE

This chapter deals with the most important Italian populist-regionalist party. It traces its origins back to a peculiar national context, analyses its organisational structures and, finally, highlights the impact of its origins and organisation on its anti European stands. The chapter de scribes, first, the conditions of emergence and development of the Lega Nord, showing its rise in a period of a deep crisis of political participation and of party politics in Italy. Second, the chapter takes into consideration the leadership of the party, its anti-establishment attitude, and its hierarchical structure – all key factors in order to account for its flexible and adaptable political strategy. Third, the chapter analyses the anti-European attitude of the party. The main argument is that the populist anti-European position represents a strategy to re-affirm the anti-system and anti-establishment character of the party, to externalise the economic and political problems, to emphasise both a "heartland" above classes and a politics of Alpine identity for the mobilisation of the electorate.

CHAPTER 5
Right-Wing Populism Plus "X": The Austrian Freedom Party (FPÖ)
Anton PELINKA

This chapter argues that the FPÖ is a populist party which is defined as an anti-establishment movement, with a right-wing ideology, and an exclusive understanding of "the people" directed against élites and "the other" (immigrants and ethnic minorities). The FPÖ, unlike other European right-wing populist parties, is a conservative party, deeply rooted in Austria's Pan-German tradition, as well as in the Austrian national-socialist experience. The chapter analyses the FPÖ's isolation, which is visible, in particular, in the European Parliament, as well as during the diplomatic boycott that 14 EU governments implemented in 2000 against the FPÖ's participation in the Austrian cabinet. Alpine themes and scepticism towards the EU are the qualities of the FPÖ which link it to the other cases analysed in the volume. However, this chapter shows that the FPÖ is something more (what the title indicates under "X-factor"): the continuity of a past which did not stop in 1945. As in other Alpine cases, this highlights the role of delayed and problematical state formation and nation-building processes.

CHAPTER 6
Mobilising Resentment in the Alps: The Swiss SVP, the Italian *Lega Nord*, and the Austrian FPÖ

Hans-Georg BETZ

This comparative chapter focuses on the ideological evolution of three main Alpine populist parties: the Schweizerische Volkspartei *in comparison with the Italian* Lega Nord *and the Austrian FPÖ. The chapter argues that within the broader family of Western populist parties, Alpine cases emphasise the entrepreneurial virtues and the work ethic. What makes Alpine populism distinct is its pronounced "producerist" bent, together with an equally pronounced emphasis on the entrepreneurial virtues characteristic of the* Mittelstand *(the middle classes). The populist ideology is described along three dimensions. First, anti-élitism and anti-establishment stands against the political class, and in favour of "more democracy". Second, ethnic and regional identity politics (anti-immigration programmes and priority of locals in the labour market). Third, the specific work ethic and economic liberalism (small producers against big business and state taxation). The chapter concludes by linking economic insecurity on the one hand, and the evolution toward a defensive ideology on the other.*

CHAPTER 7
Once Again the Deviant Case? Why the *Christlich-Soziale Union* Only Partially Fulfils the Image of an "Alpine Populist Party"

Claudius WAGEMANN

This chapter examines if, and the extent to which, the Bavarian Christlich-Soziale Union *(CSU) corresponds to the elements of an "Alpine populist party." The origins, history, and development of the CSU are outlined, as well as its success and the several conditions to which it can be attributed. Regarding the characteristics of an Alpine populist party, it is argued that the CSU only partially fulfils this type. The CSU – unlike parties with similar programmatical profiles in the other countries and regions compared in this volume – is not an opposition party but, on the contrary, has been continuously and successfully in government for a very long time. In this position, it has promoted policies of social and economic modernisation. Its pro-system rather than anti-system character make it distinct from other Alpine cases (but similar to* the Südtiroler Volkspartei*). Moreover, because of its programmatical positions and policies concerning European integration, the CSU does not completely overlap with the strategies of the other Alpine cases.*

CHAPTER 8
The *Südtiroler Volkspartei* and Its Ethno-Populism

Günther PALLAVER

This chapter analyses the strategic shift in perspectives from the "people" to "ethnos" through the example of the Südtiroler Volkspartei *in the Province of Bozen/Bolzano (South Tyrol). Since 1945 the* Südtiroler Volkspartei *has obtained the absolute majority of votes in all provincial council elections, representing roughly 80% of the German- and Ladino-speaking populations. A central key to the* Südtiroler Volkspartei*'s success lies in how it conveys the message that both linguistic groups belong to a community that shares the same distinct ethnic and Alpine destiny (*Schicksalsgemeinschaft*) with regard to the outside world. The term "homeland" (*Heimat*) is used as a symbol of the idealised and unchanged peasant community. The chapter describes how the* Südtiroler Volkspartei *uses this tensions between "us" (Germans) and "others" (Italians), the criteria on which the divide between inclusion and exclusion is based, and the consequences for the political system.*

Chapter 9
Multi-Level Populism and Centre–Periphery Cleavage in Switzerland: The Case of the *Lega dei Ticinesi*

Oscar MAZZOLENI

This chapter focuses on the recently founded Lega dei Ticinesi, *the only party to politicise a centre–periphery cleavage in Switzerland. It is maintained that the analysis of the political opportunities and the populist rhetoric of this party from early 1990s requires a multi-level approach. The* Lega *is not only a regionalist party, but also claims the right to national defence (against the EU), and expresses local demands. The conditions for the emergence of the* Lega, *its electoral success, and the present electoral decline are linked to the historical and cultural background of Ticino, the specificity of Swiss federalism, the ambivalent relationship with Northern Italy and European integration, and, finally, the participation in a consociational cantonal government. At the same time, the chapter discusses why the political opportunities for a regionalist party in the German and French parts of Switzerland are limited today, and discusses the relationships between the* Lega *and the* Schweizerische Volkspartei.

The Alpine Challenge to Identity, Consensus, and European Integration

Daniele CARAMANI and Yves MÉNY

I. Toward a European Cleavage Constellation

The analysis of the Alpine transnational region and its relationship to the process of European integration can be considered to be a case study of the emerging cleavage constellation at European level, and of the incipient formation of a European-wide party system.[1] For a long time, work on European parties and cleavages has focused on a limited number of dimensions, namely, the left–right dimension and the pro/anti-European dimension (Hix and Lord, 1997: 27–49). However, in the light of the recent deepening and widening of the process of integration, the development of several "levels" of governance (Hooghe and Marks, 2001; Héritier, 1999), and the (re-)emergence of regional, and even local, identity feelings and socio-economic models (Keating, 1998), such a framework appears inappropriate. First, it is unable to account for the different conceptions or "images" of European integration, which cannot be simply reduced to a pro/anti-integration alternative. Second, the framework is unable to take the cultural dimensions of ethnic, linguistic, and religious diversity in Europe into consideration. These elements of cultural diversity assume a striking importance with the eastward enlargement of the European Union (EU) towards territories which are still characterised by a larger cultural diversity than Western Europe (Flora, 1999: 86).

These developments require the analysis of the formation and consolidation of European-wide cleavages, namely, of social and economic oppositions with distinct sets of values and beliefs, and a sense of identity and self-consciousness which are expressed in specific political, institutional, and partisan organisations and behaviour (Bartolini and

---

[1] For another recent work stressing the analytical relevance and socio-economic and political importance of the Alpine region, see Ihl *et al.* (2003).

Mair, 1990: 215). The European-wide nature of political cleavages relates to the increasingly transnational (between sub-national units) or
supranational (within the "centre") character of oppositions and alliances in which the nation-state (in its paradigmatic Westphalian sovereign form) has lost its central position as the predominant political
arena.

It is true that a number of writings have recently attempted to adapt
theories of the structuring of party systems at national level to the EU
party system. These attempts represent an important step forward, for
they recover the rich conceptual and theoretical apparatus which, in the
wake of the work produced by Karl Deutsch, Stein Rokkan, and others
goes under the label of "comparative historical sociology". According to
this work, theories of state formation and nation-building, cleavage
structures and centralisation, constitute promising models for the interpretation of European unification. Several of these writings explore, in
particular, Stein Rokkan's macro-theory of state formation, nation-
building, and mass politics in Europe as a powerful model for interpret-
ing general processes of "system-building" (Flora, 1999: 88–91;
Klausen and Tilly, 1997). European unification can be understood as a
process of external boundary-building and of dismantling internal
boundaries – above all, judicial and economic (less so political and cultural) barriers – combined with an increasing centralisation of decision-
making structures and processes. The interaction between external
boundary-building and internal boundary-dismantling was developed
from Hirschman's twin-concepts of "exit" and "voice". In the legal
sphere, in particular, the reduction of "selective exit", mainly through
the jurisprudence of the European Court of Justice (Weiler, 1999), has
led to the development of channels for the expression of voice (institutions for the representation of various social and territorial groups) as
well as to the development of political opposition, differentiation, and
cleavages – in the form of contrasts between nation-states.[2]

The national dimension, however, is only one of the possible dimensions within a forming European-wide cleavage constellation. As Bartolini has stressed (2002: 130–55), territorial resistance to centre formation – economic, legal, and cultural – will closely interact with
functional differentiations within the new "higher level" system that is
forming. In particular, the territorial dimension over more *vs.* less EU
political control or more *vs.* less integration cuts across the traditional
class or left–right dimension – the principal functional differentiation in

---

[2]   See Weiler (1999) for this interpretation of Hirschman's scheme – and, more gener-
    ally, for the first application of the "exit" and "voice" concepts to European integra-
    tion. See Bartolini (2002) for a development of the implications for European unifi-
    cation of the interaction of the two mechanisms in a historical sociology perspective.

all European party systems. Thus, the forming of a European electorate and party system will strongly depend on whether or not the left–right dimension will impose itself over the "sovereignty dimension" (Marks and Steenbergen, 2002).[3]

Within this framework, what follows attempts to answer three main questions. First, why study the Alpine region? Second, what are the specificities of the Alpine region? Third, how does this specificity represent a challenge and to what extent does it cause a cleavage in the forming European party system?

II. Why Analyse the Alpine Region?

A. The "Case"

The Alpine region represents an ideal "laboratory" for the investigation of the various cleavages and their repercussions on the process of European integration: centre–periphery cleavages in the form of ethnolinguistic resistance to assimilation and standardisation, and economic protectionism; rural–urban cleavages between both socio-economic activities and lifestyles; religious cleavages between traditional and secularised attitudes and orientations, as well as the left–right cleavage between the "winners and losers" of integration.[4] The specificity of the Alpine region may develop into a cleavage that not only has an impact on the shape of the *internal* political space of the forming EU cleavage system (in terms of oppositions and alliances) but also on the *external* delimitations of the system (in terms of membership and identity boundaries with outside systems).

There are a number of reasons for which the Alpine region is a crucial case study. First, because of its complex and rich social and cultural composition, the Alpine region offers the entire *palette* of contrasts (Viazzo, 1990). The Alps have been a crucial geo-economic area at the heart of the European "city-belt" for centuries. The area is characterised

---

[3] Besides the main class dimension, as a further functional or sectoral dimension of differentiation, Schmitter (2000: 68) points to agriculture – a cleavage that has disappeared, or has been incorporated in other alignments, at the level of national cleavage landscapes – but which, at EU level, is re-emerging as a consequence of the important resources for the Common Agricultural Policy controlled by the EU and through alliances of the "integration losers" (economically weak producers and peripheral regions) who are threatened by the opening of markets and globalisation processes.

[4] The term is from Schmitter (2000). It relates to the expression used by Betz ("losers of modernity") in regard to the support for populist parties in Western Europe (Betz, 1998). The left–right character of this opposition consists of the positions on liberalisation and privatisation policies, reform of the welfare state, as well as of the democratic deficit of the EU.

by an exceptional richness of natural resources as well as by resources derived from the control of trade routes (in the past as well as today) across Alpine passes. Today, these are extremely wealthy areas. Second, this geopolitical and geo-economic centrality, which has a character which is distinct from any other region in Europe, has not only led to transnational collaboration between regions, but also to the supranational recognition of the specificity of the Alpine region by the EU, most notably through the INTERREG programme. Third, the entire Alpine region offers a unique patchwork of different cultures: languages (German, Italian, French, Slovene, *Reto-Romantsch*, *Ladino*, etc.), and religions (Catholic and various Reformed denominations). The level of this diversity is unique in Europe. Fourth, geography and morphology have helped to maintain – through both physical remoteness and socio-economic distance –traditional political cultures in which elements of religiosity, ecology, and community are stronger than elsewhere. Fifth, because of the fragmented nature of the societies in this region, a consociational type of political accommodation has, in many cases, developed, based upon negotiation and consensus. Sixth, a further common trait of this region is the presence of important regionalist/populist parties that developed partly from national centre–periphery cleavages, and partly as a response to the élitist consociational and corporatist type of decision-making process. Finally, in a large part of the Alpine population, we find a pronounced Euro-scepticism.

A further reason why the Alpine region represents an ideal "laboratory-case" for the analysis of cleavages in Europe and their relationship to the formation of European-wide cleavages is methodological. The Alpine region has been characterised by a delayed process of state formation and nation-building, mainly in the second half of the 19th century, with persistent border modifications even after the First World War (including frequent transfers of territories, and policies of population assimilation) that make it distinct with respect to other less central regions in Europe. Furthermore, the entire Alpine arc (from Nice and Savoie in France, to the Istrian peninsula) has, until recently, been characterised by unstable borders and by regional autonomy, in spite of different types of states and contrasting experiences of national integration – cases of delayed federalisation within former lose confederations (Germany and Switzerland), cases of strong centre formation (the French "Napoleonian" model, also adopted by Italy at its the unification in 1860), and, finally, cases of break-up of multi-national empires (Austria and Slovenia). This means that – in a comparative perspective –

it is possible to control for the "variable" timing of state formation and increase the comparability of the different cases in the Alpine region.[5]

B. What the Book Argues

Yet, the specificity of a transnational Alpine region and the potential emergence of a cleavage between alternative images of Europe is a matter of empirical investigation. The goal of this "case-study" is analytical, and the different chapters of the book aim to provide empirical support for the following argument.

- First, the high degree of territorial (political) fragmentation and cultural diversity led, during the process of state formation and nation-building, to regional resistance (centre–periphery cleavages) within centralised nation-states, or to decentralised institutional structures (in the forms of federalism and autonomous provinces) which, in turn, allowed for the survival of distinctive identities. Distinctive identities, as well as distinctive modes of production (based on the rural–urban cleavage: agriculture, control of natural resources and trade routes), are at the origin of defensive or "retrenched" cultures, with regard to both the defence of identitarian-communitarian elements and the preservation of ecological, geo-economic, and geopolitical resources.

- Second, the great political-territorial fragmentation of the Alpine territories and the strong ethno-linguistic and religious diversity that characterises their populations resulted in a particular mode of political accommodation between minorities, a "consensual" model (Lijphart, 1999), or *Proporz* democracy (Lehmbruch, 1967, 1996; Steiner, 1974), in which negotiation and neo-corporatist elements are strong, and have, in many cases, led to stability or "immobility" over the decades, to which an "anti-system" response has followed through the development of strong populist parties. The protestary reaction on the part of these parties is, first and foremost, concerned with the political (both national and international organisations), economic-financial (national and international globalisation), as well as cultural (assimilationist models) élites to which peripheral populations have only a distant relationship.

- Third, the defensive claims (economic and social) of political culture (traditional) and political expression (populism) may lead to

---

[5] In all these respects, the choice of cases allows for a comparable-cases or "most similar systems design" (Lijphart, 1975; Przeworski and Teune, 1970). The commonality of many properties between cases thus makes it possible to concentrate on a more parsimonious number of variables.

Daniele Caramani & Yves Mény

a contrast – a *challenge*, as we call it in the title – with respect to (1) the universalistic and assimilationist type of identity (the type of citizenship that developed from the French Revolution onwards), and (2) to representative democracy. Furthermore, with the progressive withering away of the nation-state as the primary political arena, these defensive attitudes may turn against (3), the EU and the current type of integration. Our argument is that this constitutes a potential cleavage in the EU, based on alternative views of identity (differentialist *vs.* assimilationist; ethnic *vs.* universalistic) and on alternative views of democracy ("direct" *vs.* representative; people's *vs.* élitist). The task of the chapters of this book is to answer the question of whether or not such a challenge exists, and if alternative views of identity and democracy do represent a potential cleavage in the forming European party system.

The chapters focus on a number of empirical cases which are specific to the Alpine region. These are parties which are either exclusively located in the Alpine region, or parties that use typical Alpine themes in the political discourse: the *Lega Nord*, the *Union Valdôtaine*, and the *Südtiroler Volkspartei* in Italy, the *Lega dei Ticinesi* and the *Schweizerische Volkspartei* in Switzerland (together with the *Katholische Volkspartei*),[6] the *Freiheitliche Partei Österreichs* in Austria, the *Christlich-Soziale Union* in Bavaria (Germany), as well as the *Ligue Savoisienne* in the French Alps. Through the analysis of party programmes, public discourse, statements by leaders, and the attitudes and orientations of their voters and members, the different chapters try to link the positions and ideologies of these parties to the peculiar socio-economic, geopolitical and geo-economic, as well as cultural characters of the Alpine region. We hope that this "case-study" will not only be a description of the Alpine region, but also turn out to be a "theory-confirming" or "theory-infirming" case study (Eckstein, 1975; Lijphart, 1971) which is able to address the broader theoretical questions concerning the emergence of cleavages in Europe.

What do the chapters show with regard to these questions? They demonstrate that there is, indeed, a specificity of the Alpine region, and that this specificity presents a challenge to both the national and the European type of identity, and to consensual democracy, leading to the an alternative vision or model of European integration, which constitutes a potential cleavage (also territorial) and overlaps with a number of other cleavages. The remainder of this introduction first presents this specificity, then presents the challenges to identity and representation,

---

[6]   The abbreviation SVP is used for the *Schweizerische Volkspartei*; the *Südtiroler Volkspartei* which usually takes the same acronym is not abbreviated in this book.

and finally presents the relationship with the other industrial and pre-industrial cleavages that are at the origin of national party systems.

III. The Specificities of the Alpine Region

A. *State Formation and Nation-Building*

The long-standing central position of the Alpine region within the European network of cities and trade routes – the European city-belt (Rokkan *et al.*, 1987) – has delayed the process of state formation in this area, not only in the states that unified and consolidated their external (Alpine) borders in the second half of the 19th century, such as Italy, Germany and Switzerland, but also in the states that resulted from the break-up of multi-national empires (such as Austria and Slovenia), and in the states that formed "early" at the fringes of the city-belt, such as France, where Alpine border modifications took place until the late 19th century, with the territorial transfers of Nice and Savoy in 1860.

Daniele Caramani's chapter describes the laborious and delayed process of state formation along the Alpine peek line. In addition, his chapter shows that the strong cultural, political, and territorial fragmentation of this area led to multi-lingual and religiously mixed populations. This had important repercussions on the "completeness" of the process of nation-building. The nationalisation of language and religion, the administrative penetration, and the economic integration of the Alpine region has, when compared with more central national areas, occurred to a lesser degree. The morphology of this region has also helped to reinforce both cultural and economic resistances, by cutting off several regions from national centres, as in the case of Ticino in Switzerland.

The similar geopolitical and geo-economic position of the different territories of the Alps across national borders, makes it possible to speak about these areas as of a transnational region. This argument is reinforced by the increasingly frequent common initiatives and collaboration across borders, between both sub-national political communities and the political parties of these areas, mainly through ideology and collaboration at European level (as, for example, the right-wing, anti-immigration political movement *Alpi-Adria*). As Michael Keating's chapter shows, this transnational character of the Alpine region appears in a large number of formal agreements and accords, such as the *Alpi-Adria Working Group*, which was founded in 1978 to deal with functional matters such as transport, environment, and research, or the Working Community of the Western Alps (COTRAO). In all these cases, collaboration is not limited to functional sectors, but is extended to overcome past divisions and to work on the co-existence of different cultures, ethnic belonging, and languages.

Figure 1. Area of the "Alpine Space Programme"[7]

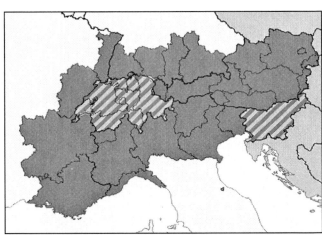

Legend: Solid = EU member states; Dashed = Non-EU partners
(at the time of the launching of the programme).

In spite of the general Euro-scepticism that characterises most of these areas, the existence of a transnational character of the Alpine region has encouraged both these territories and the EU to develop an Alpine "vision", particularly after the accession of Austria in 1995 and the beginning of the negotiations for accession with Slovenia. As Keating notes, this process was spurred by policy considerations determined by the geo-economic and communication centrality of the Alps in Europe. The Alpine Convention was signed in 1995 between the European Commission and the various states around the Alps (which also includes Lichtenstein and Monaco), and, in 2001, the INTERREG III B (Alpine Space Programme) was launched. This programme also includes Lichtenstein, Slovenia, and Switzerland, which is financed under the European Regional Development Fund, and includes both the mountainous areas (as well as the surrounding foothills and lowlands) and some coastal areas (see Figure 1). As the figure shows, the sub-national units included in the programme are not necessarily NUTS II-level units, such as the *Regioni* in Italy or the *Länder* in Austria. This has some relevance for the topics of this book, as, for example, not all of Bavaria can be considered as Alpine.[8] In the case of Austria and

---

[7]   Joint Technical Secretariat of the Alpine Space Programme: Alpenforschungsinstitut, Garmisch-Partenkirchen.

[8]   The Alpine Space Programme includes only the four *Regierungsbezirke* of Upper Bavaria and Swabia (in Bavaria) and of Tübingen and Freiburg (in Baden-Württemberg). The latter area is also linked to the Regio Basiliensis (French, Ger-

Switzerland, however (as well as Slovenia and Lichtenstein), the entire national territories are covered by the programme.[9]

B. Economic Structure

The distinctiveness of Alpine peripheral regions within national networks depends not only on religious, ethnic, and linguistic separation, but also on an agrarian economy. The development of Atlantic capitalism and successively the Industrial Revolution, as well as the development of faster and more direct means of communication have, to some extent, marginalised the position of the Alps as a communication node. The diffuse urbanisation that characterises the Alps is small, rural, and distant with regard to the main urban centres at the margins of the Alps: Milan, Turin, Zurich, Basle, Vienna, Lyon, and Munich. The rural–urban cleavage and the dependence upon external markets is reinforced by cultural barriers and geographical remoteness, and has led to strong agrarian parties which developed in concomitance with the first mobilisation of mass electorates at the beginning of the 20th century. With the exception of Scandinavia, where large agrarian parties developed with mass democracy and then transformed into broader centre parties after the Second World War, the Alpine area is the region in which one finds the strongest concentration of peasant parties until the First World War and, in some cases, after it.[10]

For more recent times, however, it is difficult to argue that the Alpine economy is an agrarian, farming, or cattle-breeding economy, especially if one looks at the rates of employment in the secondary sector. Rurality, in a society in which tiny percentages of the population work in agriculture, assumes a different meaning. First, the Alpine region seems to be better characterised as a small and diffuse urban structure. And second, rather than relying upon agricultural production (the mor-

---

man, and Swiss localities in proximity to Basle) and to the Regio TriRhena around the Rhine valley in proximity to Basle (another Euro-Region funded by the INTERREG programme).

[9] For Italy, the regions are Friuli Venezia Giulia, Veneto, Valle d'Aosta, Piemont, and Liguria, as well as the autonomous provinces of Bolzano and Trento. In France, the regions are Rhône-Alpes, Provence-Alpes-Côte d'Azur, Franche-Comté, and Alsace. In Switzerland, the regions indicated in the map are the *Grossregionen.*

[10] The development of such parties depended on the market relationship between towns and countryside with a small farming economy more exposed to the uncertainties of the market and industrial economies (Linz, 1976; Urwin, 1980). The largest of these parties is the *Schweizerische Bauern-, Gewerbe und Bürgerpartei* (today SVP). In Germany, strong agrarian parties developed mainly in Bavaria (*Bayerische Bauernbund* in alliance with the *Deutscher Wirtschafsbund für Stadt und Land*). In Austria, regional peasant parties unified in the *Landbund für Österreich*, and, in Italy, the *Partito agrario* or *Partito dei contadini d'Italia* was particularly strong in the foothills in Piedmont. For details, see Caramani (2004: 218–20).

phology of the territory makes large production difficult), the Alpine economy relies upon the exploitation of natural resources in the form of the production of energy, the control of North–South trade routes (both roads and railways), as well as the exploitation of the tourist industry. Around the tourist industry, in particular, a large number of small and medium-sized enterprises have developed, as have craftsmanship activities.

C. Regionalism

Another strong pre-industrial factor – the centre–periphery cleavage – has determined the emergence of a further specificity of Alpine politics, namely, a strong regionalism. Regional cultural and economic distinctiveness, as well as geographical remoteness, are at the origin of a number of parties which defend peripheral interests and identities. As the chapter by Caramani shows, such parties emerged especially in culturally distinct regions within the centralised states which were based on the Napoleonian model of national standardisation and integration. These are the cases of the long-standing parties of the South Tyrol (*Südtiroler Volkspartei*), described in the chapter by Günther Pallaver, of the Valle d'Aosta (*Union valdôtaine*) in Italy, and of the more recent *Ligue Savoisienne* in France. This is also the case of the most important recent regionalist phenomenon of the *Lega Nord* in Italy, which, for the first time in the Italian party system, has politicised the North–South divide. As the chapters by both Patricia Chiantera-Stutte and Hans-Georg Betz show – after an initial success that included even the main urban centres such as Milan, Turin, and Venice – the *Lega Nord* is today stronger in the Alpine valleys than it is in the largest cities. The same applies to Bavaria, where Munich and Nürnberg traditionally remain Social-Democratic cities.

But regionalist party politics also developed in political systems which – through a federal structure – opened up institutional channels of voice and electoral representation and, in principle, curtailed the emergence of regionalist parties. The chapter by Claudius Wagemann shows, for example, how the Bavarian *Christlich-Soziale Union* adopted an explicit and distinct (in the German context) Alpine style and political discourse which the party was able to combine with both a modernisation programme and successful policies with regard to economic performance, education, and ecology on the one hand, and was also able to permeate the style and the political discourse of other parties in Bavaria (namely, the *Sozialdemokratische Partei Deutschlands*) on the other. In Switzerland, the more recent and significant case of regionalism is that described in the chapter by Oscar Mazzoleni on the *Lega dei Ticinesi*, a party of the only Italian-speaking canton. His concept of a multi-level relationship between this periphery and several centres – internal (*vis-à-vis* Berne) and external (*vis-à-vis* Milan and the strong Lombard economy, and, now, also *vis-à-vis* Brussels) – reveals that the federal representation of territorially-based cultural and economic minorities is insufficient to channel regional claims.

Sub-national regionalism (according to the threefold distinction Keating makes in his chapter) is, therefore, a typical – though not exclusive – feature of the Alpine region. What we are confronted with, however, is a particular type of sub-national regionalism. First, as several chapters underline, regionalism in the Alps is a right-wing, Catholic, and conservative, anti-modernist type of regionalism, whereas, in other parts of Europe, it is associated with a more progressive character, either broadly "leftist" or declaredly Marxist: in Brittany, in the Basque countries, in Scotland, etc. Keating's chapter systematically tests two alternative hypotheses of the "new" *versus* the "old" ideal-types of sub-national regionalism, in which the former is conservative, traditionalist, localist, defensive, and Euro-sceptic, and the latter is modernising, progressive, and pro-European. The answer we get from his chapter, supported by the in-depth analyses carried out in the chapters on the specific cases, is that the "old regionalism" does, indeed, predominate in the Alpine region.[11]

Variations among cases do not reverse such a picture. Pallaver shows that the *Südtiroler Volkspartei* is, indeed, a catch-all conservative regionalist party with a strong emphasis on primitive independence, ethnicity, tradition, localism, and heroic figures. Similarly, the case of the *Lega Nord* appears in the chapters of Betz and Chiantera-Stutte as one of conservative *Weltanschauung*, with its opposition to immigration, its emphasis on fictitious ancient ethnic Celtic roots, which turned strongly anti-European. The *Lega dei Ticinesi*, too, as it appears in Mazzoleni's chapter, is a right-wing, anti-immigrant, anti-European party allied to the populist *Schweizerische Volkspartei* (characteristics that we find in other Swiss parties, such as the *Christlich Demokratische Volkspartei* in the Catholic cantons). The same characters appear in the French Alpine area with the *Ligue Savoisienne* in French Savoie and with the *Union Valdôtaine* in the Italian Valle d'Aosta (both described in Caramani's and Keating's chapters). In contrast, the Bavarian *Christlich-Soziale Union* is a case of a successful combination of conservative and traditional regionalism that emphasises Christian values, rejects the multi-

---

[11] One finds another example of conservative regionalism in another country located in the European city-belt, namely, Belgium: *Volksunie, Vlaams Blok, Rassemblement Wallon* are the main regionalist parties before the split of the major parties of the system (Socialist, Catholics, and Liberals) along the linguistic cleavage in the 1960s–1970s.

cultural society in favour of the family and the community, has an imagery which is rooted in the mountain landscape, and emphasises modernising policies, successful entrepreneurship, technological innovation, ecological protection, and educational primacy in Germany. Notwithstanding this, it is its conservative image that remains predominant.

D. Political Culture

The conservatism and traditionalism of the transnational Alpine region and of its type of sub-national regionalism is one of the elements that the analysis of the Alpine political culture has identified. Caramani's chapter argues that spatial factors of geographical distance and social remoteness have not only helped to strengthen cultural resistance, and therefore to maintain ethnic, religious, and linguistic identities, but have also helped to produce a distinct political culture in which the elements of tradition, religiosity, nature, community (*Gemeinschaft*), and locality (*Heimat*) are stronger than in other areas.[12] The remote location with respect to the main centres of industrialisation and urbanisation has, to a greater extent, preserved a type of community from processes of secularisation, atomisation, and modernisation. These values developed, first, in contrast to the basic values of the nation-state and, second, from the incipient European identity and citizenship.

Traditional values dominate over modern approaches in most domains of life. There is a sceptical rejection of modern societal developments, from social roles to social structures and social deviation. Furthermore, what, perhaps, characterises the Alpine region most is the accent on nature, which can be found in both the public discourse (and its imagery) and in several of the issues raised. The "natural" element of Alpine political culture is present from the defence of natural resources to the definition of a natural communitarian identity. Finally, an element of ethics (which clearly appears in the chapter by Betz, in particular a work ethic), is perceived both as a value and as a distinctive identitarian character that makes these "laborious" regions distinct form other regions in the respective nation-states, as well as from external social groups such as immigrants, both (Southern) Europeans and non-Europeans (immigrants fom North Africa, Middle East, and Asia).

With regard to how group identity is conceived, three well-know German terms express the "ethnic" (Smith, 1986) perception of the group in the Alpine political culture. The first term is *Volk*: the relationship between the individual, the community, and the territory is defined

---

[12] This "remoteness" is more a matter of perceptions and feelings than an objective distance in, first, small countries in which spatial distances are reduced and, second, in federal systems in which the contact with the political system is more immediate.

in natural terms.[13] The group has a natural identity with ethnic roots ("blood"), which represents a holistic entity above the individual. This natural identity, as a consequence, rejects the unnatural and artificial citizenship of the nation-state, which is suspiciously regarded as a legalistic-bureaucratic idea. The second term, *Gemeinschaft*, refers to a communitarian perception of the "true" and "real" group, in opposition to such an artificial citizenship. This term is opposed to that of *Gesellschaft*, an atomised and individualistic type of society created by processes of industrialisation and urbanisation which uprooted the original belongings and feelings of identity. There is, therefore, a reference to pre-industrial origins re-awakened through the crisis of the social organisations which replaced them after the Industrial Revolution, namely, the welfare state and social security systems.

Concerning the evaluation and judgement of the political system, its institutions, and its personnel, issues of efficiency and trust dominate. The geographical remoteness and the social distance between the community and the élites contribute to the creation of a strong scepticism towards the efficiency and honesty of the "establishment" – political-administrative, financial (national and international), and also religious. Thus, from a vertical perspective, the relationship with the élites is dominated by mistrust, which is reinforced by centre–periphery and rural–urban differences. The political system is often seen as corrupt and distant from ordinary citizens, and its personnel is criticised on standards of morality. The political arena is seen as the site of compromises and loss of "purity" (another natural element) in which the (bourgeois) values of "hard work" and efficiency are absent. However, from a horizontal perspective, the relationship within the group is characterised by trust between members, which is expressed in forms of social participation and dense networks of local membership associations.

Several chapters stress how this set of values, orientation, evaluation, and identities is increasingly perceived by the concerned populations as being under *threat*. This perception of a threat is a central element of this political culture. This threat has an *external* origin which affects all three dimensions of the political cultures distinguished above, and results in both a *defensive response*, a form of "retrenchment", and in the reinforcement of the geographical and social-membership barriers against the external influences. As a result, elements of spatial distance and social remoteness acquire a new meaning and weight. There is the

---

[13] On the distinction between "ethnos" and "people", see the very clarifying treatment by Günther Pallaver in his chapter on the *Südtiroler Volkspartei*.

idea of a form of wealth – cultural, social, and economic[14] – which is in need of protection and preservation.

The threat originates, first and foremost, from processes of supra-national economic globalisation and political integration. Financial capitalism and unemployment are seen as being "imported" (from outside) and threaten both the traditionally low unemployment rates in these areas and the work ethic that condemns "easy money" not based on daily work. In particular, this translates into protectionist attitudes, programmes, and policies in favour of agriculture, craftsmanship, small and medium-sized enterprises, and anti-taxation movements. This also translates into initiatives for the defence of the local workers on the labour market, which is further linked to the anti-immigration stands.[15] Second, globalisation processes, supra-national integration, as well as the "Americanisation" of society are perceived as a threat to ethnic and cultural identities based on the concepts of the *Volk* and *Heimat*. However, such a threat has older origins which come from the "artificial", individualistic and assimilationist citizenship of the nation-state to which an "exclusionist model" (as Chiantera-Stutte calls it in her chapter) or "exclusionary nativism" (in Betz's chapter) of regional and cultural identity is opposed. Urbanisation and industrialisation also constitute a threat to the ecology of the Alpine region. Preservation of natural purity (not just the moral and ethical purity) is needed against the physical corruption by cities. Third, the threat originates from the distant political system: geographically distant "centres" and socially remote élites ("those above") that are unaccountable to small people. The "corruption" of the establishment and its impermeability to change are seen as threats to the true power of the people. Distrust predominates in the relationship with the central state (anti-taxation movements also have this meaning), and the true democracy is threatened by an artificial "representative" democracy instead of a direct link between the leaders and the people (*Volk*). These are all processes of social, political, and economic modernisation to which the Alpine area is increasingly confronted.

---

[14] The idea of the cultural patrimony that has to be defended expresses in forms of idealisation of past heritage, through the accent on mythologies (created and used more or less *ad hoc*).

[15] This yields to reject the "immaterial economy" in favour of the "real" economy centred around small craftsmen, shopkeepers, and workers. The initiatives for "locals first" in the labour market are described in the chapters of Betz, Caramani, and Chiantera-Stutte.

E. Consociationalism

This critique of democracy is, to a large extent, linked to the development of patterns of consociational decision-making and of negotiation democracies in the Alpine countries.[16] As for other parts of Europe – above all, the Benelux countries, and, to a lesser extent, Scandinavia – the chapter by Yannis Papadopoulos shows that, in the Alpine region, consensual accommodation between segments of the society, neo-corporatist agreements between government, associations, and trade unions, the existence of multiple levels of government (*Politikverflechtung*) as well as the practice of governmental coalitions, have created a *Konkordanz* or *Proporz* (Lehmbruch, 1967) type of democracy as an alternative to majoritarian democracy based on clear policy choices and accountability sanctioned by the electorate.[17]

Consociational decision-making, negotiation and accommodation democracies, and corporatist agreements develop in response to the great social, territorial, and cultural (ethno-linguistic and religious) heterogeneity of the populations described above, and to the external threats to which small countries are confronted in the international economy (Katzenstein, 1985). Classical texts on consensual democracies – Austria, Belgium, the Netherlands, and Switzerland – have shown how the strong social segmentation of society have determined the development of a type of democracy that does not correspond to the ideal of an Anglo-Saxon type of majoritarian democracy with single-party cabinets, clear responsibilities for policy choices, accountability in elections, etc.[18] Furthermore, this literature has stressed the central role of the collaboration between the élites of the various social segments or "pillars". Political accommodation, neo-corporatist agreements, and *Konkordanz* between parties is, therefore, a process that takes place at the top level of the stratification of societies, rather than at the level of the masses. This type of democracy requires collaboration between élites.

In the Alpine region, this has been translated into a number of political arrangements, which range from the "magic formula" in Switzerland – the governmental coalition since 1959, in which all major parties are included – the Austrian system of consociationalism (*Proporz*) domi-

---

[16] The term is that of *korporative Verhandlungsdemokratien* (Lehmbruch, 1996).

[17] On consensual democracy as an ideal type opposed to majoritarian democracy, see Lijphart (1999). The elements of negotiation democracy are clearly outlined in Czada (2003): (1) *Konkordanz* between political parties, (2) federal structure, and (3) corporatist agreements between sectoral organisations.

[18] On these cases, see also Lorwin (1966), Lijphart (1968), Steiner (1974). On consociational nation-building, see Daalder (1973).

nated by the two major established parties, in Germany with the neo-corporatist agreements between Social Democrats and Christian Democrats (sometimes known as the *grosse Koalition*) with the employers' association and the trade unions, and the sharing of power in Italy known as *consociativismo*.[19] In addition – and this might be an element that further distinguishes and characterises the Alpine region with regard to other consensual democracies – the political cartelisation of decision-making processes in this region is paralleled by a multi-layered structure with several levels of government and strong regional autonomies (to which the EU level must also be added now). We find federal structures in Austria, Germany, and Switzerland, all countries which belong to the *Mitteleuropean* tradition of decentralised political systems, communal liberties, and multi-ethnic societies (a tradition that can also be found in the "pan-European" thinking that is typical of Central Europe). To this tradition, the northern regions in Italy (long under the Hapsburg Empire) also belong, in which – in spite of the centralised nature of the Italian state – one finds autonomous provinces (such as that of Alto Adige or the South Tyrol), and regions with special status.[20] This political *Verflechtung* – or vertical stratification of competences across levels of government – increases the need for negotiations, agreements, and accommodations during the decision-making process at the level of political and economic élites. It is, therefore, an important element of the consociational nature of these systems which is absent in other cases, such as the Netherlands or the Scandinavian countries.

In all these countries, this model of democracy has come under stress. The consensual type of democracy is increasingly associated with the idea of a crisis which requires radical change. To a large extent, this crisis is determined by its stable character (*immobilismo* as it has been called in Italy). First, consociationalism is associated with the power of political parties that have lost contact with the citizens. Terms such as *partitocratie, partitocrazia,* and *Parteienstaat* indicate how the loss of influence of the parties on the voters and citizens is negatively perceived by the political system, as it affects the very principle of people's democracy. Second, as Papadopoulos notes, in spite of the "inclusive" character of consociational models of democracy, a number of minori-

---

[19] Other cases are those of governmental coalitions in Belgium and *Verzuiling* in the Netherlands. As Papadopoulos notes in his chapter, also the case of France under the *co-habitation* regime might approach a consensual model of democracy. In Rokkan's geopolitical conceptual map of Europe (1981; 1999: 135–47), consociational democracies appear above all in the territorially and politically fragmented and multi-cultural city-belt.

[20] Three of the five regions with special status in Italy are located along the Alps: Trentino Alto-Adige, Friuli Venezia Giulia, and Valle d'Aosta (the other two being Sardinia and Sicily).

ties remain at the fringes of the system or are totally excluded. Thus, it is not paradoxical that movements of protest have emerged in countries such as Austria and Switzerland, and in regions such as the North of Italy, Bavaria, and the Rhône-Alpes, which are among the wealthiest in the world, and in which there is also general satisfaction with the political system as a whole. Third, the élitist character of accommodation and agreement patterns has led to a feeling of *Verdrossenheit*, low democratic quality, and high democratic deficit. There is the perception that the cartelisation of party politics and consociationalism lead to a "truncated" model of democracy (Katz, 2003: 13). Citizens and voters increasingly feel distant from the élites in a system in which the latter have a central role while the former are excluded.[21]

This crisis of a specific consociational type of democracy automatically leads to demands for change. In all the cases analysed, the theme of change is recurrent in both the general public feeling and the political discourse. In all countries in the last decade, the hegemony of the traditional coalition parties has been challenged with arguments for "renewal" and "change" of the political system, with a "replacement" of the established parties and élites. And, indeed, the parties that have exploited the theme of change have been rewarded in terms of votes: the *Lega Nord* and *Forza Italia* in Italy, the SVP in Switzerland, and the FPÖ in Austria in particular.

IV. The Populist Challenge(s)

A. Populism in the Alps

The expression of the political *Verdrossenheit* and the reaction to immobile negotiation and consociational democracies which has emerged from segmented societies and the consequent accommodation politics, is that of right-wing populist and protest parties. In this respect, the chapter by Papadopoulos is crucial in making the link between consensual and negotiation democracy (caused by the territorially and culturally segmented nature of this region and the "smallness" in the world economy) on the one hand, and the populist reaction on the other.

However, as the different chapters on single cases show, populism emerges not only as a consequence of cultural segmentation and political accommodation (and therefore from the peculiar patterns of state

---

[21] As Chiantera-Stutte remarks in her chapter, this process has been particularly accentuated since the 1970s, when an "affective de-alignment" took place beside a "structural de-alignment" (the increase in electoral volatility as a consequence of changing ideologies, economic activities, secularisation, etc.). The affective de-alignment describes the distance of the voters from the traditional political parties (the *Altparteien*, or old parties) which led to forms of political protest.

formation and nation-building mentioned earlier), but also from the distance perceived by this region between the élitist and "establishment" character of consociational politics, from the type of economic structure of this region – based on natural resources and external dependency – which, more than in other regions, is exposed to the threats of globalisation and integration (the "losers" of modernity and of integration), from the external threats to the labour market which originate from immigration, and from a type of political culture which is very strongly oriented towards an ethnic type of identity which is threatened by both the nation-state and the EU, and which is partly determined by the regionalised structure of the Alpine area.

Several of the cases analysed in the different chapters have been described as right-wing populist parties – besides also being regionalist and agrarian and/or small industry parties. Even though, on the one hand, this populist response constitutes a further specificity of the Alpine region, our argument, on the other, is not that populist parties do not exist outside the Alpine region but rather that, in the Alpine region, they are linked to historical, geopolitical and geo-economic, historical, socio-economic, and cultural conditions that make the populist response more accentuated and acute than in other parts of Europe. Not only, as noted earlier, is regionalism in the Alps more conservative than anywhere else, but also, more than anywhere else, populist parties in the Alpine arc have been able to consolidate their electorates, with a surprising electoral stability in the last 10 years, and to influence the configuration of national political systems as the *Lega Nord* did in Italy, the FPÖ in Austria, the SVP in Switzerland, and the CSU in Germany.[22]

The defensive orientations and attitudes which come from socio-economic and cultural factors give rise to an alternative and contrasting conception of both society and political organisation. This opposition we call a *challenge* – in fact, a number of challenges. There is, first, a challenge to *identity* and, second, a challenge to *consensus* politics. Furthermore, in recent years, as a consequence of the on-going process of European integration, this challenge has progressively shifted from the national to the European level. Identity and consensus are not only challenged in the usual arena of the nation-state, but are also increasingly challenged in the way these elements are transposed and used in the

---

[22] The main populist parties in Western Europe are the *Front National* in France (a similar party exists in Belgium) and the different Scandinavian "progress" parties: *Fremskridtspartiet* in Denmark, *Fremskrittspartiet* in Norway, and *Ny Democrati* in Sweden (see Mény and Surel, 2002). As for other populist parties in the countries considered here – *Freiheitspartei der Schweiz, Schweizer Demokraten, Republikaner, Alleanza Nazionale*, etc. – the regionalist element is missing. This element can be found only in the Flemish *Vlaams Blok* (presently, *Vlaams Belang*) and *Volksunie*, more similar to the cases treated here.

construction of a supra-national political system, in other words, against the EU and the current type of *integration*. Many of the "threats" are increasingly perceived as originating from the EU rather than from the nation-state: cultural standardisation, the artificial and impersonal character of citizenship, distant bureaucracy, and open immigration from non-Christian populations through the blurring of borders. This leads not only to a sceptical view of European integration but also (in more positive terms) to an alternative conception of Europe.

The remainder of this section sums ups the challenges that have been identified in the different chapters of the book, attempts to estimate the degree to which these challenges may contrast the Alpine region both with other regions and with the emerging European "centre", and discusses the relationship of this contrast with other cleavages in the European constellation.

B. Challenges to Identity

The types of membership identity at both nation-state and EU level are based on an abstract and universal type of identity. In spite of strong variations among states in Europe, political citizenship developed from individualism and the ideals of equality of the 18th century and, after the French Revolution, from the process of nation-building. The construction of national citizenship beyond the predominant local and regional attachments of the feudal/agrarian society was paralleled by the process of democratisation and equalisation of political participation (Rokkan's "National Revolution").[23] On the other hand, this type of identity also developed from the formidable socio-economic transformations of the 19th century, through the process of industrialisation and urbanisation, with the consequent uprooting of local identities, as well as the general process of social mobilisation, and the consequent atomisation of society (Rokkan's "Industrial Revolution").

As pre-industrial and pre-national identities did not disappear with the rise of nation-states and the industrial society, two different types of identities came to co-exist in Europe. On the one hand, in the peripheral areas of Europe, the conditions existed for an early nationalisation of states through a political, abstract, and universalistic citizenship. The ideal-typical case, here, is France. On the other hand, deprived of the political element of nationality, Germany maintained and consolidated an ethno-cultural meaning of the nation that did not correspond to any territorial-legal state. As Brubaker noted, "the 19th century saw the consolidation of the French and the construction of a German nation-state"

---

[23] This is the thesis of the transformation of "peasants into Frenchmen" (Weber, 1976). On the construction of political citizenship, see Bendix (1977).

(1992: 10). The German understanding had been based on the idea of the *Volk* and, without a sovereign territorial assessment, was "pre-political", organic, and cultural (*Kulturnation*) rather than abstract, legal, or centred on the political unit.[24]

First, the entire Alpine region – with the exception of the French Alps – had long been under the influence of the Germanic culture. The various chapters of the book seem to agree that strong elements of the ethnic type of identity were both concentrated and have survived in this part of Europe. The chapters by Betz and Chiantera-Stutte, in particular, show how important the "politics of identity" ("race", culture, and territory) is for the *Lega Nord*, the FPÖ, the SVP, as well as the *Lega dei Ticinesi* (the same also being true for the *Südtiroler Volkspartei*). Wagemann, too, discusses the case of Bavaria and the CSU. In all these cases, the community is seen as a *Schicksalgemeinschaft* (a community of descent) based on a homogeneous, and Germanic, culture.[25] Second, the Alpine area seems to have been less permeated by the universalistic ideals of the Enlightenment, which were mainly received in the urban centres surrounding the core of the Alps. Third, the Alpine area has been less touched by the process of industrialisation and the consequent social mobilisation which has strongly contributed to the uprooting of ethnic regional identities. The challenge that this political culture represents is not limited to the question of a national or a European identity, but touches upon concrete policy choices, namely, in the issue of immigration. The predominant type of identity in the Alpine region is "differentialist" rather than "assimilationist", and reinforces the tendency to tighten the boundaries, which is set in motion by the instinct to protect the labour market.

The challenge which these parties and these regions represents is important when discussing the "roots" and the identity of Europe. This has a disruptive potential. Populist movements are strong in the national contexts that did not solve – or did not solve entirely – their relationship with the past. This is clear in the cases of Austria, Germany, and Italy, but partly also of Switzerland and the role that it played during the Second World War with regard to Jewish refugees and their bank

---

[24] On the opposition between ethnic and territorial-political nations, see Smith (1986) and Sahlins (1989). The opposition between ethnic and political can be seen in the German maintenance of *jus sanguinis* (until recently) as opposed to *jus soli*. For a comparative analysis of the naturalisation laws in France and Germany, see Brubaker (1992).

[25] The exception is, to some extent, the Swiss SVP, in which the accent is much more on the political elements that found the Swiss national identity: neutrality, federalism, and direct democracy – even though they are often combined with ethnic elements such as the founding myth of Wilhelm Tell.

accounts.[26] Even though this difficulty is, in most cases, addressed through the short-cut of an idealisation of the past (often a distant past and a primordial and "natural" origin), it reveals how, in a Europe in which the unsolved historical questions are still numerous and painful, the populist challenge might prove to be divisive when it comes to talking about identity. Furthermore, the ethnic elements of European identity might re-emerge in the definition of the external boundaries (geographical and membership boundaries) both when it comes to adopting a common constitution and to accepting new members.[27]

C. Challenges to Consensus

The second challenge that comes from the populist parties that developed in the Alpine region concerns the type of democracy and, in particular, includes a virulent critique of consensual democracy. As Papadopoulos discusses in detail in his chapter, the consensual type of democracy is attacked by an alternative view of democracy. First, the diffusion of power among coalition partners, organisations of the various social segments, and associations of interests, as well as the vertical stratification of power between central state, federated states, and local communities sets rigid limits to popular sovereignty. Second, in consociational regimes, élites enjoy a greater autonomy than in majoritarian democracies, and the influence of the people is limited through negotiation rounds, neo-corporatist compromises, and multi-actor policy-making. In this type of democracy, the link between election outcome and government formation or policy choice is indirect. As a consequence, the informal and opaque type of democracy which is identified with consociationalism is accused of undermining the very principles of popular sovereignty. In a telling conceptualisation quoted by Papadopoulos, the growth of mechanisms of horizontal trust-building co-operation between élites is likely to result in a weakening of the vertical trust between the citizens and the élites (Benz, 2002).

However, as the chapters by Betz and Chiantera-Stutte show, the challenge that populist parties in the Alpine area pose is not limited to consensual democracy, but touches more generally upon the basic elements of *representative democracy*. The progressive emergence of networks of governance, in which public and non-public actors at multiple levels take part in the decision-making process, can be seen as a *pendant* of the crisis of party democracy, the decrease in the organisational capacity, ideological mobilisation, and decision role of political parties

---

[26] See Anton Pelinka's chapter on Austria for an analysis of this aspect.

[27] An example is the debate about the Christian identity of Europe in relation to the works of the European Convention and the possible accession of Turkey.

which has been observed from numerous viewpoints (see Mény quoted in Betz's chapter). Thus, if the populist phenomenon seems to be linked to a more general phase of the deeper democratic crisis, then this crisis seems more acute in the political systems in which social segmentation, political accommodation, and neo-corporatist practices have been traditionally stronger, as is the case of the Alpine region.

As the various chapters analysing the single cases show, the regionalist and nationalist parties considered in the book share most of the elements that make up the populist challenge to consensus and representation. As Betz notes, there is, first and foremost, an "anti-system" characteristic which becomes synonymous not so much with "anti-democratic", but, instead, with opposition to a certain type of "representative" democracy. Both the chapters of Betz and Chiantera-Stutte show clearly that this character is present in the *Lega Nord*, the FPÖ, and the SVP.[28] These chapters – and, even more so, the cases dealt with in the chapters by Pallaver and Wagemann on the *Südtiroler Volkspartei* and the Bavarian CSU – also clarify how these parties attempt and, to a large extent, succeed in combining this anti-system position with their long-standing role in government, which is at the heart of the very system that they contest, as well as succeed in combining anti-party and anti-politics discourses with their role as parties in competitive party systems.

As Betz notes in his comparative chapter, the populist right made significant gains in Austria, Italy, and Switzerland, not so much because they mobilised on the immigration issues, but rather because they promoted themselves as the advocates and defenders of genuine and "true" democracy by exploiting the contraposition between the "small people" and the powerful élites of the political financial, and cultural (also religious) establishment. This emphasis on the contraposition between small working people and the élites is closely related to the new-liberal economic positions of most of the parties analysed. Betz underscores how the growth of populist parties in Europe takes place in a moment in which there is a fundamental shift from Keynesianism to neo-liberalism (from the 1970s) as a response to the difficulties of Western European countries to regain competitiveness after the economic crisis. The heavy intervention of the state in the economy, the strong vested interest of public industries and banks, the high cost of wage employment inflated by the strength of labour organisations, and the growth of the welfare state are some of the factors which are alluded to. Only in a subsequent phase did these parties react to the extreme liberalism and, in particular,

---

[28] This anti-system character therefore includes a strong anti-party element which clearly appears in the critique to the *partitocrazia* in Italy and to the *Parteienstaat* and the *Altparteien* in Austria.

to international competition which threatened the weaker production sectors of the economy.[29]

Right-wing populist parties very early on adopted the neo-liberal creed proposed at the end of the 1970s and during the 1980s in favour of an "enterprise" culture against a so-called "parasitic culture" (a recurrent theme also in relation to identities).[30] This creed found fertile ground in the bourgeois values of individualism, merit, and hard-work against state subsidies, *assistenzialismo*, etc., which were promoted by the ever growing state bureaucracy. The removal of bureaucratic hurdles was proposed as an alternative to subsidies to largely unproductive enterprises, tax alleviation as an alternative to the welfare state, and privatisation as an alternative to state-ownership, in order to foster economic growth. Again, the theme of exploitation of the small enterprises, which would never get the same help from the state, was used in Italy (where the work ethic of the North was opposed to the corruption of Rome and the South), in Switzerland (where Blocher made himself the defender of the *Mittelstand*), as well as in other countries.

The challenge to consensual and representative democracy appears, finally, in a another typical element of populism in these parties, namely, leadership. The parties analysed here are all characterised by a similar strong hierarchical internal structure centred around the figure of the leader (Taguieff, 2001). Instead of having a function of political representation, the leader incorporates and incarnates the true identity of the group, replaces the role of political and social organisations which are regarded with distrust, and embodies the natural communitarian identity of its members. The leader has a different type of representative function which is more oriented towards the reflection or the mirroring of the members of the group. The personal style of the leader reflects the social status, the educational background, and the personal values of the members. Because of this strong link between the leader and the members, the leaders of these movements are not only long-standing but also uncontested by rival leaderships. The leader is not in discussion and opposition to him is considered as a betrayal of the entire community that he represents. Organisationally, this translates into an "internal dictatorship" (as Chiantera-Stutte calls it in her chapter) in which frequent

---

[29] This is the idea of the losers of modernisation, which was mentioned earlier and can be found in several forms, from the reaction to new post-industrial forms of social organisation (Ignazi, 2003) to the consequences of modernisation, globalisation, and European integration (Kriesi, 1999b).

[30] This corresponds to the reaction against the success of left-libertarian movements that advocate individual self-accomplishment within increasingly tolerant and multi-cultural societies (Kitschelt, 1995).

rotations of the body loyal to the leader take place, and in which open opposition to the leader can lead to "purges" and expulsions.[31]

The challenge that populism addresses is, therefore, double. From within the system, populist parties oblige the establishment, the élites, the media and, above all, the traditional parties to look at the quality of democracy, to give a critical look at what democracy has become in an increasingly multi-layered political structure, with an open economy, with blurred borders between the public and private spheres, in which influences from external cultures bring about unaccountable power by international financial capitalism, with state and supra-state bureaucracies in which the role of citizens is close to nil. Given the strong traditions of local autonomies combined with an accentuated moralism and work ethic, this is stronger in the Alpine region. From outside the system, populist parties challenge the very principle of representative democracy by replacing political representation in the meaning of Burke – a parliamentary and deliberative representation – by a sociological representation, a "mirror" between the represented and the representatives, an incarnation of the people by the leader.[32] This appears notably in the style of the leadership of these parties, and in the territorial, social, and cultural correspondence with the represented people – more strongly identifiable in the Alpine region than elsewhere.

D. Challenges to European Integration

Today, these challenges which are delineated along the two dimensions of "identity" and "representation" are transferred – in the public discourse of populist parties – from the level of the nation-state to that of the EU and, more generally, to the process of European integration. What emerges from the contributions in this book is that the Alpine region and its regionalist-populist parties are Euro-sceptic. After an initial phase in which regions – in other areas of Europe, too – saw great opportunities not only for economic but also for institutional development in the emerging decentralised setting of the EU, in a second phase the parties under investigation turned against integration, in some cases virulently. However, instead of being merely and negatively "anti-European", these parties more positively put forward an alternative conception of Europe and of integration based on ethnic and religious

---

[31] The image is that of *tribun du peuple* applied to himself by the leader of the Swiss SVP Christoph Blocher. More generally, the fonction *tribunitienne* (the term is originally from G. Lavau in relation to the French Communist Party) described by Betz in his chapter fulfils, also on the analytical level, a constructive and corrective function where the representative and democratic process are perceived as static and inefficient.

[32] On the different types of representation, see Pitkin (1967).

identity, rather than on artificial and impersonal citizenship, with more subsidiarity and federalism in place of the current centralisation and cultural standardisation, with more power for small people against lobbies at EU level (a critique of "democratic deficit" more generally addressed to international organisations). Thus, the current type of integration is strongly attacked and challenged.

A first critique is addressed to the type of European identity emerging. First, on-going standardisation and homogenisation processes are perceived as a major threat to regional identities. Second, the impersonal and bureaucratic character of the new Europe (the "monster" of Brussels) leads to an artificial and impersonal citizenship. In contrast, the regionalist and populist parties of the Alpine region advocate a Europe of the People (originally, a leftist slogan), based on the "true" ethnic identities of European populations. The threat of an external "civic" idea of citizenship had, until that time, originated from the nation-state and its nationalisation of culture and identity. Today, this threat is increasingly perceived as coming from the EU and the corresponding reaction is that of a cultural and identitarian "retrenchment" in regional settings. The reaction includes a return to the "natural" elements of identity and to a closure with regard to external influences, namely, immigration.[33] The accent on the identity of Europe is put on the variety of its "peoples" – a pan-German and *Mitteleuropean* conception – but also on its unity under a classic and Christian history.[34]

Furthermore, this citizenship lacks its democratic element. The themes against the consociational and the élitist character of national decision-making are thus increasingly used to criticise the *modus operandi* of the EU. As Papadopoulos notes in his chapter, the process of Europeanisation constitutes an additional factor that increases the multi-level character of decision-making procedures, which aggravates the problems of accountability, and stimulates feelings of dispossession on the part of citizens. Once again, the rhetoric is directed against a geographically remote bureaucracy whose personnel is accused of ignoring the real problems of everyday life. The strong influence of lobbies and interest groups in "Brussels" is seen as a usurpation of popular sovereignty in that lobbies and interest groups are beyond any and all

---

[33] This corresponds to the idea of "Fortress Europe" built on the assertion of the specific values of the European culture as opposed to other cultures, the necessity to preserve the ethnic integrity in Europe, and the stress on the internal regional plurality of peoples and cultures in Europe.

[34] The accent on Christian values also entails a strong critique on the above-mentioned consumerism and individualism of the modern industrial and urban societies, as well as aggressive capitalism and international finance.

democratic control.[35] Feelings of disempowerment are reinforced by the perception that the process of European integration has weakened the influence of voters at the level of local and national parliaments, with elected bodies increasingly losing their decision-making autonomy as well as their capacity to intervene in the economy and the labour market, and thus seeing their margin of action as being substantially reduced. In contrast, the local and national democratic circuits are being curtailed by the loss of competences and autonomy through integration while, at European level, the reduced role of the European Parliament, the consociational and negotiational nature of decision-making processes, and the role of neo-corporatist practices through lobbies and interest groups, all serve to increase the feelings of democratic deficit and dispossession.[36]

Consequently, the deepening of integration with the centralisation of competences at EU level is another point of contrast. Here, the critiques concern the administrative standardisation from above, and the rules imposed from a distant and technocratic centre. In contrast, what is advocated by these parties is an increase of the federal elements of the EU and of the principle of subsidiarity. The European federative model – the Europe of the Regions on the model of the Swiss Confederation – should replace the current centralised model as a parallel process to the creation of a Europe of the People replacing the abstract character of European identity.

V. The Impact on the European Cleavage Constellation

What is the relationship between these alternative views of identity, democracy, and European integration and other cleavages? This last point is concerned with the question of whether or not the emergence of an alternative conception of democracy, identity, and European integration represents a cleavage that overlaps or cuts across the main cleavages of the European party system that emerged from the National and Industrial Revolutions during the 19th century. For one, the previous discussion based on the various chapters of the book suggests that the emerging cleavage constellation at European level is a more complex system of the dimensions of opposition and alliances than most analyses

---

[35] More generally, these critiques are extended to all supra-national and international organisations, such as the UN, the WTO, the World Bank, and the IMF. The scepticism toward international organisation is notably strong in Switzerland, which has a long tradition of isolationism.

[36] Examples of the virulent attacks by the *Lega Nord* on the EU and its fundamentally non-democratic, technocratic, and Jacobin nature of a "super-state" can be found in Caramani (2002). Anti-European positions were also frequent in the FPÖ and the CSU (against the Treaty of Maastricht and the European common currency).

of the European political space have hitherto argued by focusing on the left–right and pro/anti-European dimensions.

The first question concerns the "renaissance" of a territorial dimension in Europe (Kohler-Koch, 1998). For a long time, the literature has argued that processes of socio-economic modernisation in Western societies have definitively led to the integration of peripheral cultural identities and economic areas within broader political contexts and markets. Theories of state formation and nation-building, as well as of the hegemony of the left–right cleavage and class alignments, seemed to indicate the disappearance of the territorial and cultural dimension (Caramani, 2004). This uni-directional determinism has only recently been questioned (Keating, 1998) and, for a long time, ethno-linguistic, religious, and territorial identities were thought to "have lost in the game of history" (Urwin, 1983: 222). Yet, the disappearance of pre-industrial cleavages and territoriality cannot be taken for granted. The survival of old identities and the emergence of new ones can lead to the reappearance of a territorial dimension at European level, not only in terms of contrasts between nation-states, but also between transnational regions, such as the Alpine one, and the new forming EU centre. Indeed, such a territorial dimension could take the shape of a centre–periphery cleavage – even though, given the geopolitical and geo-economic centrality of the Alpine region, it is difficult to speak of it as a periphery – which seems to emerge from the cultural, administrative, and democratic dimensions of the opposition between the Alpine region and the emergence of a new centre at European level.

As the different analyses show, the centre–periphery dimension overlaps with cultural dimensions. Ethno-linguistic identities play an important role in matters of local or regional identity, in contrast to the above-mentioned abstract and universalistic civic citizenship (at national and at EU level). The same is true for religiosity and the Christian "roots" of Europe in comparison with the secularising attitudes of élites. This also entails an important rural–urban dimension which makes a contrast between the important role of religion and traditional *Weltanschauungen* in rural areas, and the more secularised attitude in the large urban centres. Furthermore, the common religious heritage of the Europeans is used to define the external boundaries as a delimitation with neighbouring civilizations such as Turkey and the Islamic world in general.

Concerning the rural–urban cleavage, this is a cleavage that has disappeared, or has been incorporated in other alignments within national cleavage landscapes. At EU level, this cleavage is re-emerging as a consequence of the important resources for the Common Agricultural Policy controlled by the EU and through the alliances of the "integration losers" (economically weak producers and peripheral regions).

47

Contrasts, here, focus on the support for specific economic activities, such as agriculture (through the Common Agricultural Policy), the small and medium-sized enterprises, and shopkeepers. Furthermore, protectionists attitudes may contrast with liberalisation and privatising policies in the form of anti-redistribution positions, "locals first" in the labour market, maintenance of local wealth (taxation and ecological resources). Finally, this dimension concerns issues of protection of natural resources, from the control of transportation axes to energy sources.

How do these dimensions relate to the left–right opposition? Here, the findings support the hypothesis that the cleavage constituted by an alternative political culture and vision of European integration is cross-cutting, rather than overlapping, the left–right dimension. The development of a critical image of European integration takes place in an alliance of integration losers at the extremes of the left–right spectrum (Schmitter, 2000: 68). This alliance is composed of the extremes of the political spectrum (extreme left-wing and extreme neo-populist right-wing parties), but is also composed of other party families (*e.g.*, green parties, regionalist parties, religious parties, etc.). Here, contrasts not only concern the strong critique in terms of the democratic deficit of the EU, which relates to the anti-party, anti-establishment, and anti-lobby distrust towards élite institutions and bureaucracies, but also concern the defence of welfare provisions whose cuts (necessary because of policies of deficit reduction, low inflation, and monetary stability, combined with low economic growth and aging population) affect the weaker strata of the population.

In conclusion, therefore, the case-study carried out in this book on the Alpine region shows that the specificities of this area do, indeed, lead to an alternative vision of democracy, identity, and European integration. This alternative image represents a challenge – which is mainly posed by regionalist and populist right-wing parties – both at national and EU levels, as well as a new cleavage. This new cleavage is part of a forming European-wide constellation and interacts with other industrial and pre-industrial cleavages. *It overlaps with the main pre-industrial cleavages* – centre–periphery, rural–urban, ethno-linguistic, and religious – and *cuts-across the most important industrial cleavage* – namely, the left–right dimension.

VI. The Structure of the Book

The book divided in two parts: the first thematic part is devoted to the Alpine case as a whole, while the second part is devoted to the different cases. The three chapters in Part I (*The Alpine Case*) address a number of topics that are common to all the cases analysed in the book: political cultures and identity, cleavages, consociationalism and corporatist accommodation, regionalism and populism. In Part II (*The Alpine Cases*), the different parties and regions are analysed either through in-depth analyses or comparatively through juxtaposition with other parties. This part includes both cases of strong challenges to the existing systems (both nation-wide and from regional organisations), and cases of successful integration in the system and continuity.

PART I

THE ALPINE CASE

CHAPTER 1

Regionalism in the Alps
Subnational, Supranational, and Transnational[1]

Michael KEATING

I. The New Regionalism

Regionalism has become an important theme in European politics and the term covers a number of distinct, but related, phenomena. First, there is sub-state regionalism, a reconfiguration of politics within the state, which produces a new balance between centre and periphery and various types of institutional reform. Second, there is supranational regionalism, a concept used in international relations to refer to a grouping of states themselves. The best known example of this is the European Union (EU). Third, linking the two, is transnational regionalism, in which regional movements of the first type seek to extend their sphere of action beyond state borders through co-operation with other regions, cross-border co-operation, or by acting within the European institutional structures. This may involve larger regions such as the Nordic area, the (British) Isles or *Mitteleuropa*, which are smaller than Europe as a whole or the EU, and may lack supranational institutions. This has created a new political game, the Europe of the Regions, which has given an ideological and thematic guide to region-builders as well as providing various opportunities for action and policy-making.

Regionalism also has a number of dimensions (Keating, 1998). There is the *functional* one, stemming from changes in the significance of space for economic development, the maintenance and development of culture, and for the welfare state. Of these, the most important is the economic dimension, as new local and regional territorial production systems have emerged. Regions, previously the objects of state policy

---
[1] Monika de Frantz and Jonathan Wheatley assisted in the research on which this chapter is based, with funding from the Research Council of the European University Institute. I am grateful to Monika de Frantz and to Daniele Caramani for comments on an earlier draft.

which aimed to integrate them into national economies, have constituted themselves as actors and started to compete within the state and, more broadly, in European and global markets. Regionalism also has a dimension related to *culture and identity*, particularly in areas populated by national minorities, or with their own languages; in this sense, it is entangled with the issue of ethnic and nationality politics. There is a *political* dimension, as territory has become a more important theme for political mobilisation, and interests have been given a territorial expression. Historic centre–periphery tensions have re-emerged and new territorial cleavages have appeared. Finally, regionalism has an *institutional* expression, as all the large states of Europe and some of the smaller ones have adopted various forms of intermediate or "meso" government between the state and the municipal level (Sharpe, 1993).

This means that European regionalism is a rather heterogeneous phenomenon and that we can certainly not speak of a single European model (Le Galès and Lequesne, 1997). On the other hand, there are certain common themes. Regions have become an important level for the organisation of economic development, with the rise of local and regional economic development coalitions, including business, trade unions, social movements and governments, although the balance of social interests varies from one to another. Regional government tends to be characterised not by traditional bureaucratic administration, but by steering and co-ordination, although some regional governments have important service delivery responsibilities. The various meanings of regionalism show a certain tendency to converge, as political regionalism takes up the theme of economic development, linked to culture and identity. Minority nations and national minorities show some tendency to territorialise, as this gives them the possibility of institutional expression and recognition within the state and within Europe. These effects, however, are not constants, but variables, depending on the case in question (Keating, forthcoming).

Political regionalism comes associated with an array of ideologies, and is not inherently linked to any one of them. In the late 19th century, many regionalist movements were conservative and traditionalist, opposed to the modernising, secular state, although even in this period there were progressive regionalisms (Keating, 1988). In the 20th century, regionalism was a theme taken up by Christian Democrats in the core of Europe around the Alps as an expression of subsidiarity, community, and tradition. Another regionalism, emerging from the 1950s, was modernising, supported by business, trade union and academic élites, the *forces vives*, and often combined with support for technical solutions and planning. By the 1980s, this had matured into "bourgeois regionalism" (Harvie, 1994), a strategy for regional business élites in partnership with public institutions to promote development and competitiveness in European and global markets.[2]

In the 1960s a leftist regionalism appeared, tied to the libertarian left, the 1968 generation and, later, ecology, opposed equally to big business and the big state, and emphasising themes of self-management and "small is beautiful." For a while, the concept of internal colonialism gave these movements an ideological link to the traditional left, as well as a parallel with contemporary struggles in the Third World (Lafont, 1967). In the course of the 1970s and 1980s, the social democratic parties too started to move away from centralisation, rediscovering the decentralist and localist traditions of the early movement. Regionalism was also a way for them to recover support lost to new social movements, environmentalists, and minority nationalists. Local and regional culture, previously seen as a buttress of conservative values and ways, has been re-invented in a form of modernised tradition, and the folklore and music re-assessed to emphasise its popular and anti establishment themes. Generally speaking, there has been a growth in left-wing regionalisms and in bourgeois, modernising regionalism, although the traditional conservative version remains strong in some parts of Europe. Some movements, as we will see, succeed precisely by combining elements of different models, using place itself as the integrative factor and defying the contrast between tradition and modernity.

Regionalists tended at one time to be rather hostile to European integration, seeing the European level as even more remote and insensitive than the host state. Over the years this has changed, as regionalists see opportunities in the new supranational spaces to assert themselves and circumvent state borders. This has a practical dimension, connected with the opportunities for regions to co-operate in economic and other projects, and to act within European institutions. It also has an important ideological dimension, in giving the regionalists cosmopolitan credentials, in placing their demands in an international context, and in exploring new forms of autonomy beyond the nation-state formula altogether (Keating, 2001). The theme of Europe has become an important one for many regionalist movements, and much hope has been invested in it as a formula that would allow us to escape old arguments about separatism, self-determination, and boundaries.

Other transnational spaces have served similar purposes, including the concept of "the Isles" (or, in the Irish version, "these islands") as a de-nationalised framework for the Northern Ireland problem; the Nordic

---

[2] There is a right-wing variant on this, based on the argument that, in a competitive European market, wealthy regions no longer can, or need to, subsidise their poorer compatriots through fiscal equalisation and regional policies. Regionalism has also, on occasion, been linked to the extreme right and to populism.

area, which allows for functional co-operation and shared values without touching the sensitive theme of national sovereignty; Southern Europe, introducing a common frame within Europe; or *Mitteleuropa*, with its historic connotations and multiple meanings. One condition for the rise of such regional spaces and for inter-state and inter-regional co-operation is the very fixedness of borders in Western Europe, which allows them to be penetrated without challenging their existence.

Yet, not all regionalist and minority nationalist movements are pro-European. There is a residual Euro-scepticism, which may be on the increase especially in the Alpine region, suspicious of European centralisation and of cultural uniformity. Extreme right regionalisms do not find a place in a Europe committed to liberal values, as the *Vlaams Blok* and *Lega Nord* have both found.

This all gives great variety to regionalism and regionalist movements but, at the risk of simplification, we can distinguish two ideal types, an old and a new regionalism (Keating, 1998). *Old regionalists* are conservative, traditionalist, tied into traditional social networks, defensive and Euro-sceptic. They are, in fact, less regionalist than localist, although surveys sometimes confound the various levels. *New regionalists* are politically progressive and modernising, they interpret local culture in a less conservative mode and their reference point is the imagined community of the region, rather than the locality, and they are pro-Europe. Since grasping the regional level involves a certain abstraction, they tend to be more highly educated and politically efficacious.

There is some support for this in survey data across Europe, although differences in questions and methodology make it hard to draw firm comparative conclusions (Jiménez Blanco *et al.*, 1977; Lilli and Hartig, 1995; Dupoirier and Roy, 1995; OIP, 1997). The failure to distinguish territorial levels might also explain the surprising finding of some Eurobarometer surveys (1991, 1995) that regionalism is strongest in countries such as Portugal, Greece, and Ireland, which do not have regions; what is being measured here is really localism. As with all ideal types, we cannot overlay the distinction between old and regionalism on to real life cases, which tend to be a mixture of the two, often in considerable tension. Some of the most successful cases of regional mobilisation are the work of leaders who can precisely synthesise these discordant themes in a form of modernised traditionalism and then project this into state politics and into the emerging transnational spaces (see Wagemann's and Pallaver's contributions in this volume on the CSU and *Südtiroler Volkspartei* respectively).

II. Regionalism in the Alps

These factors can be used to identify commonalities and differences among European regional movements. The question here is whether there is an *Alpine type of regionalism*, at sub-state level, at transnational level, and in the supranational arenas of Europe, the Alpine geo-region, or some other framework. The counter-hypothesis is that there are various forms of regionalism, rooted in the individual states that have Alpine territory, or in the ethnic or linguistic divisions of the area.

There are certainly some common factors in the Alps. The area was incorporated into nation-states at a late historical stage and has political traditions rooted in empire and in political fragmentation, with an emphasis on local sources of authority and resistance to centralism. Without falling into geographic determinism, we can perhaps say that the mountainous nature of the area encourages localism and differentiation. All politics in the Alps seems to have a local dimension; there is a tradition of distinct local parties, and even the national parties need to adapt their message to local conditions. Yet, despite the isolation of many valleys, it is not a European periphery, but an area of transit. It is also the meeting place of empires, nation-building projects, and three major linguistic groups: Germanic, Romance, and Slavic. From the 19th century, with the rise of ethnic and linguistic nationalism, it was the site of a great deal of tension, and the traditional mechanisms of government came under strain, finally breaking down with the absorption into nation-states, most of which entertained irredentist designs on their neighbours. This is not favourable terrain for transnational regionalism, although with the relaxation of tensions and the new recognition of borders, there may be an opportunity to re-discover a usable past of accommodation, tolerance, and co-existence within a generally shared value framework and transnational order.

On first looking at the experience of Alpine regionalism, I was inclined to sustain the hypothesis that underlies the theme of this book, that this is a conservative, traditional, and Euro-sceptic region. There are many signs of the *old regionalism*. The concept of *Heimat* (in Bavaria and Austria), indeed, encapsulates much of this, with its invocation of place, homeland, and timeless tradition. The very ambiguity of the term, which can be applied at different spatial levels, from the local, through the regional, to the national, lends itself to an old regionalism, in which levels of belonging are nested, and can be used for different purposes, but with a similar emotive function.

Regionalism is frequently associated with conservative politics here. Tradition too is conservative, in contrast to other European regions, where neo-traditionalism, if not appropriated by yuppies and corporations, sustains the politics of protest and dissent. Ecology, too, is given a conservative bent, with the Alpine imagery of a pristine landscape threatened by modernisation, change, and European intrusion, in contrast to the leftist regionalism or many European Greens. Dialect is used freely by Conservative political leaders to connect with their followers, in a way that would be inconceivable in many other parts of Europe. There is a strong populist element connected with this, and a certain xenophobia and anti-immigrant sentiment. An emphasis is placed on the interests of small producers and the Alpine ethic of hard work and self-reliance (Betz, in this volume). We also find a regionalism of the wealthy (in Bavaria and Northern Italy), with complaints about subsidising poorer parts of the state.

There is widespread Euro-scepticism, but it differs from Nordic or British Euro-scepticism. Europe is accepted and, indeed, invoked, but at the same time held in suspicion. Supranationalism is downplayed in favour of a Europe of the nation-states *and* regions, with proper respect for subsidiarity and the repatriation of many functions currently handled in Brussels. Nor is there much transnational political co-operation. The European Free Alliance is the transnational party of regionalists and minority nationalists, allied in the European Parliament with the Greens, and strongly committed to a supranational Europe. Its Alpine members tend to be very small and marginal parties, in contrast to those from Spain, the United Kingdom, and Belgium, where they represent substantial, and sometimes governing, parties.

A. The Germanic Zone

Closer examination, however, reveals a more complex picture. Many of the features of "Alpine" regionalism apply to the German-speaking parts, with some spillover into neighbouring regions, including Italy. Even generalisations about these parts, however, must take important national differences into account.

The Bavarian CSU is a clear case of conservative regionalism, which has combined tradition with modernity. Although it reaches well beyond the Alpine regions, Alpine imagery does form a part of its make-up, although far from the whole (Wagemann, in this volume). Claims are made to deep historical roots, to Bavaria as the "oldest state in Europe" (CSU, 1993), as the basis for building an incorporating modern identity (Mintzel, 1990b). CSU discourse is full of references to *Heimat* and the role of the CSU as *the* Bavarian party. There is an emphasis on Christian values as the basis for solidarity, and a rejection of multi-culturalism (Sutherland, 2001b). As in many regionalist movements, its imagery is taken from the regional periphery and the Alpine mountains, rooted in family and community, but this is combined with a modernising economic discourse which appeals to the middle classes and city dwellers. The appeal is both rational and instrumental (*for Bavaria: with hearts and minds*); both traditional and modern (*Laptop und Lederhosen*) (Sutherland, 2001b). This is a form of bourgeois regionalism with echoes elsewhere, including late 19th-century Catalonia.

There is no rejection of Germany, but there is a distinct way of being part of a broader German family, including a strong emphasis on regional culture, dialect, and tradition. This folk Bavarianism and strong defensive regionalism helped to see off the challenge of the *Bayern-partei* and of separatist tendencies in the late 1940s and early 1950s (Parkes, 1997), but proved an obstacle to Bavarian aspirants to German national leadership until the arrival of Edmund Stoiber, whose sober technocratic image belied the stereotype (although he still lost). Germany's federal system allows the party to play the autonomist card, while making clear what the limits are.[3] The CSU is also able to play upon a certain Euro scepticism, appealing to its core vote and the farming lobby (including the many part-time and hobby farmers), while not calling Germany's role in Europe into question. Instead, the party stresses a Europe of Nations and Regions, with more subsidiarity, and has consistently called for the repatriation of important functions in competition, environmental policy, and other fields. There was suspicion about the Euro and about EU enlargement, although these came to be accepted as facts by the realistic and pro-business leadership of the party.

Some of these features can be seen in German Switzerland. Federalism allows a strong defence of cantonal interests, without suggestions of disloyalty to the nation. Themes of *Heimat* are strong, with the same flexible range of references, and regionalism is allied with social conservatism. There is the same need to integrate the mountain periphery, a source of the cultural images, with the cities and their internationalised economic base, which reflects the historical struggles "between city and country, between enlightened, rationalist cosmopolitanism and clerical, pious, democratic conservatism" (Steinberg, 1996: 84). The German Swiss identify with Switzerland (where they are the majority) and with their locality, rather than the canton, and the myth of the old self-contained community is strongest among the older, immobile, and less educated (Kriesi, 1998), suggesting an "old regionalist" or localist orientation. Euro-scepticism is pronounced among Swiss Germans, but class and urban–rural divisions are also important, with the older, rural people most strongly opposed. In the 2001 citizen-initiative referendum "Yes for Europe", the rural German cantons registered support in single fig-

---

[3] This corresponds to the pattern that one can observe in the case of the *Lega dei Ticinesi* in federal Switzerland (see Mazzoleni, in this volume).

ures or the low teens, while the cities scored in the 1920s. The German Swiss nationalism does bridge these divisions in a mixture of tradition and modernity which is reminiscent of Bavaria, but at local and regional level the contrasts are marked.

Similar themes are visible in Austria, although the state history is quite different. Nationalism until the 1950s was pan-German, while localism was rooted in traditionalist and conservative themes. With the consolidation of the Austrian state, a certain regionalism has developed in the Alpine areas of Carinthia, Salzburg, and Steiermark, building on these localist traditions. One part of this is well to the right. Jörg Haider, while not pursuing his ambitions at federal level, has taken a strong line of regionalism in Carinthia and his party was, until the 1980s, rooted in the rural and mountain areas. Haider makes great use of Alpine tradition and folklore, appearing regularly at *Frühschoppen* where he can tie his appeal to tradition and custom (Gingrich, 2002). His line on Europe was that of a Europe of Nations (*Vaterländer*) and Regions, combined with a barely concealed contempt for his Slavic neighbours (Haider, 2003), but in recent years it, like the *Lega Nord*, has turned Euro-sceptic (Pelinka and Betz, in this volume). In Salzburg, on the other hand, the *Österreichische Volkspartei* (ÖVP) leadership has been a leading protagonist of the Europe of the Regions, and has been strongly engaged in inter-regional associations, while, at the same time, excluding the *Freiheitliche Partei Österreichs* (FPÖ) from the coalition, thus breaking with the usual Austrian tradition of inclusive government at *Land* level.

In Südtirol/Alto Adige, we find the familiar themes of primitive independence, localism, liberty, and tradition. The myth of Tyrolese independence and love of liberty is represented by the heroic figure of Andreas Hofer and his resistance to both French and Bavarian domination. Politics, however, has been shaped by ethnic competition with the Italian-speaking population in Trentino which, after the Second World War, was placed in the same special-status region, to deprive it of a German-speaking majority. The representation of the German speakers is dominated by the *Südtiroler Volksparei*, a catch-all conservative regionalist party that has used the ethnic cleavage to establish a dominant position (Minarik, 1999; Pallaver, in this volume). It is a member of the European People's Party (EPP) and has some links with the Austrian ÖVP.

Without renouncing the right of self-determination, the *Südtiroler Volkspartei* has played within Italian politics to gain increased autonomy and a very favourable financial settlement. This, in turn, has allowed it to establish a clientelistic network within the German-speaking community. The *Südtiroler Volkspartei* does play to themes of traditionalism, localism, and *Heimat*, as well as to stereotypes of Germanic and

Latin characters. Its emphasis on ethnic boundaries is not merely a response to conditions on the ground, but a strategy for maintaining the sub-culture and networks that are the basis for its support. However, it has faced increasing competition since the 1990s. The *Südtiroler Freiheitlichen* is a far-right party akin to Haider's party in Austria. The *Union für Südtirol*, which campaigns on the dual themes of *Heimat* and *Zukunft*, linking past and future, is a member of the European Free Alliance. It favours a European Free State uniting the Italian and Austrian parts of the Tyrol, within a united Europe of Regions and Peoples (Union für Südtirol, 2002); this Europhilia marks it out among the Germanic parties of the Alps. Both have made some progress in local elections, reducing the *Südtiroler Volkspartei*'s hegemony over representation of the German community.

These common themes of regionalism and localism in the German areas are sustained by contact among politicians and ideological diffusion. The state context, however, is very different. In Bavaria and Carinthia, it is possible to play against the centre, whether this be Berlin, Vienna, or Brussels, a target that is largely absent in Switzerland but which the *Lega dei ticinesi* still uses. This orientation towards the state also discourages the emergence of a pan-German regionalism, although there are transnational initiatives of various sorts (discussed below). In Tyrol and Carinthia, ethnic competition has encouraged identification with the titular nation rather than autonomous regionalism, although the titular nation itself has changed over time from German to Austrian.

B. The Italian Zone

Regionalism in the Alpine areas of Italy has been dominated by the presence of the *Lega Nord,* which from its base in Lombardy reached out to incorporate other regionalist protest groups in the course of the 1990s. The *Lega* ideology incorporates many of the "Germanic" features observed above, including populism, a conservative vision of the world, and opposition to immigration. Similarly, it is rooted in older local identities, which it has tried to weave into an imagined community of "Padania" (Biorcio, 1991, 1997), while claiming ancient roots (Oneto, 1997). The demotic appeal is reinforced by the use of dialect, and a conscious contrast is made between the plain-speaking honest "Padanians" and the manipulative politicians of Rome. As elsewhere, history has been used to create a myth of liberty and primitive independence, focused on the oath taken at Pontida by the original *Lega Lombarda* to resist the Emperor Barbarossa. The *Lega* has held its position much better in the small towns and rural areas of Northern Lombardy than in Milan and the other big cities.

In some areas, it has come to dominate local representation, succeeding the Christian Democrats as representatives of the local sub-culture (Cento Bull and Gilbert, 2001), taking over existing networks or building its own. During the 1990s, the *Lega* sought to break out of the role of localist protest party, positioning itself as an ethnic nationalist party determined to create a new state within Europe. However, its attempts to make allies among the nationalist and regionalist parties of Europe failed, and, after it entered the first Berlusconi government in 1994, it was excluded from the European Free Alliance (Lynch, 1996). By the early 2000s, it had turned virulently anti-European, allowing it to tap into local populism, but leaving it no external support system for "Padania" other than the Italian state. Alpine themes do not recur much in the *Lega*'s imagery and propaganda, as its remit is far wider. Oneto's (1997) ideological construction of "Padania" notes that the Alps unite people rather than dividing them, but does not pursue the question of Alpine culture and traditions.

Severe tensions have persisted within the *Lega* over its recognition of regional diversity within the North. Venetian and Fruilian movements have consistently maintained their own identity despite the authoritarian and centralised nature of the *Lega* under Umberto Bossi's leadership. These are generally right wing and have, in some cases, drifted into the orbit of Haider. Some have adopted *Mitteleuropa* themes, a long way from the "Padanian" vision, and there is some evidence of commonality in values across Bavaria and North-West Italy (Chauvel, 1995). On the other side of the political spectrum there is a left-wing regionalism which seeks to break with the ethnic nationalism of much of Northern Italy. Riccardo Illy, an independent of the centre-left and successively mayor of Trieste and president of the region Friuli-Venezia-Giulia, has adopted strongly new regionalist themes, with a view to placing the region at the centre of its geo-economic space and exploiting the opportunities of EU enlargement. This includes promoting an inclusive regionalism, to include the Slovene minorities, a *Mitteleuropa* vision and a commitment to cross-border co-operation.

Political behaviour in Trentino-Alto Adige (see above) is strongly influenced by ethnic patterns. In Südtirol/Alto Adige, the Italian voters, confronted with the Germans, have preferred the strident Italian nationalism of *Alleanza Nazionale* to the regionalist vision of the *Lega* or other autonomist parties. In Trentino, politics was until the 1980s dominated by the *Democrazia Cristiana*, which did almost as well as the *Südtiroler Volkspartei* did in the neighbouring province. Since then, the Italian parties share most of the vote. There is a tradition of independent politics represented earlier by the *Partito Popolare Trentino Tirolese* and now the *Partito Autonomista Trentino Tirolese,* which gets between

10 and 12% of the votes. It favours a Europe of the Regions and cross-border co-operation but – fearing Tirolese or Austrian irredentism – opposes any supranational elements including the new Euro-Region (see below). The *Movimento Autonomisti Trentini* is more favourable to the Euro-Region, but is also concerned to retain the present Autonomous region and fearful of pan-Tyrolean ideas. The *Lega Nord* has found increasing difficulty incorporating these distinct elements. In the 2001 elections, it only managed 3.7% in Trentino-Alto Adige, against 12.1% in Lombardy and 10.2% in Veneto.

In Ticino, particularism is represented by the *Lega dei Ticinesi*, a right-wing, populist, anti-immigrant and anti-European party which, in 2003, allied itself federally with the Swiss People's Party (SVP). It mixes strong Swiss nationalism with regional defence, and has some family resemblance to the *Lega Nord*, except for its tendency to rail against the domination of Milan over the region. Ticino's vote in the citizen-initiative referendum on Europe in 2001 was close to that of the rural German canton's, reflecting a strongly Euro-sceptic tradition.

C. Slovenia

A visitor to Slovenia is quickly welcomed to "the sunny side of the Alps." This is both a tourist slogan and a subtle reminder that this is not the Balkans. There is a strong ethnic identity based on language and tradition that persisted during Hapsburg times even in the absence of institutional recognition. Slovene traditions are permeated with localist themes, the spirit of *Heimat* and an ideal of the uncorrupted peasantry, although in the 20th century this gave way to a nationalist spirit and eventually, in 1991, to statehood (Hladnik, 1991). Independence was linked to the project of joining Europe in advance of the other republics of Yugoslavia, and, while there is a certain Euro-scepticism shared with the German Alpine regions, there has been little question about Slovenia being part of the next EU enlargement. *Mitteleuropa* has also featured as unifying theme, but there are recurrent fears of Italian irredentism, which hindered transnational regionalism during the 1990s.

D. The French Zone

Regionalism in the French speaking areas of Switzerland, in French Savoy, and in Val d'Aosta in Italy has been less marked by Germanic ideas of tradition, locality, and *Heimat*, and has tended to be politically more progressive. These areas escaped incorporation into neighbouring states for too long, and have retained a sense of local identity as well as a transnational tradition. Savoy was an independent duchy, home of the dynasty that ruled the Kingdom of Piedmont and Sardinia. It long existed at the edge of the French orbit, and was finally incorporated in

1860 as payment for Napoleon III's support for Italian unity. France, however, had to concede a free trade zone in Haute-Savoie so that the locals could maintain their economic links with Geneva, the rest of Switzerland and, beyond that, Germany (Le Roy Ladurie, 2001). It supplemented the existing "neutral zone" created in 1815 in Northern Savoie, which represented a continuation of the Swiss area of neutrality.

This Alpine vocation has remained a feature of local culture, as has the idea that Savoy was incorporated by treaty, whose terms were subsequently violated, rendering it void. Within Savoy, the *Mouvement Région Savoie* (MRS) was founded in 1971 to campaign for a separate Savoy region. With the failure of this idea the following year, it remained in existence as a loose social movement to defend the interests of Savoy within the larger region. In 1994, the *Ligue Savoisienne* was founded by Patrice Abeille on the platform of a "sovereign state of Savoy." Their historic grievance is that Savoy was annexed in 1860 through a bogus referendum, in which the people were not given the option of joining Switzerland. They have made limited headway, gaining 6.1% of the votes in Savoie and 4.8% in Haute-Savoie (in addition to 3.7% for the MRS) in the regional elections of 1998. Both Savoy parties are members of the European Free Alliance, putting them on the progressive side of politics.

Since the 1970s, Savoy has been part of the modern French region Rhône-Alpes which, although an artificial creation, has established a certain identity as a leader in regional development, institutional development, and high technology industry (Jouve, 1998). In its case, the Alpine imagery is linked to a high quality of life, to attract qualified incomers and clean, modern industry, rather than a cultural theme or traditionalism. This is closer to the modernising or bourgeois regionalism of Northern Europe. It is also located within the French system of functional regionalism and spatial planning that produced the region in the first place, and Europe – as a challenge, a market, and a policy set – has reinforced this orientation.

The Val d'Aosta is officially the French-speaking part of Italy, although, historically, the language was a dialect of Occitan. Like Trentino-Alto Adige and Friuli-Venezia-Giulia, it has a special autonomy status conceded after the Second World War to ward off irredentist pressures. Representation is dominated by the *Union Valdôtaine*, founded in 1945, which heads the regional government. Its politics are of the progressive left and its martyr is Emile Chanoux, a Resistance fighter killed by the Nazis. It favours a federal Europe and a Swiss-type canton for its own region, and generally stresses Alpine themes. Other, smaller autonomist groups are Christian Democrat in orientation, and two of them merged in 2002 to form the *Stella Alpina*. In the Italian Parliament, the

Union Valdôtaine has just one seat, elected in a first-past-the-post constituency, putting a premium on unity. At the 2001 elections, the autonomist parties agreed on a single candidate under the heading *Vallée d'Aoste*, who won with 35% of the vote. The *Union Valdôtaine* is a member of the European Free Alliance, supporting a federal Europe of regions, ethnic groups and cultures.

French speaking parts of Switzerland have not shown the hostility to Europe found in the German rural areas and show a greater willingness to co-operation among themselves (Kriesi, 1999a; Steiner, 2001). In the 2001 referendum on Europe, the French cantons showed 40–44% support for Europe, against a national average of 23%.

III. Supranational Regionalism and Europe

The Alpine region is characterised by great social, cultural, and political diversity, but this itself is not an obstacle to supranationalism European integration is built precisely on the idea of unity in diversity and the need to come together to protect that diversity in the face of global forces. Both in Western and in Central-Eastern Europe, sub-state regionalists and nationalists have embraced the European frame as an instrument for gaining more autonomy.

This has happened in the Alpine region only to a limited extent. Euro-scepticism persists in the *Lega Nord*, in German and Italian Switzerland, in Austria and, in a milder and different form, in Bavaria. Here, the theme of Europe of the Regions is interpreted to mean that Europe should, wherever possible, keep out of the affairs of the regions. Slovenia, having achieved statehood, is more interested in a Europe of the nation-states. Ethnic competition across much of the Alps has raised defensive barriers, sustained by the self-interest of politicians and parties. In the French-speaking areas, in some of the Italian cases, and even in one German-speaking case, however, there is a clear link between European integration and regional autonomy, although as elsewhere there is a lot of vagueness as to how this is to be realised. The relaxation of border tensions since the 1990s has encouraged these movements, while the strengthening of the European level holds the prospect that opening to the outside does not carry the risk of being dominated by one's neighbours.

The EU itself has encouraged an Alpine vision, especially after Austrian accession in 1995, and with the prospect of enlargement to Slovenia and Hungary. This is driven by policy considerations, given the centrality of the Alpine region in the enlarging Europe and the importance of economic development, transport, and environmental issues. There is a plethora of initiatives of a functional and technical nature. An Alpine

Convention was signed in 1995 with the Commission and relevant states and regions, including non-members. In 2001 an INTERREG III B programme was launched, with a view to fitting the Alpine region into the European Spatial Development Perspective (see map on page 28). These top-down initiatives do not seem to arouse the suspicion and visceral opposition that they might have provoked in the past, but they are not accompanied by any great effort at affective region-building. There is no pan-Alpine spirit or ideology to sustain them or to provide symbolic rewards for politicians to participate in them.

IV. Transnational Regionalism

Transnational regionalism refers to initiatives within the Alpine area to build new political communities and to co-operate across borders. Again, the recognition of borders should facilitate this, reducing suspicions about separatism and irredentism, as should the relaxation of ethnic tensions. In fact, there is a variety of transnational experiences, but not all of them point in the same direction.

While the ideologies and attitudes surveyed above are generally rooted in local and national traditions, there is a certain transnational diffusion. Haiderism has been exported to parts of Northern Italy, where the ground had been prepared by existing local traditions and by the *Lega Nord*. A number of local politicians broke away from the *Lega* and other parties to found local movements explicitly inspired by Haider and a certain idea of Europe. In 2001 for example, a *Lega* councillor in Varese formed an electoral list *Europa con Haider*, while two *Alleanza Nazionale* leaders in Udine formed *Haider per la Libertà*. Haider (2003) himself has accorded the Northern Italians a more favourable, "Austrian" stereotype, in contrast to the Slavic Slovenes. There are links between Austrian rightists and Bavaria, diffusing the same localist, regionalist, and Euro-sceptic message. In this way, a larger market is created for rightist-populist regionalism, although this only seems to be in the Italian and the German-speaking areas. The French extreme right remains statist, centralist, and Euro-sceptic.

Again, co-operation is easier on functional matters, and becomes more difficult as it strays into cultural and political questions. As early as 1963, there were initiatives for co-operation in the region of Basle, *Regio Basiliensis*, bringing together Swiss, French, and German localities. Over time, this developed into a complex network of conferences, linkages, and working parties, including the *Regio TriRhena* and a Euro-Region funded by the INTERREG programme. It is generally cited in the literature as a successful example of functional co-operation. Another early example of transnational regional co-operation is the Alp-Adria Working Group, founded in 1978, following the settlement of border issues between Italy, Yugoslavia, and Austria. Its original members were Friuli-Venezia-Giulia, Trentino-Alto Adige, Carinthia, Upper Austria, Steiermark, Slovenia, and Croatia. Later, they were joined by Salzburg, Bavaria, and Lombardy, and, in 1986, by Ticino and two Hungarian regions (Necak, 2001). It is a light organisation without a permanent bureaucracy, and has focused on functional co-operation in practical matters such as transport, the environment, and research, keeping away from sensitive issues of nationality or language.

Even this depoliticised form, however, attracted opposition from some localist and regionalist groups. With the end of the Cold War and following the Balkan wars, it took on a new significance as a forum for regional co-operation, and there were efforts to create an imaginary space and historical image. Europe is presented as a way to overcome past divisions and recover some of the common history forgotten during the era of nationalism. The principal historical reference, however, is *Mitteleuropa*. In 1982, the Working Community of the Eastern Alps (COTRAO) was founded by German and Italian regions and Swiss cantons. Again, the emphasis is on functional co-operation, to the point that, in 1999, the six standing committees were abolished and replaced by working groups based on whatever precise task was at hand.[4]

Cross-border co-operation in the Tyrol region has developed since a treaty was signed between Italy and Austria on the subject in 1993, and the Austrian accession to the EU two years later. In 1995, the Austrian Tyrol and the Italian autonomous provinces of South Tyrol and Trentino opened a joint office in Brussels. After some years of preparation, a Euro-region was launched in 1998. Again, this is not intended to abolish the frontier or unite the Tyrolean territories, but to promote functional co-operation. Responding to fears that it would lead to a Greater Tyrol, Lorenzo Dallai, president of the Trento province, insisted that it was a substitute for such designs: "con i localismi e micro-nazionalismi vagheggiati da Haider in Austria non si costruisce l'Europa delle Regioni. Però è arrivato il momento di affrontare la gestione dei confini in chiave transnazionale". (*Il Sole – 24 Ore*, 9 December 1999).

The Alpine region has thus not developed those middle-range transnational spaces that could lift questions out of the local context while not taking them all the way to Europe. There is nothing like the Nordic area or the British Isles. *Mitteleuropa* comes up repeatedly in transnational initiatives in the Eastern Alps and the Adriatic area. It is a power-

---

4   There is also a political movement called the *Alpi-Adria*, not be confused with the transnational region. This is a right-wing, anti-immigrant group created in Vicenza, but linked to groups in Bavaria and Austria. Its policy, designed by a former *Lega Nord* "guru", Gianfranco Miglio (2001), is to create European macro-regions to replace the nation-states.

ful image but one that has several distinct meanings and a range of geographical referents (Maier, 1994). Most of them depict a transnational space, an idealised vision of the old Hapsburg empire, and a meeting place between East and West. Sometimes, the reference is a-spatial to a cosmopolitan culture before the rise of ethnic/territorial nationalism (Konstantinovic, 2001). In the Alpine context, the theme is given the whole variety of meanings and exploited by both left and right. It is a powerful image for overcoming the differences between the Slavic and Germanic groups, but does not cover the Alpine region as a whole while, at the same time, going well beyond it.

Conclusion

Regionalism in the Alps is thus strong, highly localised, and differentiated, almost forming a microcosm of Europe as a whole. Territorial regionalism is overlaid with the ethnic/linguistic cleavage that has predominated since the 19th century. "Alpine" self-images and visions of the other are not consistent across the region and are mediated by ethnic stereotypes, such as that of the orderly Germans and the boisterous Italians, and mutual contact may even reinforce these (Berghold, 1997).

Regionalism is also strongly shaped by the various state arenas, despite the late arrival of the nation-state in the region. The political and cultural dimensions of regionalism are not, however, always well articulated, and there is a tendency for larger projects for region-building in the state and European context to be undermined by persistent localism and cultural specificity. There is a growing sense of economic regionalism, much of it coming from the challenges and opportunities of the European single market. This is not always well linked to cultural or political regionalism except, perhaps, in Bavaria, where the dominant party has achieved a synthesis of localism, regionalism, nationalism and Europeanism, combining tradition and modernity. To return to the ideal types discussed earlier, there is more "old regionalism", only now it is being challenged by new regionalist themes linked to modernity and change.

There are transnational patterns, with differences between the Western and Eastern Alps and among the German, Italian, French, and Slavic speaking areas, although there is also a certain diffusion. Conservative regionalism and emphasis on tradition, *Heimat*, and locality is particularly strong in the German areas. The theme of Europe of the Regions is invoked quite a lot, but has two rather different readings, one emphasising suspicion of Brussels, the need for local control, and safeguards for regional rights and intergovernmentalism, the other much more supranational and looking to transcend the old order of nation-states. Transnational regionalism is mainly confined to functional co-operation, and is delinked from sensitive political and cultural issues and, apart from the *Alp-Adria* working group, rather recent.

As early as 1971, there were suggestions that European integration could help resolve ethnic issues on the borders of Carinthia (Nussbaumer, 1971), although this proved to be premature. In the future, this may affect politics, not by eroding existing identities, but by providing new opportunities for people at the border to negotiate and create their own identities according to context (Kaplan, 2000; Bray, 2004). With its traditions of diffused authority and late statehood, the Alpine region might seem a promising candidate for the construction of a form of post-national political order. Lacking strong state traditions or Jacobin assumptions about the locus of power, it might indeed be able to transform itself from a pre-modern to a post-modern polity without passing through the interlude of modern statehood. Such adjustment has proved more difficult for states rooted in unitary conceptions of authority and order than for those with a more pluralistic history to invoke (Keating, 2001). This is, however, a long way off. It is difficult, therefore, to talk of the Alps as a transnational region, but distinct patterns of localism, regionalism, and Europeanism can be discerned within the Alpine area.

CHAPTER 2

Populism as the Other Side
of Consociational Multi-Level Democracies

Yannis PAPADOPOULOS

I. Populism: A Reaction to "Negotiation" Democracy

Which are the major parties that are usually called "populist" today in Western Europe (Mazzoleni, 2003b)? The French *Front National*, the Swiss *Schweizerische Volkspartei* (SVP), the *Austrian Freedom Party* (FPÖ), the *Fremskrittpartiet* in Norway, the Dansk *Folkepartit* in Denmark, the *Vlaams Blok* (today *Vlaams Belang*) in Flanders, in their own fashion, the new right-wing parties in Italy (*Forza Italia*, the *Lega Nord*, and *Alleanza Nazionale*), and the remnants of the *List Pim Fortuyn* in the Netherlands.[1] What do these countries share in common? They have all developed some patterns of "consociational" decision-making,[2] a model of democracy that was also nicely portrayed by Gerhard Lehmbruch first as "*Proporz-*" and then as "*Verhandlungsdemokratien*" (Lehmbruch, 1996). One can refer here to Czada (2003), who identifies three faces of "negotiation democracy": (1) "*Konkordanz*" between political parties, (2) federal *Politikverflechtung*, and (3) neo-corporatist agreements between associations, although not all these countries display all the properties of negotiation democracies.[3]

With the exception of France, all these political systems correspond to the "consensual" model of democracy – according to Lijphart's (1999: 248) conceptualisation – with multi-party government, which

---

[1] Clearly, the *Vlaams Blok* and the *Lega Nord* have regionalist claims too, but they share populist features (anti-élitism, xenophobia, narrow conceptions of solidarity) with the other right-wing populist parties.

[2] Or, at least, patterns of consensual decision-making, that is, the concept of "consociationalism" which implies the existence of deep social segmentation as an adverse condition for governability.

[3] On the other hand, however, Italy is not very neo-corporatist, and only moderately decentralised. Moreover, the Netherlands and Scandinavian countries are unitary systems rather than federal.

entails the regular involvement of several parties in the exercise of power. Even the French exception should be qualified, as Lijphart uses long-term data (1945–96) which are not very sensitive to recent political developments. The repeated "cohabitation" by the French also produced power-sharing among the major ideological blocks, albeit involuntarily.[4] "Consociativism" not only applies to the fragmented societies of small European states, but was also considered a major trait of the "first" Italian republic, dominated by the *Democrazia Crisitiana*. And as the right-wing parties wish to distance themselves from the previous corrupt political class in the new bi-polar Italian party system, they incorporate populist elements in their discourse.

Does this have anything to do with the Alpine space? Clearly, the category of "negotiation" democracies encompasses not just the Alpine democracies, but there is much concentration of this type of political systems in the Alpine region, a concentration that can be explained historically (see below and Caramani, in this volume). This distinctive policy style of the Alpine "negotiation" democracies can be expected to generate the success of populist protest parties as a reaction to opaque decision making due to neo-corporatist practices and consociational accommodation. Thus, the nature of the political system matters for this success. The line of this argument is as follows: the more we have to do with negotiation democracies, the more this deviates from the common perceptions of how democracy should legitimately function. In order to be legitimated, democracies need to be viewed primarily as majoritarian systems, which offer the crucial possibility not only of being authorised through the election of office holders, but also of successively identifying and sanctioning those responsible for policy choices. As negotiation democracies deviate from this clear legitimate pattern, discontent of a populist nature is likely to grow there.

II. Consociational Cartelisation, *Verdrossenheit*, and Populism

Several sociological or cultural explanations have been put forward for the emergence and success of populist parties. Right-wing populism has, for instance, been viewed as a reaction to new post-industrial forms

---

[4]   France is the country that fits least well the model of negotiation democracy, with a system of interest intermediation which is less integrative than the neo-corporatist pattern, and with a long-standing centralist tradition. It should, nevertheless, be noticed that more fine-grained policy studies (such as the works of the *Centre de sociologie des organisations*) came to the conclusion that negotiation was an important component of centre–periphery relations in this country even before de-centralisation, and social historians (for example, Offerlé, 1995) show that some policy choices were delegated to interest groups as early as in the end of the 19th century.

of social organisation (Ignazi, 1999), or more specifically related to the apprehensions of the losers of modernisation, globalisation, and European integration (Kriesi, 1999b), or viewed as a reaction to the success of "left-libertarian" movements that advocate individual self-accomplishment within increasingly (too much for some) tolerant and multi-cultural societies (Kitschelt, 1995).

Without dismissing such explanations, this chapter starts from a different point, namely, that of populism being the privileged expression of *Politikverdrossenheit* (discontent with politics) *vis-à-vis* established parties (Schedler, 1996). *Verdrossenheit* is related to, and strengthened by, the convergence between these parties, a phenomenon that was emphasised by the theses of the growth, first, of "catch-all" and, then, of "cartel" parties (Katz and Mair, 1995),[5] which is particularly visible in consociational democracies. This implies that the vote in favour of populist parties should, above all, be interpreted as a vote of protest, which does not mean that this is necessarily a negative vote, nor that this vote is not also ideological (probably above all anti-immigrants).[6] This also means that consociational practices are (quasi) a pre-requisite for the growth of strong populist parties as a reaction to them, but not that they are a sufficient condition for this. In particular, factors belonging to the political offer should be considered, as is suggested for instance by Coffé (2004) who explains the lack of populism in Wallonia (as opposed to Flanders) not only by the absence of any regionalist claims, but also by the lack of charismatic political entrepreneurs.

Although the increase of *Politikverdrossenheit* is a general phenomenon, negotiation democracies are particularly likely to produce *Politikverdrossenheit*, and hence are particularly vulnerable to populist critique. Thus, the success of populist protest and anti-establishment parties should also be related to the *systemic properties* of these political systems. This is a rather novel approach, although it is not the first time that consociationalism is challenged at the margins of the ideological spectrum. A few decades ago, the challenge came from the left. Radical left-wing organisations used to criticise strongly the "accommodative" practices of social-democratic parties and labour unions, and new social movements used to criticise the inefficiency of the "conventional" action repertoire of established organisations. And this was accompanied by an intellectual critique that consociational arrangements were a solution coined by political élites in order to consolidate and perpetuate their

---

[5] On the "cartel-party" thesis, see also the critique by Rudd Koole (Koole, 1996), and a rejoinder by Katz and Mair (1996) in the same issue of *Party Politics*.

[6] Empirical research shows that these two kinds of motivations are not exclusive: see Van der Brug *et al.* (2000).

control over their reference groups (for example, the cultural segments or "pillars" in the Netherlands: see Scholten, 1980).

However, in comparison with the various other systems of democracy throughout the world, consociational solutions are highly valued today, notably for the political management of deeply divided societies. Arend Lijphart, for instance – the father of the consociational theory[7] – has always seen and continues to see consociationalism as a possible export-product which is likely to enhance the quality of democracy (see, for instance, Lijphart, 1999).[8] Without negating the merits of consociational solutions,[9] this chapter wishes instead to point out a weakness in this political model, namely, its democratic deficit which makes it vulnerable to populist critique. Such a weakness is seldom emphasised, with the notable recent exception of Richard S. Katz who maintains that "both consensus democracy and the cartel party thesis appear to lead to models of representation that are highly truncated, and that might perhaps be described as a throwback to a pre-democratic era [...]. The objective of government on behalf of the people remains, but without the effective ability of the people either to decide for themselves what that means, or to reward and punish those who claim to be acting as their trustees" (2003: 13–14).

In fact, Lijphart underestimates the negative effect of the cartelisation of political life in consensual regimes. He argues that satisfaction with the quality of democracy is wider in these countries, which is probably due to the inclusive character of their political regime (Lijphart, 1999: 275–300). Yet, apart from the fact that Lijphart's assessment of the quality of democracy does not necessarily coincide with that of the electorate of the protest parties, it can be objected that there will always be a sufficient number of people who are excluded in these systems to fuel populist protest, and that these people will have more intense resentment for their unjustified exclusion from the otherwise integrative polities. This is also the reason why populism emerges in countries where, as a whole, the majority of the public is fundamentally satisfied with the functioning of democracy in spite of the global trend towards less confidence in élites and in established institutions (Norris, 1999; Pharr and Putnam, 2000). The vast majority are satisfied because consociational systems are inclusive but a minority

---

[7] For a recent assessment of this theory, see the issue of *Acta Politica* devoted to "Consociationalism and Corporatism in Western Europe" (37, 2002) and, for a synthetic account, Andeweg (2000).

[8] For a similar approach on the Swiss model of power-sharing, see Linder (1994).

[9] These solutions presuppose, however, the historical sedimentation of consociational norms of behaviour (Lehmbruch, 1996).

is nevertheless dissatisfied and due to the lack of opposition populist parties can easily capture these dissatisfied voters.

III. Three Sources of Populism in Consociationalism

Three systemic properties can explain the existence of a strong social demand to increase the "populist" component (in other words, the genuine influence of popular, i.e., majoritarian sovereignty) in representative democracies in general, and all these properties are particularly present in consociational Alpine polities.

A. Obstacles to Popular Sovereignty

The first property is related to the mitigation of the populist principle by a "liberal" (Riker, 1972) or "constitutionalist" (Leca, 1996) principle: popular sovereignty is subject to limits, above all, in order to protect the "negative liberty" of citizens (for example, minorities). Such limits find their institutional crystallisation in the establishment of "checks and balances" systems which are deemed to induce reflection and deliberation, and to raise countervailing powers (of second chambers, courts, central banks, and autonomous agencies insulated from political pressure) to the majoritarian rule embodied in parliamentary sovereignty.[10]

As a matter of fact, a strong dose of liberalism, or constitutionalism, is a core ingredient of the institutional architecture in consociational democracies, and such principles also guide their everyday practice. Not only is power-sharing the rule between political parties[11] and interest groups, but – again according to Lijphart's own classification – their institutional architecture is usually complex and fragmented, and includes counter-majoritarian institutions. In some cases, the institutional architecture includes in addition vertical diffusion of power across several decisional units through decentralisation or federalist arrangements. Vertical diffusion of power aggravates the lack of accountability generated by the problem of "many hands" (too many actors involved in decisions). Contrary to the formal doctrine, decentralisation and federalism, more often than not, imply shared competencies and negotiations across decisional levels (*Politikverflechtung*), instead of a strict separation of competencies (Schmidt, 1997: 250–51), so that confusion in the division of roles between political actors is further exacerbated.

---

[10] For an account of such developments and their impact on populism, see Mény and Surel (2002).

[11] This is also related in some cases to the high degree of societal fragmentation (for example, pillarisation in the Netherlands or cultural heterogeneity in Switzerland). In purely numerical terms or because of sub-cultures being too remote from each other, single-party majority dominance is not a viable option.

Hence, limits to responsiveness can be perceived as restrictions to government by and for the people, and problems of accountability due to the "overcrowding" of policy-making can be perceived as impediments to the exercise of democratic control. The sources of these two problems should not be amalgamated. Responsiveness refers to the substantial content of policy choices that must conform to voters' wishes, whilst accountability is related to the availability of adequate instruments which oblige policy-makers to report on their deeds, and enable policy-takers to respond with electoral sanctions (Bartolini, 1999: 448–49). But both problems provide fertile soil for the expansion of anti-élitist attitudes and ideological doctrines, which can even become the "master frame" of political cultures in the political systems under consideration in this volume.[12]

B. Consociationalism as Élitism

The second property is related to what was very clearly described by Bernard Manin (1997) as the structurally aristocratic, inherently oligarchic or inevitably élitistic, character of representative democracy. The latter relies on the mechanism of elections, which implies the professionalisation of politics (see also the Schumpeterian model of democracy, or Gaxie, 1993). This does not mean that consociational regimes are more oligarchic *per se* than, say, majoritarian democracy, but élites enjoy more autonomy in the former. For instance, they negotiate among consociational regimes for the composition of governmental coalitions – this can sometimes take months – and policy-making is often the outcome of compromises at the top, as suggested by the neo-corporatist literature. This stands in sharp contrast to the populist ideal of (majoritarian) popular preferences being voiced in elections, and being thereafter translated into policies by the incumbent party without any intermediation that would reduce the transparency of such a process. According to Scharpf (1993: 27), the normative attractiveness of the majoritarian ideal "derives from the circular connection between the full dependence of government on the citizenry, and the equally full governmental control over all aspects of state activity having an impact on the citizenry" (our translation).

In coalition formulas, there is no straightforward link between the outcome of elections and its impact on government formation. Policy choices that involve negotiations – "amicable agreement *vs.* majority rule" according to Jürg Steiner's (1974) formula for Switzerland – between the incumbent parties again cause the problem of "many hands". As it is hard to predict on the grounds of party manifestoes what

---

[12] As Diani (1996) put it to explain the successes of *Lega Nord* in Northern Italy.

is going to be decided by the future government, elections are devalued. The lack of a vigorous opposition and of power alternation (as in Austria's *Grosse Koalitionen* or as in the Swiss "magic formula") is an aggravating factor. Not only does consociationalism entail more élite autonomy, it also entails less élite competition: even the conditions of the minimalist Schumpeterian model of democracy are not fulfilled.[13] The clientelistic allocation of spoils among party members and friends as a "material base of consent" as Adam Przeworski (1985) put it in quite another context – which is more pronounced in countries such as Italy, Belgium, and Austria – is another aggravating factor. Under such conditions, élite consensus is perceived by those who believe they do not benefit from it as a self-referential or, even worse, as a collusive and self-interested game which takes place at the expense of third parties.

All this is, indeed, puzzling for common sense perceptions of how democracies should work, which are grounded in ideological discourses produced by democracies themselves. It is, therefore, understandable that such a configuration can lead to reactions of, at best, disinterest, or, at worst, cynicism or resentment (Betz, in this volume). This is not exactly the same as to hold that populism increases due to a lack of élite responsiveness, which is the populist "indigenous" claim. Lijphart, for instance (1999: 287–88), is able to show (using two measures) that the distance between governmental choices and voters' preferences is shorter in coalitions than in one-party government systems. Nevertheless, populism grows because élites can be perceived as being involved in plots and as being remote from the citizenry, or, in the worst case, show complete disregard for the objective degree of responsiveness to their policy choices. As Katz and Mair (1995: 24) pointed out, the demand of right-wing populist parties to "break the mould" of established politics is particularly effective in mobilising support.

C. Accountability Problems of Co-Operative Forms of Network Governance

The third property is related to the growth of co-operative network forms of "governance" in which public agents act in close concertation with non-public organised actors and experts who possess resources that state bureaucracies do not have (in terms of knowledge, the trust of reference groups and constituencies, organisational capacity, and so on). Such resources allow these actors to exert a sort of blackmailing power *vis-à-vis* the state, so that their collaboration becomes necessary for

---

[13] The relationship between the presence of a *Machtkartell* in countries such as Austria or Switzerland, the legitimacy problems caused by the absence of alternation, and the rise of populist and anti-system parties has also – albeit cursorily – been pointed out by Grande (2001: 206).

"steering" by the state and for the implementation of public policies. Co-operative forms of governance in élitist networks – often informal and opaque and thus non-accountable, selective, and prone to capture by rent-seeking interests (Benz, 1998; Papadopoulos, 2003) – are good candidates for the criticism of political entrepreneurs who build their careers by denouncing the usurpation of popular sovereignty.[14] Here, the problem is not only the lack of responsiveness,[15] but also the lack of transparency and, as a result, accountability too.

The shift from "government" to "governance", as it is usually called in the relevant literature (Pierre, 2000; Pierre and Peters, 2000; Rhodes, 1997), may be new in majoritarian democracies of the Westminster type. It has been attributed to recent phenomena, such as an increased social and problem complexity, major deficits in public spending, the success of new public management doctrines, globalisation, etc. However, network governance is a long established feature in negotiation democracies. Several explanations, all of a functional nature, have been put forward for the precocious advent of tight élite co-operation in these countries:

- a *cultural* one, the argument being that social fragmentation – for example, pillarisation – necessitates bargaining and deliberation among sub-culture élites to avoid centrifugal trends and disintegration (this is the core of consociationalism *à la* Lijphart, 1968 or Steiner, 1974);

- an *economic* one, the argument being that openness to international markets induces domestic co-operation and exchanges so as to compensate for vulnerability and thus acquire competitive advantages (Katzenstein, 1985);

- an *institutionalist* one, the argument being that a complex architecture with veto points under the threat of which policies are formulated and implemented – such as direct democracy in Switzerland – is a strong incentive for élite collaboration to avoid policy blockades (Neidhart, 1970).[16]

---

[14] This argument is also presented in more length in Papadopoulos (2002).

[15] As it is framed by Olson's (1982) theory of distributive coalitions, or by moral hazard problems due to informational asymmetries which are emphasised by principal-agent and delegation theories.

[16] This part of the argument has some similarity with Kitschelt's (1995) argument that convergence due to centripetal competition between the major parties leaves space at the margins for populism. However Kitschelt's argument refers to the arena of partisan politics. Reference is made here to a more general "ethos" of co-operation that includes administrative élites and interest groups as well, and to the role of co-operative procedures the opacity of which can be subject to criticism.

Network governance, in turn, exerts negative effects on the legitimacy of democracy. At first glance, such a hypothesis seems to be contradicted by evidence from Anderson and Guillory (1997), who found that in consensual democracies the "losers" (i.e., the voters who voted for opposition parties) are less dissatisfied with democracy than in majoritarian systems. The data that these conclusions rely on are, however, out of date (from a survey dating back to 1990), and precede the success of more radical anti-establishment parties that exploit their oppositional condition. The growth of mechanisms of horizontal trust-building between élites – often under the protection of secrecy – is, in effect, particularly likely to lead to a deficit of vertical trust between citizens and élites, a trade-off that is noticed by Benz (2002), who focuses on democratic problems of "governance" in general. In a similar vein, with regard to neo-corporatist arrangements, Scharpf (1997) maintains that intersectoral compromises can lead to intra sectoral conflicts between organisational leaderships and the rank-and-file, a conflict which is conceptualised by Schmitter and Streeck (1999) as the result of a gap between the "logic of influence" prevailing among organisational élites and the "logic of members".

What Peter Mair (2002) describes as a general phenomenon is particularly true for consociational systems: representative democracy is primarily party democracy. Although this entails cross-country differences (the degree of "partyness" of political systems varies, but this is hardly measurable), this form of party democracy has become eroded today. Governance by networks is part of this wider trend of erosion of party democracy. According to party specialists, the so-called "cartel" parties (which are blossoming particularly in consociational polities) have become governing agencies instead of channels for the aggregation of their clienteles' interests. At the same time, the links between voters and party leaderships have greatly distended, as suggested by works on "political alienation", *Verdrossenheit*, and the like. Furthermore, the locus of effective policy formulation and implementation tends to shift from the democratic-representative (parliamentary) arena to other (administrative and corporatist) arenas which are only loosely coupled to it, and in which neither parties, nor electoral processes, nor finally voters play any major role.

Network governance with its multi-actor configuration and the blurring of the public-private divide increases the deficits in accountability which originate in the problem of "many hands". On the other hand, such phenomena increasingly tend to become the target of media attention – as a result of the self-referential logic of the media system that induces the search for "scoops" and the disclosure of "scandals" – and thus tend to become visible and subject to criticism in the public space.

The role of the media contributes to populist success, and the shift towards an "audience democracy" (Manin, 1997) particularly affects network democracies in which secrecy and informality are crucial ingredients to consensual policy-making, and in which the media take up the role of the generally missing opposition.[17] The media logic also promotes a number of norms of political behaviour that deviate from the "network governance" pattern, and which are congruent with the populist one: personalisation, use of catch-words and simple arguments, confrontation instead of compromise, or the denouncing of politicians in order to appeal to the public and appear as independent and critical (Swanson and Mancini, 1996; Pfetsch, 1998; Blumler and Kavanagh, 1999).

One might expect that the general shift to negotiated policy-making which approximates to the consensus model ("network governance") – including the Westminster democracies (Rhodes, 1997) – is, in general, likely to favour the propagation of populist ideas (notwithstanding obstacles to the success of smaller parties in systems which operate under a majoritarian logic, mainly plurality electoral systems. An additional factor would be the increased multi-level character of decision-making. Due to Europeanisation and internationalisation, "multi-level governance" is, in effect, no longer a distinctive attribute of federalist national systems. It aggravates problems of accountability and stimulates feelings of dispossession because in order to overcome blockades due to the complexity of the institutional architecture (joint decision-making, veto points, and so on), co-operation is required at élite level and this often takes place in circuits which lack transparency. Finally, contrary to what happened in small countries according to Katzenstein (1985) about two decades ago, external pressure no longer generates domestic consensus, but instead seems to induce cleavages between societal segments which are internationally oriented and segments which are domestic-oriented, with the latter tending to support populist parties that criticise élite willingness for openness and that offer protectionist policies. The concluding remarks, however, point out some of the limits of this populist trend.

IV. Can Populism Be "Consociationalised"?

It is worth noting that there is a paradox in the relationship between consociationalism and populism. Consociationalism, with its integrative politics, nurtures populism because populist parties can claim the mo-

---

[17] For an empirical assessment of the limits put to Swiss corporatist practices in social policy (summit agreements between the major interest organisations) that result from increased mediatisation, see Häusermann *et al.* (2004).

nopoly of purity, the representation of "ordinary" people, opposition, and can argue that they enhance accountability. At the same time, however, consociational systems mark the limits of populism. Functioning on an integrative code, they are often able to absorb opposition parties into their logic. Such parties are offered opportunities to govern more easily than in more exclusionary systems, and, once they are involved in governmental politics, at least four damaging things may happen to them:

- They are induced to behave "responsibly", which may create acute internal rivalries, as in the Austrian FPÖ, and probably in the near future within the Swiss SVP;
- They must make compromises with the other (more moderate) parties which are part of the governmental coalition;
- Given the complexity of problems and the scarcity of resources, they are unable to accomplish their usually unrealistic electoral pledges ("over promising") or to implement their simplistic solutions;
- They, themselves, end up becoming involved in the opaque network governance complex.

Clearly not all systems in which populist parties were successful are equally integrative. French political life remains bipolarised and Kitschelt and McCann (2003) correctly argue that the Swiss SVP finds it easier than the Austrian FPÖ to be represented in the federal government and, at the same time, to play an oppositional role thanks to a more favourable opportunity structure provided by referendum instruments. But maybe the more a system displays consociational features, the more it can be favourable to populist protest in its first phase, and be able to successively neutralise it in a second phase. On the other hand, the "de-radicalisation" of opponents that is expected from their integration into the power spheres is no easy task. A recent historical study on the shift in Swiss federal government from single-party to multi-party cabinets (Bolliger and Zürcher, 2003) demonstrated that the opponents (the conservative party at the end of the 19th century) joined the federal executive only after having undergone a moderation process, while this is not (yet?) true for populist parties. Besides, it was quite a long time until any further integrative effects deriving from the shift in governmental patterns were noticed. A more general lesson that can be drawn, then, is that negotiation democracies may be better equipped to cope with the "stress" caused by populist opposition, but this requires the co-operation of populist leaders themselves, and it may take quite some time until any substantial positive outcomes are felt in terms of governability.

CHAPTER 3

Natural Cultures

The Alpine Political Culture and Its Relationship to the Nation-State and European Integration

Daniele CARAMANI

This chapter deals with the question of a transnational political culture in the Alpine region, which expresses itself in a similar way in a number of countries regardless of national borders. The geographical remoteness, the type of economic activity, mainly based on agriculture and small commerce, the persistence of religious attitudes and traditional forms of society and family, the type of identity based on *Heimat* and *Gemeinschaft* elements – combined with a strong emphasis on the "natural" element of the community – all contrast with the prevailing globalisation and supranational integration trends. As a consequence, these areas and populations perceive themselves to be under threat and have developed a defensive political culture. This chapter investigates the socio-economic and geopolitical conditions at the origin of this perception, their cultural implications, and their political expression.

The main political expression of this defensive political culture is the development of neo-populist and/or regionalist parties, which are particularly strong in the Alpine region. In some cases, this concerns long-standing parties which have been continuously present since the beginning of competitive elections, such as the Bavarian *Christlich-Soziale Union* (CSU), the *Südtiroler Volkspartei* (in the German-speaking Italian region of the South Tyrol), and the *Union Valdôtaine* (in the French-speaking Italian region of Valle d'Aosta). In other cases, however, new parties have recently emerged, for example, the Italian *Lega Nord* (the Northern League),[1] which developed out of several regionalist movements at the end of the 1980s, the *Ligue Savoisienne* since 1993 and the Swiss *Lega dei Ticinesi* (in the Italian-speaking Swiss canton Ticino).

---

[1] The main new regionalist parties in Italy were the *Lega Lombarda* (Lombardy), the *Liga Veneta* (Venetia), and *Piedmont Autonomista* (Piedmont). On these early northern movements, see Diamanti (1993), Mannheimer (1991), and Fix (1999: 126–43).

Finally, old parties transformed themselves ideologically towards na-
tionalism and populism as in the case of the Austrian *Freiheitliche
Partei Österreichs* (FPÖ) and the Swiss *Schweizerische Volkspartei*
(SVP).

These cases are interesting not only because they represent a recent
evolution in Alpine areas, but also because they are – to different ex-
tents – part of a more general growth of new right-wing populist movements in several other European non-Alpine countries, such as Belgium,
France, and the Scandinavian countries.[2] In both the Alpine and the non-
Alpine cases, the populist character of these parties is accompanied by a
more general orientation towards "anti-modern" and traditional values
(concerning issues such as family or immigration) which, in some cases,
are linked to persistent religiosity. The Alpine and non-Alpine cases
further share a sceptical view of European integration. In spite of these
commonalities between Alpine and non-Alpine cases, this chapter argues that there is a distinct Alpine character within the more general
"anti-European" cultures.

The topics discussed in this chapter represent a case study which can
be carried out for other "transnational regions". The breakdown of
Communist rule in Central and Eastern Europe, as well as the process of
European integration and the successive weakening of the normative
role of nation-states has created new spaces in Europe, in both the ideological and the territorial dimensions. The decline of the hegemony of
the left–right dimension has led to a re-awakening of interest not only
for political attitudes and values, but also for trends of "new regionalism" with the (re-)emergence of pre-industrial ethnic, linguistic, and
religious dimensions which have not been totally absorbed in the left–
right dimension in the course of state formation and nation-building
processes (Caramani, 2004). Thus, new ideological dimensions and the
"renaissance" of territorial politics may constitute important aspects
with regard to the formation of a European cleavage constellation.[3]

This chapter presents an exploration of these issues and, more generally, wishes to contribute to the debate on the impact of the diversity of

---

[2]   These parties are the *Front National* in Belgium and France, the *Vlaams Blok* (presently *Vlaams Belang*) and *Volksunie* in Belgium, the *Fremskridtspartiet* and the
Fremskrittspartiet (the two Progress Parties in Denmark and Norway), and *Ny Democrati* in Sweden. Other populist parties in the countries considered in this chapter
are, for example, the *Schweizer Auto-Partei* (now *Freiheitspartei der Schweiz*), the
Nationale Aktion (now *Schweizer Demokraten*), the German *Republikaner*, the right-
wing *Movimento Sociale Italiano* (now *Alleanza Nazionale*). On the populist party
family in Europe, see Mény and Surel (2002).
[3]   See, for example, Keating (1998) and Loughlin (2001). On the "renaissance" of the
territorial dimension in Europe, see Kohler-Koch (1998).

political cultures on the process of European integration today, namely, with regard to institution-building, cleavage constellation and party systems, and centre–periphery relationships. In a moment of decisive thrust towards political integration, the cultural diversity of Europe acquires an entirely new weight and meaning. The type and degree of homogeneity of political cultures become fundamental elements of the analysis of the formation, the consolidation, and the performance of a supranational system.[4] Yet, although political culture affects both the type of demands towards the political system and the responses of political élites, the relevance of this diversity for the European integration process has been largely overlooked. This chapter starts with an overview on state formation processes and the creation of party systems in the Alpine region. It then moves on to the Alpine type of political culture in terms of threat from outside and defensive response. Finally, it addresses the question of party populism in the Alpine region with special reference to European integration and the interaction with other cleavages.

I. State and Party-System Formation in the Alpine Region

A. The Geopolitical and the Geo-Economic Position of the Alps

The Alpine region is a transnational region that is characterised by the long-standing central position that it has possessed since the times of the Roman Empire within the European network of main trade routes. It covers several sub-national units (Northern Italy, South-East France, North-Western Slovenia, and parts of Bavaria) as well as national entities, such as Austria and Switzerland.[5] The central position of the Alps in the European trade network was strengthened with the dissolution of the Roman Empire, when it became crucial to control the mountain passes between the commercial Italian cities (the maritime powers of Venice, Genoa, and Pisa, as well as the banking centres of Florence and

---

[4] Originally, the concept of "political culture" was employed in its basic function, that is, the survival and workability of democratic institutions after their breakdown in the inter-war period. Among the early contributions of this time, the most widely known volumes are by Almond and Verba (1963), Almond and Powell (1966), and Easton (1965). After democratic consolidation, however, the concept was abandoned by the literature.

[5] As far as Bavaria is concerned, this has to be restricted to its Southern, more Alpine, half. These are the most Catholic areas of Bavaria, which are located between the Danube and the Alps. The Alpine parts of Bavaria are located mainly in Upper Bavaria, Swabia, and parts of Lower Bavaria. Liechtenstein is also an entirely Alpine country. However, it is excluded in this chapter because of its small size and exceptional institutional system.

Milan) and the flourishing North at the mouth of the Rhine (the Flemish cities and the Hanseatic League).[6]

The central position of this region in-between the Northern Italian communal network and the core of the old Germanic Empire along the Rhine led, as in the rest of the European "city-belt" (Rokkan *et al.*, 1987; Rokkan, 1999), to a high political fragmentation that hindered the emergence of a strong centre which was able to unify these territories. As a consequence, in comparison to cases of "early" state formation such as Britain, France, Spain, Russia, Denmark, and Sweden, all of whom were at the fringes of the city-belt, state formation in these areas was delayed until the 19th and early 20th century. This delay most notably concerns the two large cultural areas composed of Italy and Germany, both of which achieved national political unity only in 1861 and 1871 respectively. Switzerland, too, was transformed from a loose *Staatenbund* to a sovereign *Bundestaat* in 1848, but was further centralised only with the Constitution of 1874. State formation in Austria is, on the other hand, the result of the break up of the multi-national empire after the First World War, when the tensions between different nationalities (Bohemian, Hungarian, various Slavic, Polish, etc.) reached their peek. In the Alpine region, national borders were modified up to the late 19th century, even in France, with the transfer of Savoy and Nice from the newly constituted Italian state in the 1860s.

Not only did the strong political fragmentation delay processes of state formation in these areas but, in addition, the cultural fragmentation led to multi-lingual and religiously mixed nations and, consequently, to "incomplete" processes of nation-building along the Alpine relieves. The morphology of this region has reinforced the cultural specificities. Both Germany and Switzerland have been religiously diverse countries since the Reformation and the subsequent religious wars in the 17th century.[7] Furthermore, the linguistic diversity has survived in a number of

---

[6] The control of mountain passes was not only particularly relevant in pre-national processes of state formation in Switzerland, but also in the cases of the Earldom of the Tyrol (soon absorbed by the Hapsburg monarchy) and the Duchy of Savoie, which covered both the Italian and the French side of the Alps before Italian unification (1861) and the transfer of the western territory to France.

[7] In Switzerland, the religious confrontation, in some cases, led to territorial divisions (as in the case of the two Appenzell), while, in other cases, it resulted in multi-religious accommodation (as in the case of Glarus). In contrast with the language diversity, the religious dimension in Switzerland has been present since the foundation of the federal state in 1848, after the *Sonderbundkrieg* between the secularised élites (from the Protestant cantons) and the resistance of Catholic cantons. Despite the crisis that hit the Catholic camp after its defeat and its political disorganisation until the end of the 19th century (Gruner, 1969) the Catholic *Christlich-Demokratische Volkspartei* (CVP) has always been an important element of the Swiss party system.

regions: French in the *Suisse romande*, Italian in the Swiss canton Ticino (and partly in Graubünden, where *Reto-Romanisch* is also spoken), German in the Italian province of South Tyrol, French in the Valle d'Aosta, and *Ladino* in parts of Italy, as well as Italian in parts of former Yugoslavia.

Urban sites developed at the fringes of the Alps, both in the north and the south. Mainly because of the geological morphology – but also because of the development of Atlantic capitalism in the 16th century and the rise of overseas empires such as Britain, France, Portugal, the Netherlands, and Spain, and the commercial decline of Northern Italy – Alpine areas remained based on agricultural and pastoral economy. As for the most significant cases of agrarian politics in the Scandinavian countries, peasants' political organisations were movements for the defence of small or medium units of production. Their development very much depended on the market relationship between the towns and the countryside.[8] This type of weak small farming economy was more exposed than others to the uncertainties of the free market economy of urban environments, and produced a deep urban–rural cleavage in these areas.

B. Development of Political Parties in the Alps

These rural–urban, ethno-linguistic, religious, and centre–periphery oppositions were expressed in the political sphere in concomitance with the mobilisation of mass electorates. With regard to the economic and cultural relevance of agriculture in the Alpine region, the first mobilisation of mass electorates was paralleled by a comparatively strong presence of various peasants' organisations and farmers' parties. The largest of these parties is the *Schweizerische Bauern-, Gewerbe- und Bürgerpartei* – today the *Schweizerische Volkspartei* (SVP) – which is traditionally strong in the large Protestant canton of Bern, in the former peasant league of the Grisons, as well as in Eastern Switzerland (Thurgau).[9] In Germany, too, strong agrarian parties developed in Bavaria, in particular, the *Bayerischer Bauernbund*, in alliance with the *Deutscher Wirtschaftsbund für Stadt und Land* during the Weimar Republic, later

---

[8] See, in particular, Linz (1976) and Urwin (1980: 160–205). The classical analysis of the role of the peasant world in political revolutions is by Moore (1966), and includes most of the vast existing literature on agrarian politics.

[9] In the Catholic cantons in Switzerland small farming was closely tied to the urban economy (Lipset and Rokkan, 1967a). The distribution of land appears from data presented in Russett (1964), and Taylor and Jodice (1983). The largest inequalities can be observed in Italy, Spain, Greece, Austria, and the United Kingdom (Gini index between 80.3 and 71.0). However, the Gini index indicates smaller farming structures for Denmark, Switzerland, Sweden, Belgium, Finland, and the Netherlands (Gini index between 45.8 and 60.5). For more details, see Caramani (2004: 218–20).

renamed the *Deutsche Bauernpartei*. In Austria, the various regional agrarian parties unified in the *Landbund für Österreich* in 1922. In Italy, the *Partito Agrario* (*Partito dei Contadini d'Italia* after the Second World War) was particularly strong in Piedmont.

The opposition between rural and urban interests was reinforced by cultural barriers. Autonomous organisations for the defence of agrarian parties developed in contrast to the secularised attitudes in the urban world (in alliance with nation-builders). This factor accounts for the differences with Catholic regions in which peasant parties and organisations outside of the Catholic-conservative front rarely developed to a meaningful extent. Large agrarian parties formed not only in the Protestant countries of the North, where the religious dissident and non-conformist movements emerged in the countryside in opposition to urban moral standards, but also in the Protestant cantons in Switzerland (mainly Berne), the more secularised *Länder* in Austria (Carinthia and Styria), as well as in the (northern) regions of Bavaria which are separate from Upper Bavaria, Lower Bavaria, and Swabia. Furthermore, the development of agrarian parties was facilitated by the federal structure of the state in these three cases. With regard to the territorial dimension or, in other words, to centre–periphery relationships, France, Germany, and Italy assume a specific position among the Alpine countries, because the Alpine parties in these countries are territorially concentrated. Although this also applies to the Swiss *Lega dei Ticinesi*, major regionalist parties in Austria and Switzerland are absent.

In Europe, parties for territorial and cultural defence appeared in the course of the main thrusts of nation-building. Such movements were aimed against the attempts at administrative (fiscal) and military penetration by the emerging nation-states' centres, as well as against the attempts at cultural standardisation. The likelihood of the emergence of regionalist opposition to centre-building and the chances of success in voicing discontent largely depend upon the degree of remoteness of the areas, which means:

- the degree of *geographical remoteness* with regard to the main nodes of the networks of communications (this is particularly true in the case of mountain geological morphologies);
- the degree of *cultural distinctiveness* (mainly language and dialects, but also religiosity *vs.* secularised attitudes); and
- the degree of *economic dependence* from outside systems (external markets for agriculture).

The Italian case offers perhaps the best example of such a resistance among the countries analysed in this chapter. After the unification of Italy in 1861–70, the modernisation of the state and the construction of national identity followed the ideal-typical Napoleonic form with strong centralisation and the absorption of linguistic diversity (French and Slavic initially, and later German with the annexation of South Tyrol after the First World War) within a national linguistic standard which developed out of one regional language. This national model was opposed not only in the former Kingdom of the Two Sicilies, which was annexed by the House of Savoy, but also in the policies of "Italianisation" in the Alpine border regions, which were sometimes brutally implemented (as during the Fascist period), and enhanced by immigration and language imposition.

In the Alpine regions, tensions have persisted up to recent times.[10] After the Second World War, autonomous regions were created within the new centralised Republic: the two largest islands, and the three border regions of Valle d'Aosta, Trentino Alto Adige (the South Tyrol), and Friuli-Venezia-Giulia. Whereas the longer process of state formation in France led to the almost complete disappearance of linguistic minorities, in Italy these regions remained linguistically distinct with French, German, and *Ladino* (equivalent to *Reto-Romanisch*) still being used. German parties have existed in Italy since the First World War, first under the name of the *Deutscher Verband*. The *Union Valdôtaine* developed after 1946, when the Valle d'Aosta was transformed into a single-member constituency. A somewhat similar pattern applies to the *Ligue Savoisienne*, created in 1993 from diverse autonomist and nostalgic aristocratic groups which had existed since the early 1970s. French *Savoie* had been part of the Duchy (later Kingdom) of Savoy since 1416, with Turin as its capital from 1562 onwards. It was ceded to France in 1860 (under Napoleon III) in exchange for support in Italian unification. This transfer was approved by a plebiscite. In 1792, French *Savoie* had already been annexed by France with the enthusiastic support of the local population, but was again transferred to Piedmont after the Congress of Vienna (1815). Today, the *Ligue Savoisienne* claims that the Treaty of 1860 is not valid. However, contrary to other cases such as the South Tyrol, there are no ethnic or cultural grounds on which regionalism can be based.

In Germany, the process of state formation (which was contemporary to that of Italy) took place on different grounds. In Italy, the unifying centre (Piedmont) could afford to create a centralised state without the need to federalise the country, given the strong imbalance between the developed North and the backward South. In contrast, German unification was carried out from a landward military periphery which faced old

---

[10] South Tyrol is the territory which was characterised by the highest degree of violence until the adoption of the *Paket* in 1972, which established a proportional accommodation between German and Italian language communities.

established states (including Bavaria),[11] politically progressive areas (the Rhine region under the influence of French political culture), as well as strong commercial and industrial centres (the old Hanseatic cities, on the one hand, and the Ruhr district, on the other). Consequently, a federal solution could not be circumvented. Very much like the creation of the Swiss Confederation, the balance between territorial units, the long-standing role in the international system, and the rooted cultural features, led to a federal solution which opened up institutional rather than partisan channels of "voice" (Hirschman, 1970; Rokkan, 1974). Both in Germany and Switzerland, the regional dimension is no longer politicised, in other words, it does not express itself in specific parties for regional defence (if one excepts the recent case of the *Lega dei Ticinesi*, or the marginal case of the *Südschleswigscher Wählerverband* on the border with Denmark).[12]

As far as the religious dimension is concerned, Germany and Switzerland are – together with the Netherlands and Northern Ireland – the only religiously-mixed cases in Western Europe. Whereas the outcome of the Reformation led to homogeneously Protestant territories in Scandinavia and to homogeneously Catholic territories in the countries of the Counter-Reformation (Southern Europe, the Hapsburg Empire, and France), a mixed religious structure prevailed in the large number of small political and sovereign units from the Swiss Confederation up to the United Provinces of the Low Countries, and also to the "British Isles."[13] In these areas, the formation of secularised liberal states in alliance with Protestant churches (similarly to the national churches of the North) was opposed by the Roman Catholic Church. Thus, in both Germany (*Zentrumpartei*) and Switzerland (*Katholische Konservative*), we find strong Catholic parties after the creation of the nation-state.[14]

---

[11] As a consequence, a number of specific Bavarian parties have existed since the introduction of universal and equal voting rights in 1871: the *Bayerischer Bauernbund* during the Empire period and the *Bayerische Volkspartei* during the Weimar Republic (which in 1928 merged with the *Zentrumpartei*).

[12] The radical border shifts and population movements after World War I and II also contributed to the "homogenisation" of the German population. In particular, this concerns Alsace-Lorraine and the former territories of Eastern Prussia (today Poland).

[13] The principle established by the Peace of Westphalia (1648), according to which the prince decided the religion of his territory, led to a mosaic of Catholicism, Reformism, and Calvinism in the fragmented city-belt.

[14] Several Bavarian cities (for example, Nürnberg and Augsburg), and the Bavarian North (Franconia) were strongly influenced by Reformist movements in the 16th century. As a consequence, the *Sozialdemokratische Partei Deutschlands* received stable electoral support in opposition to the CSU (which was seen as too Catholic) in the early years after the Second World War. For this reason, even though the CSU has nearly completely regained territory over the years (Mintzel 1990, 1995;

Consequently, the Alpine region appears as a culturally fragmented area, both religiously and linguistically. This has led to strong centre–periphery tensions in countries such as Italy, and to territorially fragmented political structures in countries such as Germany and Switzerland. The Austrian case differs in this respect, since it is the result not so much of federalising/unifying processes, but of the break up of one of the three large multi-national empires which dominated Central and Eastern Europe, instead.[15] The independence of the different "nationalities" which constituted the former *Kronländer* within the Hapsburg Empire also led to a culturally homogeneous (in both religious and linguistic aspects) Austrian Republic.

II. The Alpine Political Culture

What is the consequence of these historical processes on the political culture of the Alpine region? To answer this question the remainder of this chapter follows the different columns of Figure 2: (1) the dimensions of political culture, (2) the specificities of the Alpine culture, (3) the perceptions of threats and (4) the answers to threats and, finally, (5) their impact on the European cleavage constellation. Starting with the first column of Figure 2, political cultures are, broadly speaking, sets of values and beliefs about social constructs. Following the classical definition, political cultures involve cognitive, affective, and evaluational orientations about the political system (Almond and Verba, 1963; see also Almond and Powell, 1966: 50). Three main elements of the political system are considered next (Easton, 1965: 21–33):

- First, political cultures are related to the goals of the political system, its *orientations* concerning values, beliefs, and priorities. In particular, the morally and religiously traditional attitudes *vs.* the modern and secularised attitudes are reflected in the relevance which is attributed to both specific social institutions (such as the church and the family) and social norms and roles (the role of women in the labour market, social hierarchies, etc.). These orientations find their expression in the support for specific issues and in the demand for particular public policies which should have priority on the public agenda.

Wagemann 2000: 116–28, and in this volume), the CSU cannot be seen as a strict Catholic party.

[15] The break up of the Hapsburg, Tsarist, and Ottoman Empires was simultaneous after the First World War. This period represented the main thrust towards the formation of nation-states in Central Europe, although the rise of the Soviet Union further delayed national construction in a number of satellite countries until the late 20th century (see Caramani, 2003).

- Second, political cultures are related to the definition of social groups and the *political community*. Group *identities* lead to feelings of belonging (territorial, ethnic, and religious) with respect to a certain group, thereby distinguishing the "us" from the "them", and the "outside" from the "inside". Political cultures can, therefore, be distinguished by their degree of closure or openness towards other social groups, be it territorially (different or broader territorial system) or functionally (moral deviation, immigrants, etc.),[16] and by the type of horizontal bonds between citizens (*Gemeinschaft vs. Gesellschaft*). This involves strong elements of trust (and distrust) which are determined by the social and geographical distance between groups (Banfield, 1953; Fukuyama, 1995; Putnam, 1993).

- Third, political cultures are defined through attitudes and orientations towards political *institutions and personnel*. This dimension of political culture implies expectations and eva-luations about the functioning of the political system. Cognitive and evaluational orientations are expressed in differentiated degrees of *support* for institutions and political authorities. This is directly related to the perception of both the efficiency and honesty of specific institutional bodies (incumbents) and orga-nisations (parties, trade unions, etc.).[17] These attitudes translate in different levels and styles of participation, ranging from passive to active, and from individual (clientelistic) to member-ship (associations).

---

[16] For the distinction between territorial and functional membership, see Rokkan *et al.* (1987: 17–25).

[17] A great wealth of recent survey data have emphasised the tendency towards increasing distrust towards established political parties. As a consequence, the literature from the 1970s has described the development of "anti-party" movements and discourses both in left-wing social movements and in right-wing populism. See Schedler (1996 and 1997). For recent contributions on France and Italy, see Torcal, Gunther, and Montero (2002), on Germany, see Bevan (1995).

Figure 2. The Alpine Political Culture and Its Political Significance

Dimen- sions of Political Culture	"Alpine" Cultural Characters	Sources – Perception of External Threat	Defensive Political Expression	Sceptical Relation- ship to EU Integration
Orientations	*Tradition*	*Modernisation*	*Preservation*	*Rural–urban cleavage*
Attitudes, values, beliefs Preferences, priorities, policies	Religiosity Nature Work ethics	Secularisation and urbanisa- tion Financial capi- talism, globali- sation, unem- ployment	Family structures, social roles Protection- ism, SME, local first Protection of ecology	Common Agricultural Policy Transporta- tion policies Natural resources
Identity	*Ethnic*	*Civic*	*Retrenchment*	*Cultural cleavages*
Definition of group: Us *vs.* them Insiders *vs.* outsiders	*Volk Gemeinschaft Heimat*	Assimilationist model (nation- state) Supra-national integration and Americanisa- tion	Differential- ist model (anti- immigration) True identities: Ethno- linguistic, territorial, religious	Ethno- linguistic: Europe of Peoples and Regions Religion *vs.* secularisa- tion External borders
Institutions	*Distrust*	*Distance*	*Populism*	*Left–right cleavage*
Expectations and evalu- ations about political system; degree of support	Distrust in élites: Efficiency Honesty	Geographical and social remoteness Partitocracy, corporatism, coalitions, immobility, *Verflechtung*	Anti- party/anti- establishment discourse Electoral support from losers of modernity Incarnation	Democratic deficit Welfare state Liberalisa- tion and privatisation

The second column of Figure 2 identifies the distinctive characters of the Alpine political culture. If one were to identify a common denominator for the different defining elements of this political culture, it would be the idea of a *threat from "outside."* The Alpine political culture is mainly a *defensive* set of attitudes which are reflected in the relationship with the "outside environment". This can be illustrated by the image of the valley as a *closed social system* which is cut off from the external world.[18] The geographical-spatial dimension of "closure" (communication networks) has been emphasised above. This idea of closure, however, can be extended to other dimensions, such as the aspect of a social defence of communitarian identities, religiosity, and traditions against the secularisation of urban centres, the ecological preservation of the purity of landscapes, and the economic (agricultural) protectionism against urban free market. The following section attempts to describe these dimensions of *distance*, *closure*, and *distinctiveness* of the Alpine political culture.

A. Orientations

First, *traditional* values and orientations dominate over modern approaches in most domains of life. This is best reflected in the role of religious beliefs and practices. Not only is more importance attributed to religion (regardless of whether one is Catholic or Protestant), but religious practice is also connected with everyday life activities. The counter-concept to this emphasis on tradition is *modernity*. Be it for religious reasons or for a general anti-modern approach, this political culture often leads to a rejection of any changes that are perceived as threats to traditional forms of life, and entails sceptical views about modern societal developments: in particular, these include social roles (the role of women in society), social structures (the weakening of the family structures in favour of new forms of partnership), and the acceptance of alternative or deviating ways of life.

Second, *nature* is a distinctive element of the Alpine political culture, compared to the other political environments in which party populism has emerged. The importance of nature is very much related to the fear that the pure and uncontaminated Alpine landscape could be destroyed through contact with the "impure" urban and industrial aspects of modernity: the natural heritage is seen to be in danger and, therefore, needs to be defended against any kind of external attack. Again, this reflects a defensive political culture against threats from outside. It goes without saying that this "purism" is somehow ambi-

---

[18] The concept of closed systems is present in the classical sociological writings from Weber to Parsons and Rokkan. For an application of this category to extreme right-wing parties, see Perrineau (2001).

guous. The insistence on the defence of the purity of the Alpine landscape sharply contrasts with the exploitation of tourism. However, policy issues which are concerned with this goal of the protection of the resources of nature are not limited to environmental policy. Transportation policy (the *Transit* across Alpine passes and tunnels) has become a major issue both in domestic political discourse and in bi-lateral and multi-lateral international negotiations.[19] The natural aspect is strongly linked to the type of agricultural economy of the Alpine regions, and to the tourist industry, which relies heavily on natural and geographical resources. The small-level of agricultural production and the high-quality of its natural products makes this type of activity vulnerably to external effects (climatic and economic) and leads to considerable call for protectionism against the outside, for example, with regard to the Common Agricultural Policy of the EU.

Finally, one of the more recurrent themes of this culture is that of *work ethics*. Physical hard work is considered to be one of its character-ising (and functional equivalent) features, and makes it possible to dif-ferentiate one group from other groups, which are defined as lazy or as parasites. There is a strong emphasis on the real or material economy of small artisans, peasants, and shopkeepers, in opposition to the immate-rial or virtual international finance. These work ethics are often ex-tended to the social values of "civicness" or even, "civilisation" *tout court*: cleanness, decency, order, efficacy, etc. As Betz notes, "[w]hat makes Alpine populism distinct is its pronounced 'producerist' bent, together with an equally pronounced emphasis on the entrepreneurial virtues characteristic of the *Mittelstand*" (Betz, in this volume: 165-66). The equation between identity and work appears in opposition to immi-grants from Third World countries or Southern European countries (as is the case in Austria, Germany, or Switzerland), but also in opposition to national sub-groups (as in the case of Southern Italians in Italy).[20]

B. Identity

Processes of globalisation and supra-national integration, together with the uncertainties which accompany them, have led to a defensive attitude which can be labelled "*identity retrenchment*", namely, the

---

[19]   There has even been an attempt to make transportation issues part of package deals. For example, there was the opinion in Austria that the Austrian Chancellor should have signed the enlargement treaty of the EU only if the EU solves the *Transitprob-lem* according to the Austrian wishes. The same issue often arises in direct democ-racy consultations concerning European integration in Switzerland.

[20]   In the case of the two centralised states (France and Italy), the regionalist movements stress the amount of hard work done which allows several other regions (namely, the capital cities Paris and Rome) to survive while doing less work.

search for secure roots in a world that has become increasingly uncertain. In the Alpine regions, the element of identity appears very clearly and can be illustrated through three well-known German words: *Volk*, *Gemeinschaft*, and *Heimat*. The relationship between individuals, territory, and community is, again, defined in *natural* terms: the *Volk* is a natural entity which is superior to the sum of its members. This holistic idea embodies the primordiality of the community with respect to social and cultural "constructs". The natural identity of these regions is seen to be threatened from outside and needs to be reaffirmed. The overwhelming of the primordial naturality of the people by an artificial and "unnatural" idea of society is perceived as the main source of threat.

The second frequently used German word, *Gemeinschaft*, is considered as being under threat because of the processes of economic modernisation and a form of state-building which transforms non-industrial communities into *Gesellschaften*. On the one hand, the *Gemeinschaft* aspect of this type of identity is radically opposed to the idea of the atomised and individualistic society that formed during the Industrial Revolution. With the erosion and the weakening of social classes, which was determined by the advance of a post-industrial phase of economic evolution, pre-industrial ethnic and religious affiliations regain vigour. This process was also stimulated by the changes or crises of the social organisations which are linked to the industrial society, namely, the welfare state. This leads to the rediscovery of other, more traditional, forms of social organisation, such as the ethnic identities, family, and religious affiliations mentioned above.[21] On the other hand, the *Gemeinschaft* aspect of this type of identity is opposed to the legalistic, universalistic, and political idea of citizenship. In contrast, this type of identity is based on elements of ethnic roots and "blood".[22]

Third, the specificity of the Alpine type of identity can be expressed through the concept of *Heimat*. Novels and tales of the Romantic period regularly select life in the Alps as a central theme. Once again, the idea of protecting the *Heimat* reappears. This is reflected in the defence of distinctive ethno-linguistic identities (dialects), which may lead to a general rejection of "others" who do not speak or do not understand the local dialect (for example, the rejection of North Germans in Bavaria, or East Austrians in Vorarlberg), as well as to a particular rejection of foreigners, who are seen as invaders of the culturally-closed *Heimat*. This

---

[21] See the distinction between "new" and "old" regionalism in Keating (in this volume).

[22] This has recently become very important with regard to the crisis of national identities (for example, in Italy in the 1990s). In Austria, the relationship to *Pangermanismus* has always been problematical. This is less so in Germany, where the ethnic and natural element has historically been predominant (Brubacker, 1992), especially compared to French or Swiss (neutrality and direct democracy) political citizenship.

protectionism results in anti-immigationist views. Clearly, the definition of identity is related to the issue of nature. Ethnic communities and the *Heimat* are seen as *natural* things, and not as social constructs. Or, to use the oxymoron of the title of this chapter, they become "natural cultures".

C. Institutions

The third dimension of political cultures consists of the attitudes and orientations towards political institutions and authorities. This dimension relates to the expectations and evaluations about the functioning of the political system, which is expressed in different degrees of support for and trust towards institutions and political personnel. The geographical remoteness and the lack of communication networks contribute to the scepticism towards the efficiency and honesty of the established parties and incumbents. The political system is often seen as corrupt and distant from the citizens, and its personnel are criticised for not maintaining high standards of political morality. The centre–periphery and rural–urban cleavages deepen the distance with the capital, the administration, and the headquarters of political actors. Additionally, a certain lack of expertise in the administration with regard to the affairs of the remote areas reinforces the perception of distance with the decision-making centres. Furthermore, the monetary wealth which has been achieved through the culture of "hard and honest work" has to be defended against "those in power". Politics and the state are seen as an arena in which compromises result in a loss of the original purity.

This results in general anti-state and anti-establishment propositions. The state, and any other structure, such as religious organisations, political parties, and interest associations, are viewed with scepticism. Instead, a developed economic liberalism, regional autonomy, and low taxation are seen as devices to protect them from outsiders (or, rather, from "those above"). Furthermore, it also results in alternative forms of social participation in these areas, namely, dense networks of local membership associations (*Vereinswesen*) which compensate for the lack of identification with other institutions. The *Vereine* also serve as political, social, and cultural forums. However, their focus on tradition, nature, and other elements of the local culture reinforces the tendency to gather in *Vereine*, instead of contributing to institutions or other political actors, such as national political parties and interest associations.

The issue against the bureaucratic nomenclature of the state is clearly stronger in the case of centralised countries such as France and Italy, and appears less in the three federal countries of Germany, Switzerland, and Austria. France and Italy adopted the same type of centralised state with something perceived as a "cast of bureaucrats" appointed from the centre and alien to local life (the *préfet* or *prefetto*). However, the protest is also directed towards other élites, namely, economic ones. This also concerns the increase in the discontent with the tourist industry, which is accused of ruining the landscape, social life, and local traditional craftsmanship.

In conclusion, the perception of a threat to economic prosperity, social traditions, group identity, and the ecological equilibrium, all of which are seen to originate from the *external* (national and international) environment, is characteristic of this political culture. The response to this threat is a retrenchment back to established social schemes. These schemes are considered to be "natural". Thus, *Volk, Gesellschaft,* and *Heimat* are as "natural" as the uncontaminated landscape that surrounds them. Modernity, on the other hand, is associated with artificial constructs (from industrial production modes to abstract citizenship) and destructive elements, such as tourism and transportation, as well as with ways of life that break up the natural nucleus of the family and the community.

III. A Defensive Partisan Expression

This political culture perceives itself as being under threat. The dimensions of this threat are summarised in the third column of Figure 2. The responses to the sources of these threats are given in the fourth column. For reasons of space, the following expands upon the two columns.

The specific political culture which the previous section attempted to describe in its basic elements is reflected in the political style, discourse, and the programmes of the political parties. Although these parties are specific to the Alpine region in France, Germany, and Italy, Alpine themes, discourses, and programmes have also come to the forefront in national politics in Austria and Switzerland. First, this means that, even though parties such as the FPÖ or the SVP are not limited to a certain region, they show characteristics which are similar to those of the regionalist parties in the other countries. Second, this also means that the other major parties in Austria and Switzerland – as well as in Bavaria – tend to adopt a similar style and discourse.

This is clearly visible in the Austrian case. The *Volkspartei* ÖVP represents the active Catholic part of the population. Similarly, the ÖVP is deeply rooted in the agricultural world. Thus, two of the above mentioned characteristics of the Alpine political culture are covered by the ÖVP and not by the FPÖ. This may mean that some aspects of the Alpine populism are also part of the strategy of the ÖVP. However, this is not true for the issue of European integration. This ambiguity with regard to Alpine populism in Austria is further enhanced if one considers that the *Bundesland* which has the highest electoral support for the FPÖ (and, at the same time, an exceptionally low support for the ÖVP) is Carinthia which, on the one hand, is Alpine but, on the other, is also integrated within another European macro-region, together with North-East Italy and West-Slovenia. This "spill-over" of Alpine strategies, however, is not necessarily limited to Austria and Switzerland.[23]

However, this chapter does not consider the discourse and programme of these major parties. Instead, the following attempts, first, to single out some features of the style, discourse, and programmes of the regionalist/populist parties of the Alpine areas and, second, to focus on one aspect of it, namely, the attitude towards European integration. Alpine political culture is expressed politically through (1) populist elements, (2) protest attitudes, (3) a protective and defensive character, (4) specific voting behaviour, and (5) its strong connection to the leadership. This section develops these points.

With regard to *populist attitudes*, they include the accusation of the distance between the people and the élites (mainly political élites, but also economic ones or religious institutions). There is a clear conflict line between the "small people" and the "powerful bosses".[24] The established élites are seen as betraying the interests of the people; this leads to a general distrust of the entire political system and, most particularly, to distrust in party politics. In the public discourse, political élites are negatively presented and are embodied in the feeling of the alienation of the individual from the political system. The state, its institutions, and political parties are perceived and presented as "enemies" of the ordinary people. This is expressed in forms of rebellion such as anti-taxation stances which, not just symbolically, are seen as the intrusion of the state into the private sphere.

This mistrust towards the state and the institutions can be observed in the cases of the *Lega Nord*, the FPÖ, the SVP, and the *Ligue Savoisienne*, which all emphasise their distance from the establishment, which they heavily criticise. Instead, they present themselves as pure and new,

---

[23]   In Bavaria, for example, the SPD leader Renate Schmidt tried to gain a position as an alternative non-CSU leadership figure in the 1990s by adopting a "Bavarian" discourse and political style (Mintzel, 1999: 123). This danger was well recognised by the CSU, which oriented the party propaganda towards undermining Mrs. Schmidt's image as an alternative Bavarian leader. She was presented as a politician who, as a "stranger", abused local Bavarian traditions in order to defeat the CSU, which regarded itself as the true conservator of Bavarian traditions (Wagemann, in this volume).

[24]   For a summary of these populist features, see Taguieff (2001). The rhetoric of the opposition between *le peuple et les gros* has been described by Birnbaum (1979).

and as not contaminated by the immoral practices of politics.[25] In the cases of the *Lega Nord* and the *Ligue Savoisienne*, we find strong irritation with the fiscal system and the centralised state bureaucracy by which the resources of the region are seen to disappear. In the French case, the *Ligue Savoisienne* claims that the wealth of the region could be comparable to that of Luxembourg or a Swiss canton if the French state did not extract and re-distribute its resources.[26] The same discourse applies to the discourse of the *Lega Nord* (*"Roma ladrona"*). The wealthy North would be one of the richest regions in the world and would have no unemployment if its wealth were not re-distributed to the backward regions of the South of Italy.

A second feature of the political expression of a specific culture is that of *protest*. The parties under research here are part of a family which is usually considered to be supported by protest voters.[27] One of the common elements of the cases considered here is the relationship to a (delegitimated) political system which is seen as immobile and unable to renew itself.[28] The political system is seen as being devoid of the necessary dynamics and dominated by established forces that are only interested in maintaining power. In Austria, the great coalition and the *Proporzsystem* between the SPÖ and the ÖVP has dominated political life for most of the time since the Second World War. In Switzerland, although the SVP has long been part of the "magic formula" governmental coalition, it has repeatedly accused the system of being fossilised. Furthermore, the SVP has frequently used institutions of direct democracy in order to threaten the other political parties by directly addressing the "real" people's will. In Italy, the *partitocrazia* was

---

[25] Leading FPÖ officials even agreed to a *codex* (not always respected) of appropriate behaviour which – among other things – established a maximum level of income for politicians.

[26] This especially applies to natural resources, such as energy coming from Alpine dams and also to tunnel fees. The *Ligue Savoisienne* proposed highway fees in their department on the basis of the Austrian and Swiss models.

[27] See, for example, Betz (1994 and 1998a). However, in a recent publication, van der Burg and Fennema (2003) argue that there is little empirical evidence that these parties are supported by a protest or rebellion vote. Furthermore, there is an ambiguity with the participation of these parties in governmental coalitions: the FPÖ is – for the second time – in coalition with the ÖVP, the *Lega Nord* is part of the Berlusconi government, the SVP is part of the "magic formula" coalition in Switzerland, and the CSU is part of the lasting government alliance with the CDU.

[28] This is the thesis of Taggart (1996), according to which populism in Western Europe has been favoured by the long social-democrat hegemony and by the neo-corporatist practices and consociational style of democracy (see also Papadopoulos 1992 and in this volume). This also has close links with the discussion about the "democratic deficit" at EU level (see below). The Italian term *immobilismo* also denotes the incapability of the political system to change and renew itself.

determined by the long domination of Christian Democrats, with the Italian Communist Party dominating as the opposition party, until the corruption scandals in 1993. In Savoie, the protest is expressed against the high bureaucratic centralisation of the French state and its control over the fiscal system.

Third, the political expression emphasises the *protective and defensive character* of the political culture. As already mentioned, the defensive position concerns both identities and interests. There is the exasperation of the threat from outside. The "naturalisation" or "ethnicisation" of the community leads to strong opposition to immigration, which is perceived as affecting only the ordinary people and not the élites.[29] The naturalisation of the political community clearly appears in the case of the *Lega Nord* (Gomez-Reino Cachafeiro 2001). The ethnic (supposedly Celtic) origin of the people of "Padania" (a name which was coined by the *Lega Nord* for the North of Italy) is opposed to the artefact of the Italian nation-state. The ethnic nation is seen as the real nation with a natural linguistic identity and territory, which is opposed to the fake juridical and political nation-state which is combined with an artificial or external linguistic standard. Consequently, there is an emphasis on local languages or dialects, the changing of names of villages, etc. The FPÖ too emphasises the correspondence between ethnic peoples and natural geographical boundaries, most recently in the discussion about bi-lingual German-Slovenian signposts in Carinthia.

The homogeneity of the ethnic community should be preserved by the reinforcement of the *jus sanguinis* and a stricter control of immigration. Natural linguistic ethnic borders also appear in the claims of the South Tyrol. This also affects the development of the idea of a Europe of the People, as we will see below. These defensive attitudes and the naturalisation of the group are also related to pseudo-historical issues. Most particularly in cases in which the historical roots of the group are doubtful (for example, in the cases of the *Lega Nord* and the *Ligue Savoisienne*), a symbolic effort is made to legitimise the existence of the movement. The annual gatherings on the sites of historical battles in the case of the *Lega Nord*, its invention of a Celtic identity, the creation of a *Guardia Nazionale Padana*, the proclamation of an independent parliament, the creation of an anti-historical geography ("Padania"), are attitudes similar to those of the *Ligue Savoisienne*, which has invented identity cards and number plates, or has defined the Rhône as the natural border between Savoie and France.

---

[29] This type of discourse is often shaped by frequent references to the founding mythology, for example, Giussano da Pontida in the case of the *Lega Nord* or Wilhelm Tell in the case of the SVP. This is similar to other populist parties (for example, the French *Front National* and the figure of Jeanne d'Arc).

Thus, the Alpine areas and their political parties are not assimilationists; instead, they are differentialists (Brubaker 1992). In the case of the *Ligue Savoisienne*, we find opposition to the assimilationist idea of the French Jacobin utopia. In Switzerland, the protectionist attitude long expressed by the refusal of the people to join international organisations (such as the United Nations or the EU). These were considered as threats to the foundation stones of Swiss identity (federalism, direct democracy, and neutrality). As will be seen below, this threat is also perceived as originating from the on-going European integration. In all these cases, party programmes include a "national preference" (be it nationally or regionally defined) as far as the labour market is concerned (locals first).[30]

Fourth, *electoral support* for these parties stems, above all, from those voters who have been called the "losers of modernity" (Betz, 1998a: 52). They are mainly small entrepreneurs, non-qualified independent workers, workers in small-sized firms, small farmers, shopkeepers, etc. More specifically to the Alpine case, quite a few supporters are linked to the tourist industry, working in (or owning) hotels, restaurants, and skiing facilities. These sectors are subjected to the uncertainties of globalisation processes more than others. Even though the Alpine region is comparatively rich and wealthy and is only marginally affected by unemployment, the on-going change is seen as a bigger challenge for rural and remote areas which are confronted with the opening up of society, than for urban centres which have always been at the centre of exchange networks.[31] This also has wide-reaching consequences for the economic programmes of these parties, which contain strong liberal features (such as the already mentioned anti-taxation stances), but which are, at the same time, protectionist when it comes to the defence of their own agricultural production from the competition of world-wide markets.

The geography of electoral support, in most of the cases, follows the rural–urban pattern; one exception is the *Lega dei Ticinesi*, which receives most of its votes in the cities (Lugano and Locarno). Several of the Alpine parties have agrarian origins. For example, the SVP was created as a merger of a rural splinter-group of the Liberal-Radicals in

---

[30] This happens to different degrees. While the *Lega Nord* and the FPÖ are quite clear about it (the FPÖ initiated a referendum *Österreich zuerst* and the *Lega Nord* made similar proposals concerning the labour market in Italy), the CSU is less explicit. See Gibson (2002) on anti-immigration parties.

[31] Not all Alpine areas are wealthy. This concerns some valleys in Northern Italy, but also Ticino, which was historically a peripheral and economically fragile canton in Switzerland. Thus, the economic crisis is one of the causes of the rise of the *Lega dei Ticinesi* (Mazzoleni, in this volume).

1919 in the mostly rural canton of Berne and the Democratic Party (a left-wing splinter of the Liberal-Radicals in the 19th century). Although the new party had its strongholds in cities such as Zurich and Schaffhausen, it is weak in the Alpine cantons of Schwyz, Uri, and Unterwalden,[32] and its main electoral support comes from large agricultural cantons such as Berne, Graubünden and Vaud. The party is mainly confined to Protestant cantons, while the Catholic Party has mobilised the peasant population in the Catholic cantons.[33] The Bavarian CSU, as mentioned, was preceded in the *Reich* and Weimar periods by agrarian formations. The CSU is still a party of the countryside, while cities such as Munich and Nürnberg are historically dominated by the SPD. The *Lega Nord*, with the exception of the period between 1993 and 1998, when it managed to conquer the mayorships in several large urban centres,[34] is stronger in the pre-Alpine valleys to which it retrenched after its decline, when it quit the first Berlusconi government in 1994. This is in line with the supportive attitudes towards the rural and ecological values of the Alpine political culture for the conservation of the purity of the landscape, the defence from the invasion of the traffic of heavy lorries along the North–South axes, and the threats to agricultural production.

Finally, the political culture is expressed by elements of strong *leadership*. Clearly, this is closely connected to the populist character of these parties.[35] The emphasis on the natural character of the community and the distrust towards political and social organisations (parties, unions, but also ecclesiastic organisations),[36] finds its expression in the role of the (almost) life-time leaders who *incorporate* the values of the community. Instead of having a function of political representation, the leader embodies and incarnates the true identity and the will of the group. The group, in turn, is reflected in the leadership figures. It is no surprise that the leaders of these movements are not only long-standing

---

[32] However, these are also the cantons in which the opposition to any opening up of Switzerland is relatively strong, as has been shown in referendums for joining international organisations. In Ticino too the strongest opposition to the integration of Switzerland into international organisations can be observed in Alpine valleys.

[33] This has similarities with Carinthia, a Protestant island in which the FPÖ is particularly strong.

[34] This occurred in the wake of the corruption scandals of the Socialist Party which dominated the urban centres in the North of Italy. The *Lega Nord* was one of the first active parties to condemn corrupt practices and to support the trials against their leaders (notably, Bettino Craxi and his Socialist Party in Milan).

[35] According to Taguieff (2001), this is a common dimension of populist parties.

[36] An example of this can be found in the frequent attacks of the *Lega Nord*'s leaders against the "Vatican" and the Catholic Church as an institution, and against its hierarchical approach to social life, which has increasingly become alien to the people (Caramani, 2002).

personalities, but are also uncontested by rival leaderships (Chiantera-Stutte, in this volume). Challenging the leadership would mean bringing the legitimacy of the existence of the group itself into question. Giuliano Bignasca, the leader of the *Lega dei Ticinesi*, was even appointed life-long president at the foundation of the party in 1991. Jean de Pingon in Savoie has been the leader of the *Ligue Savoisienne* since it foundation. Often, the leadership is even detached from formal party roles. This has been the case of the former FPÖ leader Jörg Haider after the year 2000, when he formally resigned as leader of the FPÖ. The same can be observed in the case of the Swiss SVP, even though Christoph Blocher was, for a long time, formally only head of the Zurich section of the party. Umberto Bossi of the *Lega Nord* has been party leader since the times of the *Lega Lombarda*, which was founded in the 1980s.

IV. The Relationship to European Integration: Europe as a Source of Threat

The last column in Figure 2 shows how the defensive elements of this political culture are transposed at two levels. First, the *European supra-national state* replaces the nation-state as the main source of threat both in the countries in which the Alpine parties have a sub-national base and in the small Alpine countries of Austria and Switzerland. Second, a further threat is added, namely, a threat coming from *outside the European borders*, which threatens what are considered to be the common elements of the European culture and historical heritage. This second aspect goes back to the notion that Europe is composed of natural ethnic nations which occupy historical territories. Thus, the process of the institutional construction of the EU has to reflect the fundamental characteristics of Europe as a whole.

On the one hand, the regionalist and nationalist movements of the Alpine regions perceived the opportunity and the incentives for an institutional translation of their claims for more autonomy and self-determination from the beginning of the process of European integration onwards.[37] For territorial minorities, the development of a supra-national political system offers the possibility of circumventing the national state both for economic development and for the affirmation of own identities. On the other hand, however, instead of reflecting a "Europe of Peoples" which represents ethnic and cultural elements of nations, on-

---

[37]   See Tarrow (1994) for the concept of "opportunity structure." Brubaker (1996) develops and defines the concept of "structure of incentives" for the mobilisation of cultural and territorial differences within the fluid institutional framework of the new Europe more precisely. See also Gomez-Reino Cachafeiro (2001) and Kitschelt (1986).

going standardisation and homogenisation processes, implicit to European integration, are perceived as a major threat to regional identities.

The threat of the overwhelming of an artificial national identity has been replaced by an artefact of political-intellectual European citizenship. Once again, the rhetoric is directed against a (geographically and substantially) distant bureaucracy, against powerful lobby-groups which are beyond democratic control, and against financial capitalism which is hostile to the interests of small and medium-sized enterprises. Thus, a rather defensive position has replaced the initial openness towards the new opportunities offered by European integration for a number of issues. On the one hand, development programmes and EU agricultural policies are seen as opportunities for several Alpine regions while, on the other, there is also a clear perception of the threat stemming from international competition and the opening up of markets which have been well protected from external influences for a long time. Furthermore, there is a considerable threat to national and regional identities, imposed by the impersonal and bureaucratic character of the new Europe.[38] The true Europe should not be the bureaucratic "monster" of Brussels, but a people's Europe.

In contrast, these parties advocate a Europe based on the "true" ethnic identities of the European populations. One of the common elements in the vision of the organisation of Europe is the federal legacy of *Mitteleuropean* political thinking. This is, for example, expressed in the clear proposals for an Alpine federalism (as in the case of the *Ligue Savoisienne*), and for broader systems of regional autonomies based on the model of federal states. This tradition goes back to the pan-European thinking typical of Germanic Central Europe which was represented by thinkers of the Hapsburg Empire (who are often mentioned in the public discourses), such as József Eötvös, František Palacký, Carlo Cattaneo, Karl Renner, and others.[39]

Several political strategies of the Alpine populist parties have been transferred from the national to the supra-national EU level. The rejection of both an artificial abstract identity and of the idea of being colonised from an external centre have been transferred from national to

---

[38] For example, the leader of the *Lega Nord* has repeatedly criticised the European super-state guided by non-elected technocrats. He spoke of a Stalinist super-state and of a "Western Soviet Union" and called for resistance against Jacobin Europe (Caramani, 2002: 136–39). In Austria, the anti-European stance of the leader of the FPÖ on the occasion of the accession of Austria to the EU led to the split of the *Liberales Forum*. The Bavarian CSU also regularly expresses its criticism of Brussels. The Bavarian Prime Minister Edmund Stoiber was explicitly opposed to the Maastricht process and the common European currency.

[39] On this tradition of thinking, see Batt (2003).

European level. The identity retrenchment is directed against a (geo-graphically and socially) distant entity which is, however, no longer national, but European. The threats which were previously represented by the nation-state are now represented by the EU. Thus, it is not sur-prising that the regions and the parties under research here present them-selves as being opposed to European integration, as well as to participa-tion in international organisations in general.[40]

However, this view of Europe is not simply a sceptical one, but also a view which represents an *alternative* form of integration. Europe itself is seen as a natural entity, both geographically and in its ethnic plural-ism, which is based on specific Western and Christian values, and whose identity is today threatened from outside. This common identity, however, co-exists with the plurality of cultures: this is the idea of a *Europe of Peoples*. Against centralising tendencies, these movements oppose stronger elements of subsidiarity and federalism: a *Europe of Regions*. Again, we find the themes of distance and retrenchment against both the Americanisation of European society and the immigra-tion from Islamic countries and Asia. The idea of a *Fortress Europe* has been created to replace the former protectionist role of the nation-state. Finally, these movements propose a more democratic Europe with direct participation countering the influence of technocrats and lobbies. Thus, rather than being merely anti-European, these movements are against the currently dominant idea of Europe, and propose a different, more pan-European or *Mitteleuropean* idea of Europe.

V. European-Wide Cleavages

Does such an alternative vision of European integration constitute a *potential political cleavage* within the forming European-wide cleavage constellation and party system? In other words, does an alternative vi-sion of European integration constitute a potential dimension of conflict together with the other two main lines of conflicts which previous re-search has considered (namely, the left–right and the pro/anti-integration dimensions)? This last part of the chapter addresses the question of whether or not such a distinct culture, stemming from a specific social

---

[40] In the 1986 referendum, the Swiss voted against joining the United Nations. In the 1990s, this was followed by a number of other referenda in which the participation of Switzerland to the European Economic Space (1992) or in bilateral agreements with the EU were turned down. However, the SVP is the only Swiss party which was openly opposed to the participation of Switzerland in the United Nations until the fi-nal acceptance of membership in 2002. This is reinforced by the important socialisa-tion agency which is constituted by the Swiss army and the myth of the strategy of the *réduit alpin* in the event of a foreign invasion (on Swiss isolationism, see Kobach, 1997).

base and its partisan-organisational expression, lead to a new dimension in the EU party system.[41] Second, this part addresses the relationship between this dimension and other cleavages. To what extent does this emerging cleavage between alternative images of European integration *cut across* or *overlap* with other socio-economic and political oppositions in the European cleavage constellation, in particular, with the centre–periphery opposition, the rural–urban cleavage, religious differences, and the left–right dimension.

The previous discussion suggests that the emerging cleavage constellation at European level is a more complex system of dimensions of opposition than most analyses of the European political space have argued by focussing on the left–right and on the pro/anti-European integration dimensions. The opposition caused by a different conception of European integration not only introduces a new potential cleavage with regard to the type of integration, but also relates to cleavages that formed during the National and Industrial Revolutions – in other words, processes of state formation (centralisation and secularisation), nation-building (standardisation of language and religion against peripheral resistance), and democratisation. Furthermore, a more complex vision of the emerging cleavage constellation at European level stresses the territorial dimension as a relevant dimension of the political space.

The *territorial* dimension which is intrinsic in regionalist movements, as well as the very existence of a transnational Alpine region, may well give rise to a *centre–periphery* configuration in which territorial resistance to the centralisation of decision-making procedures, cultural standardisation, and fiscal-economic penetration, express themselves both sub- and transnationally. Contrasts here focus on the development of alternative models of integration in peripheral regions which are geographically cut-off from the main decision-making centres and communication axes; economically marginal in that they are prevalently agricultural economies; and culturally distinct in terms of ethno-linguistic minorities. Thus, conflicts could emerge with regard to the levels of economic subsidies, the degree of regional autonomy in the new constitutional framework, and subsidiarity. The territorial dimension will closely interact with functional differentiations within the new "higher level" system that is forming. The territorial dimension over the

---

[41] These terms refer to the three dimensions distinguished by Bartolini and Mair in their definition of socio-political cleavages: (1) an *empirical* element which identifies the social referent in terms of social structure (class, race, etc.), (2) a *normative* element, namely, sets of values and beliefs, a sense of identity and self-consciousness, and (3) an *organisational-behavioural* element, which refers to the political, institutional, and partisan expression of social and normative differences (Bartolini and Mair, 1990: 215).

type of European integration cuts across the traditional class of left–right dimension – the principal functional differentiation in all European party systems. It has been argued that the forming European electorate and party system will strongly depend on whether or not the left–right dimension imposes itself on the "sovereignty dimension" (Bartolini 2002).[42] Furthermore, sub- and transnational regions may join the sovereign nation-state in resisting EU centre formation (economic, legal, and cultural).

The centre–periphery dimension entails strong *cultural* connotations. First, the ethno-linguistic identities might play an important role in matters of local or regional identity, in contrast with the above mentioned abstract and universalistic conception of citizenship (at national and at European level). Second, religious contrasts might, on the one hand, focus on religious *vs.* secularised orientations within the EU and, on the other, focus on the common religious heritage of European *versus* "neighbouring civilizations" such as Turkey (Huntington, 1996). In both cases, this has a strong implication for the definition of a European identity, be it assimilationist or differentialists (with consequences on immigration and free movement policies).

Concerning the first cleavage produced by the Industrial Revolution – the *rural–urban* dimension – as a further functional or sectoral dimension of differentiation, Schmitter (2000) points to agriculture – a cleavage that has disappeared, or has been incorporated in other alignments, in national cleavage landscapes – but which is re-emerging at EU level as a consequence of the important resources for the Common Agricultural Policy controlled by the EU. Contrasts here focus on the support for specific economic activities such as agriculture (through the Common Agricultural Policy), small and medium-sized enterprises, shopkeepers, etc. Furthermore, protectionists attitudes may contrast with liberalisation and privatising policies in the form of anti-redistribution positions, "locals first" in the labour market, maintenance of local wealth (taxation, ecological resources, control of transportation axes, etc.). Finally, this dimension concerns issues such as the protection of natural resources, from the control of transportation axes and energy sources.

How do these dimensions relate to the *left–right* opposition, the other cleavage produced by the Industrial Revolution? In this case, one can make the hypothesis that the cleavage constituted by an alternative po-

---

[42] According to Marks and Steenbergen (2002), the interaction between cleavage "residues" from the 19th and 20th century – especially the left–right dimension – and the pro- *vs.* anti-European dimension will also determine the nature and shape of the European-wide party system. The relationship between dimensions depends upon their respective relevance and whether they will overlap or cut-across one another.

litical culture and vision of European integration is cross-cutting, rather than overlapping, with the left–right dimension. The development of a critical image of European integration takes place in an alliance of "integration losers" (Schmitter 2000: 66–71). This alliance is composed of the extremes of the political spectrum (extreme left-wing and extreme neo-populist right-wing parties), as well as other party families (for example, green parties, regionalist parties, religious parties, etc.). Contrasts here not only concern the strong critique in terms of the "democratic deficit" of the European Union, which relates to the anti-party, anti-establishment, and anti-lobby distrust towards élite institutions and bureaucracies, but also in terms of the defence of welfare protection, whose cuts (necessary for policies of deficit reduction, low inflation, and monetary stability, and in combination with low economic growth and an aging population) affect the weaker strata of the population.

Conclusion

The presence of a distinct "image" of integration has an impact at three levels. First, it represents an important dimension in the emerging European-wide cleavage constellation and party system. For a long time, ethno-linguistic, religious, and territorial identities were thought to "have lost in the game of history".[43] At national level, they have been overwhelmed by the dominance of the left–right dimension (Caramani 2004). However, the survival of old identities and the emergence of new ones can lead to the re-appearance of territorial and cultural dimensions at European level. The Alpine political culture and its complex relationship with the process of European integration may represent such a dimension. The identification of a transnational region could also lead to new centre–periphery configurations. For a long time, the literature has claimed that processes of socio-economic modernisation in Western societies would necessarily lead to the integration of peripheral cultural identities and economic areas within broader political contexts. Theories of state formation and nation-building, as well as the dominance of the class cleavage and left–right alignments as the predominant cleavage at European level (Hix and Lord 1997: 27–49) have turned the attention away from the territorial and cultural dimension, and this unidirectional determinism has only recently been questioned.[44] However, the disap-

---

[43] The expression is taken from Urwin (1983: 222).

[44] The transition from traditional (primordial) communities to modern societies was associated with the breakdown of territory, ethnicity, and religiosity as central elements of the political process especially in the 1950s–1960s. As alternative to this main stream of integrationist theories, see, for example, Connor (1972), and, more recently, Keating (1998). For a recent analysis, see Fox (2002).

pearance of pre-industrial cleavages and territoriality cannot be taken for granted.

A second question is whether or not the emergence of a Eurosceptic culture will lead to a cleavage which reveals the diversity of the views concerning the type of integration (as opposed to the pro/anti-European dichotomy discussed above). This relates to questions of "which Europe" we should have (Jachtenfuchs, Diez, and Jung, 1998). Highlighting the different perceptions of Europe also means contrasting completely different ideas of Europe, of states, of political systems, and of communities. This also implies different expectations about the definition of European citizenship. European territories differ not only with regard to national cultures and ethnic, linguistic, and religious identities, but also in the types of state traditions and citizenship, which entail both political nations based on a legalistic notion of citizenship, as well as universalistic values and ethnic nations (Brubaker, 1992; Smith, 1986).

Third, the existence of such a cleavage might have an impact on the institutional framework of the EU. What will the role of the regions be in the future? Will regions overcome nation-states in their importance? How should the role of the regions be conceptualised in the future? Regarding these questions, it becomes clear that conceptualising a sub- and transnational political culture, and estimating the political responses to it is much more than an area-restricted analysis. The Alpine political culture and the populist answers to it can serve as guidelines for an analysis of public support towards a European polity and identity.

PART II

THE ALPINE CASES

CHAPTER 4

Leadership, Ideology, and Anti-European Politics in the Italian *Lega Nord*

Patricia CHIANTERA-STUTTE[1]

The Italian *Lega Nord* is a party without any roots that are embedded in a significant political tradition. It was born recently and began to grow in the time that followed the turmoil of *Tangentopoli*, when in the 1990s all major Italian political parties were involved in corruption scandals and subsequently disappeared or underwent transformations. Although many political experts have suggested that the success of *Tangentopoli* was due to the people's protest against the old corrupt parties and that it was therefore bound to dissolve with the stabilisation of the new political configuration (Constabile, 1991; Pasquin, 1995), the *Lega Nord* not only survived all the political changes and crises in the Italian system, but it even became part of the Berlusconi governments both in 1994 and in 2001 and has now a fairly relevant position in governmental policy-making. Moreover, the recent results of the elections for the European Parliament (EP) – in which the *Lega Nord* received five per cent of the votes – have shown that the party has to be considered as a rather successful and consolidated party.[2]

Its good results and its long-lived success constitute a puzzling question if the *Lega Nord* is to be defined as a classical ideological party. It is difficult to classify it into left–right categories because it does not have any strong political traditions or any coherent ideological positions. Its programmes are a patchwork of right-wing themes, including ecological and anti-globalisation issues, and its political alliances are always changing. It is even more difficult to find the reasons of its duration.

---

[1] I wish to thank Domenico Comino and Alberto Sciandrafor for helping me to understand the mechanisms and the story of the *Lega Nord*. I am also grateful to Daniele Caramani and Yves Mény for their suggestions on this chapter.

[2] It must be said that five per cent is a very good result for the *Lega Nord*, which contests only the northern part of Italy. In some northern regions, it receives more than the ten per cent of vote.

The *Lega Nord* is part of a broader phenomenon. Many of the populist parties that gained key positions in the European political system in the same period – such as the FPÖ in Austria, or the *Front National* in France – share some of its features: its "anti-system" character, its appeal to the "people", understood as a closed community, its racist attacks and its violation of some well-accepted "rules of the game" in the political life. The refusal to define a political programme along ideological lines, together with its self-representation as a "new movement" and the mobilisation of the electorate achieved by strengthening the fear of foreigners, are all features shared by many post-ideological parties, which have to build their identity outside the old left–right cleavage.

Yet, even though one of the keys to the success of the *Lega Nord* is, paradoxically, due to its new use of political propaganda, its anti-system campaigns, and its language – i.e., the use of dialect – as well as to its internal organisation (all features that seem to define it as an "anti-ideological" movement), its consolidation cannot be explained in these terms alone. The *Lega Nord*'s electorate is far from being volatile; it is "faithful" both to its leader and to its party in spite of the frequent oscillations and changes in the *Lega*'s programmes. The consistency and the faithfulness of the *Lega* voters can only be explained if we suppose that there is a core ideology that consolidates the process of identification of its supporters with the party and thus makes the political mobilisation possible.

One element of the core ideology is the heartland, i.e., the so-called Padania, which is seen as the "construction of an ideal world, but, unlike utopian conceptions, [...] constructed retrospectively" (Taggart, 2000b: 67). In the *Lega Nord*'s rhetoric, the so-called Padania, which includes the Alpine regions, constitutes the heart of the people's identity. The link between Padania and its people, represented by the *Lega Nord*'s leaders, is shown by the use of dialect by the political leaders. Yet, the *Lega*'s political style is new and successful not just because of its use of the northern dialect, which is only understood by the so-called Padani, or for the invention of Padania, whose inhabitants are qualified by superior work ethics; its structure and organisation also play an important role. Even though the *Lega Nord*'s ideology seems to be vague, and the political positions taken by the leadership are not coherent, the leader represents the main point of reference for the electorate and for the whole organisation.[3]

---

[3] To investigate the structure and the ideology of the *Lega Nord*, I have used primary and secondary literature and my interviews in December 2001 with the former party member Domenico Comino, former minister for European policies under the Berlusconi government in 1994, and Alberto Sciandra, former secretary of the *Lega*

In this chapter, I will attempt to explain the main features of the so-called "*Lega Nord*" phenomenon." First, I will trace its origins back to the peculiar Italian context and investigate its anti-system character and structure, in order to explain the success of its model, and to analyse the interdependency between its hierarchical organisation on the one hand, and its flexibility and ability to overcome political crisis on the other, and consider its position concerning the EU and international politics. Second, on the basis of these elements, I will argue that the *Lega Nord* is a right-wing populist party.

I. The Conditions of Emergence of the *Lega Nord*

The roots of *Lega Nord*'s success have to be traced back to some peculiar features of Italian history: (1) the so-called "national question", (2) the Fascist heritage, and (3) the *immobilismo* (the lack of change) which dominated Italian politics after the Second World War.

The long lasting fragmentation between different regions dominated by diverse and foreign monarchs, and the late unification of Italy (1861) are at the origin of the cultural and economic division between the North and the South. The so-called "southern question" emerged after the unification, and has continued to exist until the present day (see Caramani, in this volume). The term designates the problem of the internal integration between the North – which is economically developed and culturally akin to the Mitteleuropean area – and the South, which remains a periphery that is far away from the economic centre, was dominated by landlords until the Second World War, and failed to develop because of clientelism and the inadequate forms of financing from the central state. This problem is still far from being solved. Concerning the social structure, the South had to recover from the "amoral familism", which made it impossible to introduce a universalistic idea of citizenship (Banfield, 1958). The economic and social gap between North and South has not only been reinforced by the emphasis placed by many intellectuals on the fundamental "cultural" separation between the Mitteleuropean North and the Mediterranean South (one example is Romano, 1994), but also by racial prejudice against Southern Italians (Gramsci, 1951: 13–14; Sniderman, 2000: 13 ff.).

The *Lega Nord* used the gap between Northern and Southern Italy in order to mobilise voters against an enemy – the Southerners – and consolidate the party's identity. The "northern question"[4] raised by Bossi

---

Nord section in Cuneo and member of the national (i.e., regional, as the regions are defined as nations in the party statutes) *Lega Nord* parliament in Piedmont.

[4] The term was coined by Gomez-Reino (2002) and it is an inversion of term "Southern question" used to indicate the economical backwardness of Southern Italy.

was built on three issues: (1) political corruption, (2) taxation and economic resources, and (3) immigration from North Africa and from Southern Italy. In addition, the *Lega Nord* perceived the people from the North as being exploited and colonised by party bureaucrats from Rome, and also threatened by delinquency caused by Southern Italians (Gomez-Reino Cachafeiro, 2002: 181–94).

The juxtapositioning of the honest and hard-working North with the lazy South was the pre-condition for the integration of the different regional Leagues into the *Lega Nord* in 1991. The collaboration between seven regional leagues (*Piemont Autonomista, Liga Veneta, Lega Lombarda, Union Ligure, Alleanza Toscana, Lega Toscana, Movimento per la Toscana*, and *Lega Emilio-Romagnola*), which were merged to form the *Lega Nord*, was based on the renunciation of the claim for regional autonomy in favour of the construction of a "united North" (Gomez, 2002: 92 ff.), and on the understanding of "nations" – i.e., regions – as areas sharing common values and one culture. In this view, the Northerners were seen as Europeans, i.e., sharing the productivity and the civic values of Mitteleuropean Western nations against the Southerners.

Another specific element of Italian history lies in its Fascist heritage and the failure of the political and intellectual élites to come to terms with this heritage. In spite of the political trials of Fascists, the ruling political élites avoided taking any responsibility for the past (Setta, 1993). Moreover, instead of looking for, and eventually punishing, Fascist collaborators, all political parties aimed at the *conciliazione nazionale* (national reconciliation). Thus, many political and cultural figures who had collaborated with Fascism, as well as the entire administrative Fascist bureaucracy, were not affected by the democratic transition. In the meantime, parties which openly admitted their continuity with Fascism, such as the *Movimento Sociale Italiano* (MSI) founded in 1946, were able to emerge immediately after the Second World War. The birth of this party, which was mainly made up of former Fascists, went nearly unnoticed in the political sphere and in public opinion.

In this regard, the continued use of racist *clichés* by leaders of the *Lega Nord* can be linked to the lack of a deep confrontation between Fascism and its racial policies, and Italian public opinion. The stress on the division between North and South, and the aggression against the "old migrants" – Southerners who emigrated to the North – overlaps with the attacks against the "new immigrants", the so-called *extra-comunitari*. And the racist attacks against the "black race" and the stress on the ethnic difference between North-Italians and South-Italians follow two patterns: a relatively simple racist one, and a more complex one based on cultural differentialism. The proclamation of a clash of civilisations (Bossi, 1993: 205), the invitation to help the poor countries, and, at the same time, to close the frontiers to immigrants (*Programma per le elezioni europee 2004*: 10 ff.) are all based on a "naturalised" representation of culture in which culture works as a natural attribute that determines and binds the individuals, in a similar way to how a race is interpreted in racist ideologies. This deterministic view of culture and race is the ideological pre-condition for the refusal of multi-cultural and multi-racial societies (Gomez-Reino Cachafeiro, 2002: 133 ff.).

The third specific element of Italian history is the so-called *immobilismo*, a constant feature of the Italian political life from the end of the Second World War until the 1990s. *Immobilismo* means that nothing substantially moved and nothing changed in the political equilibrium since the Second World War. The Christian Democratic party was the governing party until 1992, in coalition with the Socialists since the 1960s. The Communist Party remained as the strong opposition during this long period, even during the 1970s and the 1980s, a period of right-wing and left-wing terrorism. These two parties, *Democrazia Cristiana* and *Partito Comunista Italiano* (DC and PCI), dominated the political scene – together with the Socialists, who were in government coalitions with the former – and thus the small parties, the *Partito Repubblicano Italiano* and the *Partito Liberale Italiano*, and the MSI, the residual former Fascist party, did not have any real political chance.[5] Thus, the right-wing was assimilated into the large Christian Democratic party, which consisted of different wings (*correnti*) – stretching from the left to the right. This politically strong and stable system was partly reinforced by secret organisations, such as *Gladio*, which was directly linked to the American secret services working to prevent the expansion of Communism in the strategic Italian peninsula. The *Tangentopoli* scandals, which began in 1992, brought about the final political de-alignment and the dissolution of nearly all the old political parties – except for the Communist Party, which underwent a process of change due to the international crisis of socialism of some years before, basically from 1989 onwards.

Bossi's movement achieved its present position after *Tangentopoli*, when citizens felt they had been deceived by the old parties: the *Lega Nord* succeeded because it was different from the other parties, i.e., it had no history and represented itself as expressing the people's voice. Moreover, the attacks against the old political parties – for example, a campaign called *forcolandia* against corrupt politicians in the 1990s and

---

[5] An interesting example of a new kind of party, "radical chic" with some populist traits, is offered by the *Partito Radicale*, founded in 1955 but renewed by the charismatic leader Marco Pannella in 1962.

slogans such as *Roma ladrona* – were its fundamental ways of mobilising the masses.

The *Lega Nord* launched a moralistic campaign after *Tangentopoli* in an attempt to recruit new party members, and chose persons who had a "clean" political background. This shows that the selection of the *Lega Nord*'s candidates was very strict at the beginning: no one with any political experience in other parties was accepted. This rule received the enthusiastic approval of the party base in the years of *Tangentopoli* and earned them the people's votes. The affiliation to the *Lega Nord* was described in an interview with Domenico Comino, a former leader of the League, as a "process of rational choice": those who seriously wanted to enter the political arena could exploit the possibility offered by the *Lega Nord* of acting directly in politics. People saw a new and honest movement in the *Lega Nord*, in contrast with the other parties, which were corrupt and "closed" with respect to their recruitment strategy.

II. The *Lega*'s People and Their Enemies

The *Lega Nord* is an "anti-statist" party (Kitschelt, 1997) not only with regard to its critique of state parties, but also with regard to its attacks against every institution in the national and international political system. This aggression follows two fundamental patterns: first, the conspiracy theory and, second, the critique of the old and corrupt institutions – in which the "new", represented and invoked by the *Lega*, seeks the moral "renewal" of political life.

The *Lega Nord*'s emphasis on its difference from other parties and from Italian politics before *Tangentopoli* is related to its relative freedom in front of Italian national and international commitments and history. Its attitudes towards international institutions have always been changeable and, in its political propaganda, they have hardly been respectful of international commitments taken by the Italian state. Examples, here, include its sceptical attitude towards the introduction of the Euro, and the refusal by the *Lega Nord* through one of its major exponents – the Minister of Justice Roberto Castelli – to support the European warrant of arrest (Caramani, 2002). This attitude also characterises the consideration of the Fascist past. Bossi has never taken into account the political "rules of the game" agreed upon by European countries after the Second World War, especially the significance of building the European Union based on democratic values. Concerning the EU, the *Lega Nord* changed its position from being a supporter of it to being Euro-sceptics.

At the same time, the shift of position with regard to the EU cannot be seen separated from the process of the creation of the community, i.e., the people of Padania. The regional Leagues were born in the 1980s as "defenders" of the local minority cultures and dialects against "Roman colonialism". Thus, they searched for EU protection. The Leagues protested against the central state dominated by Southern Italian politicians and found a positive model in the EU at two levels: first, at the institutional level as an "institutional promoter" and, second, at the symbolic level as a model of identification (Diamanti, 1993a). Until 1991 the EU constituted an important opportunity structure which favoured the emergence of the regional Leagues: the EU could acknowledge the legitimacy of their claims to have special financial treatment and protection, which was different from other Italian regions. The Leagues' aim was to obtain a special status for their regions, like that of Trentino-Alto Adige and Val D'Aosta (Keating, in this volume). Moreover, the EU represented a model of identification for the Northern people: they identified themselves with the productivity and the civic qualities of Mitteleuropean countries and, by the same token, emphasised their differences with Southern Italian "Mediterranean" people.

In the next phase of the *Lega Nord*'s development, from 1991 to 1996, Europe represented a symbol rather than an institutional promoter. The campaigns for the acknowledgement of ethnic diversities were reduced, and the different regional Leagues were unified under the *Lega Nord*, with a strong Alpine character. The union of the different regionalist Leagues under the patronage of the leader Umberto Bossi proceeded with a clear ideological shift, i.e., the stress on the common identity of all Northern Italian different ethnicities as "European" and as the "productive part of Italy". The "new" Northern identity was characterised by a common economic and cultural attitude, and not by ethnic features. The internal homogeneity of Northern Italy was "naturalised" and represented as an "eternal culture" (Bossi, 1992: 151; Oneto, 1997) that was characterised by typical bourgeois qualities – that is, productivity, honesty, and morality. These were described by Bossi and other leaders as stable and even as a "the political genes" belonging to the Northern civilisation (Corti, 1995; Betz, in this volume).

An ideological constellation based on a mixture of issues – cultural differentialism, the threat of a clash of civilisations, the identification with "Europe", and the defence of small people – all characterised the *Lega Nord*'s discourse from this moment on, as can be seen in this text by Bossi:

> The *Lega* defends marginal cultures, the small peoples with their traditional patrimony that must not be frozen, but kept alive by respecting the roots that are the essence of humanity. This tolerant vision is essentially European,

and as such must be asserted today more than ever, *vis-à-vis* the diffusion of the cultures of intolerance and integralism sustained by an imperialist and macro-national logic. Islam, on the one hand, and American colonisation on the other, threaten the great European culture that has in Padania a stronghold, and in the South a battle field. (Bossi, 1993: 203)[6]

In the third phase (from the coalition with *Forza Italia* and *Alleanza Nazionale* in 1999 up to the present), the *Lega Nord* has adopted the issues and attitudes that characterise right-wing parties without neglecting the territorial issues. It has promoted campaigns against the "mondialisation" (this is the word traditionally used to define globalisation processes by the right-wing parties) and campaigns in favour of the protection of traditional values, i.e., morality and family. Bossi has increasingly become the defender of bourgeois morality against capitalism, "Americanism", and "massification". Concerning religion, recently and particularly after the terrorist attacks of 11 September 2001, the *Lega Nord* has even asserted the superiority of Christian values over Islam (*Programma per le elezioni europee 2004*), whereas the first *Lega Nord* had had a strong anti-clerical attitude.

This third phase shows an increase in mobilisation through symbols and rituals which reinforce the feeling of belonging to Padania and recall the ancestral origins of a Padanian community: for example, the foundation of the Parliament of Padania and of the *Guardie Padane* or Green Guards, and the baptism of party members with water from the river Po. The increase of cultural activities, such as the founding of the newspaper *La Padania* and the publication and diffusion of books about the so-called Padania's origins are part of this process of the creation of the (imaginary) territory and concept of Padania (Biorcio, 1997: 94). Mythological issues are used in various publications which argue the natural and cultural superiority of the people of Padania. Some *Lega Nord* publicists even claim that the racial origins of the people living in Northern Italy can be traced back to the Longobards and the Celts, and that this civilisation has remained relatively "pure" in comparison with the rest of Italy (Oneto, 1997), and some groups in the *Lega Nord* use pagan symbols, such as runes.

The enemies of the *Lega Nord* are Islam, the EU, America, and the globalisation process. The new strategy of the *Lega Nord* consists of denouncing all threats to its "national sovereignty" and to the people's power: globalisation, international capitalism, as well as the danger caused by the stronger role of international organisations. In this way, the *Lega Nord* shows itself to be more than a party dealing with federalism and with the interests of the North Italian regions. It enters into

---

6   All quotations have been translated by the author.

international political discussions and deals with issues which are shared internationally and transversally by the whole political spectrum and, at the same time, continues to promote its anti-system campaigns. For example, one of the international themes appropriated by the *Lega Nord*, which cuts across the left–right dimension, is ecology and sustainable development (*Programma per le elezioni europee 2004*).[7] At the same time, the *Lega Nord* continues to present itself as a "moral party", which defends both people's rights and the rights of different peoples to live differently (Bossi, Discourse at the Party Congress in Venice in 2000). The Europe of Peoples promoted by Bossi is juxtaposed to the "type of Europe that the Left proposes: a super-state, a federation like the Soviet one, based on the reduction of the national parliaments' sovereignty" (Bossi, Discourse in Pontida, in 2001).

The explanation for the *Lega Nord*'s opposition to the EU must be found in its typical anti-system attitude: Euro-scepticism is a strategy, i e, a conscious action to preserve the party's identity and its image, and thus to keep on mobilising its electorate. More precisely, the *Lega Nord*'s Euro-scepticism must be explained as a new "platform" from which to continue the anti-system propaganda as well as a way of supplying a new form of politics of identity which is capable of re-mobilising the masses. The development of anti-EU scepticism does not represent a reactionary attitude; on the contrary, it is an attempt to become an actor in the international political system. At the same time, attacks against the EU replace the fight against the national government which took place before it participated in the government coalition.[8]

In the *Lega Nord*'s campaigns, the EU constitutes one of the main scapegoats to explain the economic crisis. EU politicians – accused of being socialist and aiming at total world power through multi-nationals – are, according to Bossi,

> stupid illuminists [who] not only want to impose through their laws how we should live, but also to block our economy. They have opened up the barriers between nations, eliminated the customs, and now those countries, that pay their workers less and use slaves, do not respect the environment and humanity, are more competitive than us. The market mystic assures us that we will all be richer and richer. But, in the meantime, we will be dead if we do not use a word that is hated by the stupid illuminists: protectionism. The

---

[7] See also Caramani, and Caramani and Mény (both in this volume) for the ecological campaigns of other populist parties.

[8] This seems to contradict the model proposed by Aleks Szszerbiak (Szczerbiak and Taggart, 2000b) in which protest parties that move into the political mainstream are likely to abandon strong Euro-scepticism. The *Lega Nord* does not seem to have abandoned its Euro-sceptic attitude. On the contrary, it has stressed it even more.

free market, the bankers, the illuminists have failed. Politics and popular sovereignty re-emerge. (Bossi, 2003)

The recent programme for the European election of 2004 shows all the features of the *Lega Nord*'s Euro-scepticism. Bossi and his party have turned their liberal pro-market campaigns into an anti-market and protectionist defence of the Italian economy and interests. Moreover, in the new party rhetoric, the usual attacks against the European bureaucrats and technocrats, who do not represent European citizens, are the counterpart of the idea of the strong identity of the different European peoples and regions. European culture has to be preserved against the threat of terrorism, against a clash of civilisations (in particular, against Islamic aggression) and against the economic decline which would follow massive immigration from the poor countries (*Programma per le elezioni europee 2004*). The EU has to be restricted not only geographically – Turkey is rejected as a possible member – but also politically: the Europe of Regions, proclaimed as the best model for a possible European order, has to be based on territorial communities, which can, at any moment, withdraw from the EU. "Regional interest" has to be introduced together with the "communitarian interest" in order to protect regional/national industry from more competitive products, to protect agriculture from the introduction of GMOs, and to implement typical regional products. Europe should even reduce its control of economic issues – the introduction of the Euro is held to be responsible for the economic crisis – and of justice. The only function left to the EU is defence against terrorism and control of immigration. Thus, the only Europe worth building is "fortress Europe", closed against external enemies, such as terrorists and immigrants (*Programma per le elezioni europee 2004*).[9]

In summary, the Euro-sceptic campaigns by the *Lega Nord* have four aims:

- First, to re-affirm the *anti-system* and anti-stability character of the party, even if and when it participates in the government. Thus, it wants to state its coherence and continuity with the past and to represent a "differentiated position" from the other political partners in the government.
- Second, to *externalise* economic and political problems: the blame must not be directed at the government but at external agencies.

---

[9] The idea of Europe of regions in not new, but it is a theme that has been elaborated by Bossi from the beginning of the movement. Here, the collaboration between Bossi and exponents of the FPÖ, such as Andreas Mölzer and Jörg Haider, in order to support their vision of the Europe of regions is of interest (Hatzenbichler *et al.*, 1993).

- Third, to re-affirm a *"heartland"* – above class differences – and *politics of identity*, capable of mobilising voters.
- Fourth, to participate in *international political discussions* and partially get rid of the regionalist heritage.

III. The Party Organisation

A. Leadership

The party identity in the "in-group" is based on the identification of an enemy, not only the racial one or the immigrants, but also – and primarily so – political enemies. The political opponent is not seen as a political competitor, but rather as a moral enemy, a traitor of the "real people" who are represented only by the *Lega Nord* and its leader. The internal enemies, i.e., opponents within the party, are expelled because of their conspiracy against the leader. The hostility against internal opponents has to be linked to the aggressive character of the ideology which is dependent on the charismatic leader, who personifies the party and the "people". The link between the "exclusionary" idea of the people, propagated by the *Lega Nord*, and some structural components, in particular the model of the people inside the party and its internal hierarchical structure, are worthy of investigation. In this perspective, the lack of a well structured organisation together with the unlimited power of the leader has to be seen as a pre-condition for the party's ideological flexibility and for its internal cohesion.

The possibility of "shifting the enemy", i.e., of externalising the internal social-economic problems from the national to the international level, is linked to the flexibility of the party ideology: the party leader decides the target that must be used in order to mobilise the party's electorate and to create a separation between "us" and "them" (Pallaver, in this volume). The shifts relating to some positions and attitudes – for instance, its oscillating collaboration and non-collaboration with Berlusconi's coalitions – do not break the "continuity" or the internal cohesion of the party, which depends above all on the identification of the party in the leader. Moreover, as we have seen, the anti-system attitude is maintained even when the party "is in the system" through the continuous mobilisation of the masses against other institutions – the international organisations, the EU, America, Islam, and so on.

Three conditions ensure the continuity of the party's strong leadership:

- The leader is out of discussion – there is no alternative way of leading the party and therefore he is relatively free to draw the programmatic lines alone.

- He presents himself as the continuity in the party and as the "new" against the "old".
- He is seen as the only one who can face the other parties and the international institutions.

First of all, the *Lega Nord* – or, rather, its leader Umberto Bossi – is tremendously skilled in using the media and attracting the attention of the public opinion by behaving scandalously. For instance, Bossi's anti-Southern campaign was a means of breaking the conformity, gaining the attention of the masses, and representing the new movement as something completely different and provoking.[10] Bossi is, therefore, an example of the new political entrepreneuralism (von Beyme, 1996) in which the personal style of the leader, a self-made man, skilled in using scandals and saying "what real people think", has a central role.[11]

B. Members

The absolute control over the party is obtained through the reduction of the party staff and organisation, as well as through its complete domination by the leader. This strategy is made clear by the emphasis on keeping the *Lega Nord* as a movement rather than as a party. Moreover, Bossi created the personalisation of the party and its de-institutionalisation in different ways: by establishing clientelistic networks of individuals with personal connections to him (Gomez-Reino Cachafeiro, 2002; Tambini, 2001),[12] through the recruitment of party functionaries who had no previous political experience and who constituted a "body" that was loyal to him, through frequent rotations and "purges", through the informal prohibition of any real discussion or critique during the party assemblies, and through the link with aggressive organisations that are faithful to him, such as the *Guardia Padana*.

The *Lega Nord* has never had a large organisation. Prior to the formation of the *Lega Nord*, its predecessor, the *Lega Autonomista Lombarda*, was a do-it-yourself organisation (Bossi and Vimercati, 1992: 42; Tambini, 2001: 90 ff.; Gomez-Reino Cachafeiro, 2002: 141 ff.) with a loose structure, and consisted of the members of the newsletter *Lombardia Autonomista*. From 1992 onward, with its growing success,

---

[10] In an interview published in *Oggi* (21 December 1992), Bossi declared that his racist campaign was promoted to attract journalists.

[11] The strong leadership and the hierarchical internal party structure are not the only prerogatives of populism. One should think of the parties which existed before, such as the Italian Socialist Party (PSI) under Bettino Craxi. However, what is new is the degree of the development of these features and their link with the "flexible" and apparently thin party ideology.

[12] See the diary of Gianfranco Miglio, intellectual former member of the *Lega Nord* (Miglio, 1994).

the *Lega Nord* expanded and began to recruit party members as well as to build a better organisation as a mass-party, while simultaneously trying to maintain the characteristics of a movement.

The party organisation is simple and hierarchical consisting of five layers: federal, national, provincial, district, and communal. Even though the movement portrays itself as "open" to the people, it is not a mass party, but rather closed and acutely centralised.[13] The Federal Congress is the most powerful body, which elects the party secretary and the president. Bossi, the federal secretary since its origin, is the absolute leader of the party. According to the party statute, the secretary co-ordinates and directs all party organs and represents the unity of the movement (Art. 16 *Statuto della Lega Nord*; Gomez-Reino Cachafeiro, 2002: 144). The first layer of members, *soci semplici*, have no right to vote. The promotion to *socio ordinario*, having a right to vote, is complex and difficult: the proportion is five members without voting rights to one with rights. The promotion consists of a process of co-optation: the future *socio ordinario* has to be proposed by the communal section to the district section and by the latter to the provincial section. This very complex procedure means, first of all, that a party member who wants to become active and to gain influence must have good relations with all representatives at all party levels, and also that all party layers have to agree on the promotion.

Bossi is certainly the charismatic figure who personifies all the hopes and expectations of the party members. Internal democracy is non-existent; this is evident both in the poor quality of the debate in the congresses, in which all motions are pre-selected and can only be read if they are in line with the party leader's opinion, and in the recurrent "purges" against members who threaten Bossi's leadership. Bossi has eliminated all his old party friends and supporters who could have represented an alternative to him: Franco Rocchetta, Irene Pivetti, Domenico Comino and his group from Cuneo. Rocchetta affirmed in a interview in 1994 that Bossi "wants to transform the *Lega Nord* into a party like those in Eastern Europe".[14] This opinion is shared by many former members. Due to his habit of criticising Bossi's leadership, the former Minister for EU Relations in the first Berlusconi government, Domenico Comino, was literally thrown out of the party in 1999 during a riot in

---

[13] The relative closure of the movement as well as the principle of the complete control by the leader were suggested by the only party intellectual that the *Lega Nord* ever had in its ranks, Gianfranco Miglio, who supported this form of centralisation only for the first period of the party formation, and not after its consolidation. As Miglio admitted, Bossi aimed to keep the centralistic structure in the party forever (Miglio, 1994).

[14] Interview with Franco Rocchetta, in *Repubblica*, 1 August 1994.

which some of his followers were violently attacked. Gianfranco Miglio, the only well-known intellectual who was a member of the League for a long time, was also obliged to leave, when Bossi refused to give him a substantial role in the government in 1994.

The *Lega Nord* "is" Bossi. The relations between Bossi and his collaborators are personal, based on a kind of code of honour, and the threat of being accused of "betrayal" becomes a very difficult experience for a *Lega Nord* member. A highly emotional and also financial investment characterises the *Lega Nord* membership: every *leghista* who was elected to Parliament had to give 2,000 Euros per month to the party – and, even at the foundation of the *Lega Nord*, the membership contribution was more expensive than in other parties. One of the bodies planned by and directly dependent on Bossi is the *Guardia Padana*, who apparently works to keep order during demonstrations, but whose real task is to control party members. The future development of the *Lega Nord* remains, however, a puzzling question after the illness of its leader and his eventual retirement.[15]

The *Lega Nord* makes it possible for every member to get a very intrusive but, at the same time, a warm form of identification. One could say that the first *Volk* – homogeneous, loyal to the leader, compact – which is created by the *Lega Nord*, is the *Volk* inside the party. A *Volk* in which individuals are not welcome: as one of the *Lega Nord* members said, "[n]o one should have a face in the *Lega Nord*: no one should make propaganda for himself showing his photo. Members are not individuals: they are the party. Only the leader has a face" (personal interview with Domenico Comino).

Conclusion: The *Lega Nord* as a Right-Wing Populist Party

The *Lega Nord* represents a form of making politics, a political style which is determined by the conditions of the contemporary world of mass communication, which focuses on a territory and on the regeneration of the people, understood as a homogeneous entity which speaks through its leader. The main characters that emerge from the analysis of the *Lega Nord* are: the exclusionist model of identity, the appeal to a *Gemeinschaft*, the protection of the territory, the naturalisation of culture, its anti-system attitude, and its thin ideology. These features seem

---

[15] Due to Bossi's stroke on March 2004, the *Lega Nord* underwent a serious crisis, which did not have any impact on the European elections of June 2004, in which the *Lega Nord* received five per cent of the vote. The problem of finding an alternative leader is, however, a crucial current issue: no one seems to be capable of attracting the masses and of giving a unity to the party apart from Bossi. This is shown in the attitude towards the government crises after the elections, when the party leaders still depend on a Bossi for the important decisions, in spite of his illness.

to characterise the *Lega Nord* neither in terms of a populist party, nor exclusively following the right-wing or the territorial cleavage. Instead, it is useful to use the territorial cleavage together with the right–left cleavage and look at their relationship as overlapping cleavages. The *Lega Nord* is therefore populist, as it bases its claims on the defence of a territory and a culture, and has a typical right-wing conception of the "people". All these features must be investigated not only with regard to internal politics, but also in their relationship to international politics. In other words, the *Lega Nord*'s development has to be considered also in the light of the process of Europeanisation: it is on this level that the *Lega Nord* maintains its mobilising force and its anti-system character.

The *Lega Nord* shares its chameleonic nature with populism as, like all populist parties, it is "heavily coloured by its context" (Taggart, 2002: 70) and is characterised by "a style of political rhetoric" (Kazin, 1995: 3). Moreover, it shows one of the most evident features of many populist discourses, i.e., the attack against every existing institution and against some well-established international organisations. Yet, the definition of the *Lega* as "populist" is formal because it only asserts that the *Lega Nord* is a "political actor" which exploits the political tensions generated in Italian politics, without considering its specific modes of action and discourses (Schmidtke, 1996; Diamanti, 1996).

What could be defined in this regard as the "content" of the *Lega Nord*'s populism is the basic orientation of the political programme, which forms a "core" identity or, rather, gives the old party "militants" what they would, more or less, like to hear from the party leaders, i.e., the "reasons" for their long lasting trust. There are some features that define the "people" (*Volk*) *represented* by the *Lega Nord* – represented in a double sense, first, as an indication of a group of people, and, second, with regard to the process of political representation – which, in the same way, indicates the "enemy". As seen above, the counter-model of the *Lega Nord* can vary: at the beginning, it was the Southerners, the immigrants and the government parties who were the enemy; recently, it has become the EU and liberalism, "the system" or what the *Lega Nord* calls the homogenising way of thinking (*Programma per le elezioni europee 2004*). These targets recall a positive representation of the heartland and of the community, seen as the source of sovereignty.

The *Lega Nord*'s idea of "the people" is exclusionary and derives from the "stable character" of the qualities defining the *Volk* (race, culture as race, territorial belonging) as well as from the oppositional nature of its definition, i.e., the aggressive nature of this collective identity. By evoking the common traits shared by the people, the populist leader mobilises and even "creates" the people in opposition to the "non-people" – as shown in the process of the creation of the so-called

Padania, the idealised land where the *Lega Nord* originates. This process
is clear in the transformation of every political question into an issue of
the definition of an inside against an outside, in which the inside is the
people, uniting all the classes, professions and ages, and the territory,
and the outside is a vague antagonistic concept.

The plea for the defence of the people is typical of right-wing political discourse. Following this model, the people are homogenous, relatively "pure", not to be contaminated with other cultures and peoples: an
exclusionary representation, based on a very narrow definition of
people's culture, which originates from the ethno-nationalistic nature of
the regional Leagues.[16] The people's culture is seen as something stable
and natural: a second nature, which it is impossible to get rid of. Moreover, as it happens with culture, people's interests are seen as im-
mutable, as incapable of being the object of agreement and negotiation.
The interests shared by the people of Northern Italy are seen as an *a
priori* category: they cannot be weighed against other interests. They
constitute the people's identity – like people's dialect and customs. As
Gomez-Reino Cachafeiro observed about the *Lega Nord*, "[t]he use and
distribution of economic resources was claimed not on the ground of a
neo-liberal agenda of 'more or less state', but as a matter of political
rights, questioning the whole edifice of the Italian state. The *Lega Nord*
did not claim the reduction of the tax burden *per se*, but the claim was
made on the basis of the political rights of the North" (Gomez-Reino
Cachafeiro, 2002: 99).

The territorial claim, which at national level is translated into the request for federalism, at the European level becomes a rejection of EU
enlargement and of the growing influence of the EU in national politics.
At this level, not only does Bossi try to gain visibility for the *Lega Nord*
as an international political actor, but points to the idea of the Europe of
Regions, which would qualify the so-called Padania and the North as
one territorial region, which is nearer to all the other Alpine regions,
than to Southern Italy.[17] The Europe of regions would be an alternative
model to the European Union and to the Europe of Fatherlands, proposed by De Gaulle and supported by some of the right-wing parties,
such as *Alleanza Nazionale* in Italy. This model, which aims at co-
operation between Alpine regions, and is centred on the assumption of
the uniqueness of the Alpine "culture", would represent a novelty in the
political field because its challenge to the existing international and

---

[16] See Pallaver (in this volume) for the definition of *Volk* and *ethnos*.
[17] The idea is not so recent. It is the "ethnic" re-interpretation of an old project by
Gianfranco Miglio, which divided Italy into three parts (North, Centre, and South)
and saw a strict collaboration of the Mitteleuropean northern part with Europe
(Miglio, 1992: 29 ff.; 1994: 9).

national institutions would depend on a possible agreement between Alpine populist parties.[18] In this way, the processes of deepening and enlargement of the EU seem to orient the political agendas of some populist parties – including that of the *Lega Nord*. The future question is whether populism will be capable of blocking or deviating the current process of European unification.

---

[18] Some efforts aiming at the collaboration between populist Alpine parties were made by the FPÖ's intellectual leader Andreas Mölzer and by Haider, when, in November 2001, Mölzer met with the political leaders of the populist right-wing parties in Burg Kranichberg, in order to co-operate to support a new group in the European Parliament (Schiedel, 2001). The issue was even the FPÖ slogan at the 2004 European elections, when Mölzer was the FPÖ candidate. The right-wing exponent Mölzer, who launched a campaign against the FPÖ first candidate Hans Kronberger, was elected to the European Parliament, with a programme which aimed at uniting all European populists in a Euro-sceptical party in the EP.

CHAPTER 5

Right-Wing Populism Plus "X"
The Austrian Freedom Party (FPÖ)

Anton PELINKA

The *Freiheitliche Partei Österreichs* (FPÖ), or Freedom Party of Austria, represents an exceptional phenomenon among European party families: among all the parties represented in the European Parliament (EP) which are not members of any of the traditional "party families" or party groups, the FPÖ is the most successful. The FPÖ has been very successful nationally and yet, at the same time, it has been extremely isolated both internationally and at European level.

This has to be seen in direct connection to the FPÖ's specific character:

- The FPÖ is a "populist" party because it claims to represent and to mobilise "the people" against the élites.
- The FPÖ is a "right-wing" populist party because it claims to defend specific ethnic, national, or cultural identities against foreigners and against the very idea of a European federation.
- The FPÖ represents an old tradition, part of Austria's traditional political culture – the Pan-German *Lager* or camp, which also includes the tradition of Austria's national-socialism (NSDAP).

This third aspect – the FPÖ's traditional character – is the factor "X" that appears in the title of this chapter. The party is deeply rooted in Austrian history. Its collective memory goes back to the times when the Austrian Nazi party grew out of the Pan-German camp in the early 1930s; the years of Nazi rule when a significant segment of Austrian society identified with Hitler's regime; and the post-1945 period when the FPÖ was founded as the protest of former (many of them high-ranking) NSDAP-members against a political order that seemed designed to make people forget about both Austria's and the Austrians' involvement in Nazism. The factor "X" distinguishes the FPÖ from other right-wing populist parties which do not have this kind of collective memory. There is, of course, a certain parallel between the FPÖ and

131

the Italian *Alleanza Nazionale* (the former *Movimento Sociale Italiano*) – a party which was collectively linked to Italian Fascism. The parallels and the differences between the FPÖ and *Alleanza Nazionale* are the same as the parallels and the differences between German (and Austrian) Nazism and Italian Fascism.

I. The FPÖ: Isolated in Europe

Most of the significant European parties belong to specific "party families". There is a European party system already in existence in the EP. This system consists of European parties and party groups which reflect the different traditions of European politics (Hix and Lord, 1997: 21 ff; Johansson and Zervakis, 2002). The European People's Party (EPP) is the umbrella for Christian Democrats and Conservatives, while the Party of European Socialists (PES) unites the different national social democratic, labour, and socialist parties. The European Liberal, Democratic and Reformist Group (ELDR) represents the different shades of liberalism. The Greens/European Free Alliance represent the pro-EU Greens, while the European United Left/Nordic Greens cover the post-communist parties and the anti-EU Greens. Some of the parties considered to be "right-wing populist" – such as the Danish People's Party and the Italian *Alleanza Nazionale* – co-operate with some very specific parties (such as the Irish *Fianna Fáil*) in the group of Europe of Democracies and Diversities or EDD (Day, 2000: 232 ff.).

Among the 626 Members of the European Parliament (EP) elected in 1999, only 26 do not belong to any of the party groups within the EP: 5 out of these 26 members are the representatives of the FPÖ. The FPÖ does not fit into the European party system in the same way that some of the other rightist parties, such as the French *Front National*, the Belgian *Vlaams Blok*, or the Italian *Lega Nord* do (Day, 2000: 238). The EP includes right-wing parties organised in a specific party group – the EDD – as well as the right wing parties outside the group structure of the EP. At European level, the parties which are usually characterised as "right-wing populist parties" are not organised in a unified way. There is no "party family" of the European right-wing. The contradictions between the different kinds of nationalism and ethno-centrism seem to prohibit any real integration of the different parties of the far right. The FPÖ, in particular, is not even linked in any systematic way to the other parties of the far right – nor is it linked to any of the moderate party groups.

One of the reasons for this might be that the FPÖ cannot be fully explained in terms of "right-wing-populism". Its isolation in the EP is just one aspect of the party's specific character that was especially underlined in the hour of its greatest triumph – in 2000 – when the FPÖ seemed to dictate Austrian politics and when Europe, represented by 14 EU governments, reacted harshly to the FPÖ's success. Among the isolated parties of the European far right, the FPÖ has been by far the most successful. In the Austrian national elections of October 1999, the Party got 26.9% of the votes – the second biggest share of all Austrian parties (see Table 1). At the beginning of 2000, the FPÖ formed a coalition with the Christian Democratic and Conservative *Österreichische Volkspartei* or Austrian People's Party (ÖVP). As a result of this alliance, the FPÖ gained control of over 50% of all cabinet positions. Half of the Austrian government was in the hands of the FPÖ.

This was the background to the bilateral "measures" that the other 14 EU-governments declared against the Austrian government in February 2000: the "EU 14" considered such a decisive government role of the FPÖ a danger both to "European values" and to the very existence of the Union. And, even after lifting the measures in September 2000, the EU 14 based their decision on a report which declared the FPÖ to be a party with extremist tendencies (Karlhofer, Melchior, and Sickinger, 2001; Hummer and Pelinka, 2002).

The FPÖ's attitude towards European integration had already changed significantly before the measures of the EU 14. Before 1990, the FPÖ had been "pro-European" in the sense that it openly favoured EC-membership as an alternative to the pattern of "permanent neutrality" established in 1955. But when the *Sozialistische Partei Österreichs* (SPÖ) or Austrian Socialist Party, then in a government coalition with the ÖVP, decided to apply for EC-Membership in 1989, the FPÖ abruptly changed its position. The party became the main voice of Austrian opposition against EU-membership and, after Austria's accession to the EU in 1995, the main voice against the deepening of the union (for example, in occasion of the adoption of the European Monetary Union, EMU) and enlargement of the EU, especially with respect to the enlargement of 2004 (Pelinka, 2004).

The reason for the FPÖ's shift from a distinctly pro-European attitude to a tentatively anti-European position lies the dramatic change in the FPÖ's electorate in the 1990s. Until 1986, the party represented five per cent of the votes, and the typical FPÖ voter was bourgeois and/or rural. Starting in 1986, the party grew rapidly into a 20% plus party, and increasingly came to represent the "modernisation losers" (Betz, 1994) – the less educated, blue collar, urbanised voters, who were negatively impressed by the impact of Europeanisation and globalisation (see Betz and Caramani, both in this volume).

Table 1. The Rise and Fall of the FPÖ

General elections	FPÖ votes (%)
1983	5.0
1986	9.7
1990	16.6
1994	22.5
1995	21.9
1999	26.9
2002	10.0

Source: Plasser and Ulram (2003: 194).

These negative attitudes *vis-à-vis* the EU fit into the general pattern of "Euro-scepticism" that existed on the eve of the 2004 enlargement and during the work of the EU Constitutional Convention. With the significant exception of the Nordic countries, hostility towards the shaping of a European federal system has become a phenomenon of the European right (Harmsen and Spiering, 2004). In this respect, the FPÖ is part of a broader picture. But, together with the *Lega Nord*, it also shares the shift from a rather pro- to a more anti-position as far as the deepening of the EU is concerned (see Chiantera-Stutte, in this volume). Sometimes, the EU is seen positively – whenever "Brussels" is seen as an antidote to "Rome" or "Vienna". But the general agenda of European integration and the shaping of a European identity seem to be alien to both.

As a party in government, since February 2000, the FPÖ was either unable or not willing to transform its anti-EU attitude into policies. Despite strong rhetoric against the "Eastern enlargement" (especially against the membership of the Czech Republic), the FPÖ did not try to block the process of enlargement. Although it expressed deep Eurosceptic resentment, underlining its isolation within Europe, the FPÖ in government was incapable (or unwilling) to stop the ongoing processes of integration.

After the national elections of November 2002, the FPÖ lost about 16% of its vote. The percentage of FPÖ votes sank to a mere 10%. However, as most of the votes lost by the FPÖ went to the ÖVP, the ÖVP/FPÖ government coalition was renewed in 2003, albeit with a much weaker FPÖ share of cabinet positions. Since then, the FPÖ is no longer an outstanding example of the success of right-wing populism in

Europe. But this decline has not changed the general "nature" of the party – and certainly has not changed its isolation in Europe.

II. The FPÖ as a Populist Party

During its rise in the late 1980s and 1990s, the FPÖ was playing the populist card successfully. It claimed to speak for "the people" and against the political class and the "establishment" more generally. By positioning "the people" against the élites, the FPÖ tried to integrate all the diverging interests of class, gender, religion, and generation groups. In other words, during this period, the FPÖ – which had, until 1986, been a small bourgeois party with a specific (Pan-German) tradition – tried to become a catch-all party.

In the period of its rise to significance, the FPÖ's attitude was very much the attitude described and analysed by Robert Dahl. "Populism" was not defined as being opposed to democracy in general, but as being opposed to the very essence of *representative democracy*: political parties and interest groups, and to all the intermediary actors placed between "the people" and the leader (Dahl, 1956: 34 ff.; Mény and Surel, 2002: 7 ff.; Papadopoulos, in this volume). The FPÖ attacked the specific political culture as developed in post-1945 Austria: (1) inter-party power sharing arrangements ("grand coalitions") and neo-corporatist networks ("social partnership"); (2) it opposed the Austrian version of "consociational democracy" and the consensus model as developed between the Catholic conservative tradition (represented by the ÖVP); and (3) it opposed the social democratic ideology represented by the SPÖ (Pelinka, 1998: 15 ff.).

This strategy succeeded for two reasons. First, as the party of the Pan-German camp which, due to its involvement in the Nazi regime, had had no significant impact on Austrian politics in 1945 and the years after, the FPÖ was not part of the Austrian consensus-oriented political culture. The FPÖ could attack without betraying its own positions. The FPÖ was able to use its outsider position to portray the dominant political culture, in which it did not have a part, as grossly outdated and as a system working only in the interest of a small group who were exploiting "the people". Thus, the FPÖ was able to use the classical populist pattern "those above – and us below". Like the Greens, who were elected to the Austrian parliament for the first time in 1986, the FPÖ could not be held responsible for all the real or not so real evils of post-1945 Austrian politics.

The second reason was that the attacks on consociational democracy coincided with a decline of traditional political loyalties. The two major parties (the SPÖ and the ÖVP) were increasingly unable to bind and mobilise the voters, especially the younger generation. The resulting electoral volatility became one of the main assets of the FPÖ's populist agenda. The "old" parties were increasingly considered to be unable to adapt Austria to the rules of a Europe that was following the path of economic and social deregulation. The ability to "renew" Austria was the major claim the FPÖ had made for itself – despite the SPÖ/ÖVP coalition's major success, namely, Austria's entry into the EU in 1995. During this period, the FPÖ was seen as a modernising force, which broke through the paralysed and paralysing structures of a cartel-like political system. Thus, the FPÖ seemed to be the force of renewal in the Austrian political system (Crepaz and Betz, 2000; see also Betz, in this volume).

This populist agenda clearly distinguished the FPÖ from other European parties which – for some time – were seen as parallel cases: the German *Freie Demokratische Partei* (FDP), deeply rooted in the tradition of European liberalism, was part of (West-) German political culture from the very beginning of the *Bundesrepublik*. Between 1949 and 1998, the FDP was always a partner in the coalition governments – with the exception of the years between 1957 and 1961, and those between 1966 and 1969. The FDP played the role that the FPÖ was unable to play, namely, it was able to be in the central and pivotal position of the political system. The Swiss *Fresinnig-Demokratische Partei*, an even more traditional liberal-radical party, was the defining party of Swiss democracy from 1848, the foundation of the *Bundesstaat*. The specific Swiss version of "consociational democracy" is the very product of this party's understanding of democracy. Unlike the FPÖ, neither of the German or Swiss liberals were ever outsiders. On the contrary, they were always the most "inside" of the insiders.

The FPÖ's outsider role in Austrian politics after 1945 is directly linked to its roots. In 1945, members of the NSDAP were officially excluded from the political process in Austria. However, in 1949, most of the former Nazis were re-integrated into politics, and allowed to vote and participate fully in the democratic process. But when, in 1949, the *Verein der Unabhängigen*, or League of Independents, (VDU) was established to give the former Nazis a voice, most of the written and unwritten rules of Austrian politics were defined; and most of the access to power was already controlled: by the moderate rightist ÖVP and the moderate leftist SPÖ. And when, in 1955, even the leading figures of the Austrian NSDAP rejoined the political process and established the FPÖ in 1956, as a successor of the VDU, the new party had good reason to view Austrian politics as a closed shop.

One expression of the FPÖ's exclusion was the tendency of Austrian politics either to opt for "grand coalitions" or, whenever possible, for one-party governments. Until 1999, Austria had been governed for 21 years (from 1945 until 1966) by a coalition of ÖVP and SPÖ, 17 years by one-party governments (1966–70 ÖVP, 1970–83 SPÖ), only 3 years by a "minimum winning coalition" (SPÖ/FPÖ 1983–86), and thereafter 13 years by a "grand coalition" (SPÖ and ÖVP) again. As the third party, the FPÖ was not really able to break through the rules of the political culture as established after 1945. The feeling of being an outsider, of being excluded from the political culture of post-1945 Austria, was used by the FPÖ to repeat the general populist pattern: "we" and "them"; "we" the people, and "we" speaking for the people; and "them" who are at the top and responsible for all the evils that "we" have to bear (Reinfeldt, 2000).

This attitude of being an outsider may also explain the party's success with blue collar-voters (see Table 2 below). The rise of the party during the 1990s was the result of the FPÖ's successful appeal to the younger, lesser educated, and – especially – male voters (see Table 3 below). By distancing itself from the *status quo*, the party was able to attract voters who were traditionally associated with leftist parties. Thus, as a populist party, the FPÖ became a proletarian party – and lost its "bourgeois" appearance. By transforming itself from a traditional party to a populist party, the FPÖ became the party of angry voters, who were angry about the trends of modernisation, and angry about the feeling of being left behind (Müller, 2000).

This also explains the fact that the FPÖ – especially in the years of its rise between 1986 and 1999 (see Table 1 above) – had become a more urbanised party. Before 1986, the party's strongholds were more in the rural parts of Austria, in Carinthia and Salzburg, and Upper Austria. Until 1986, the FPÖ could have been seen as the Austrian version of an Alpine protest phenomenon. But starting in 1986, the FPÖ began to make deep inroads in Vienna in particular. In 1983, at the last general election before Haider became party chairman, the FPÖ received 4.4% of the votes in Vienna. In 1999, the year of the FPÖ's greatest success, the percentage of Viennese voters voting for the FPÖ was 24.8. With this, it became the second largest party in Austria's capital (Plasser and Ulram, 2003: 205).

III. The FPÖ as a Right-Wing Populist Party

A. *The Orientation of the FPÖ*

The FPÖ uses its populist and anti-élitist agenda for right-wing goals. It directs "the people's" anger not only against the "them" who are "above", but also against the "them" who are "outside" – meaning outside of the realm of "we" the people. Its rhetoric and policies are formulated against the real existing foreigners – immigrants, asylum seekers, and refugees. Moreover, they are against potentially relevant and even not existing foreigners – against the people who *could* come to Austria because of European integration, globalisation, and criminal conspiracies (conspiracy theories is a further parallel with the *Lega Nord*; see Chiantera-Stutte, in this volume). The FPÖ is not a leftist populist party – that would mean an inclusive and transnational understanding of "the people". Instead, it is a rightist populist party with an exclusive understanding of "the people". The FPÖ is vertically aggressive – against the "them" who are above; and it is horizontally aggressive – against the "them" who are outside.

This tendency has been demonstrated by different popular initiatives (*Volksbegehren*). In 1993, the FPÖ organised an initiative to increase the legal hurdles that immigrants have to face in Austria significantly. And in 1997 it was responsible for an initiative which tried to prevent Austria from joining the EMU – the very symbol of the "deepening" of European integration. Both initiatives had – in terms of the number of signatures – only a moderate success. And in both cases the majority of the National Council (the Austrian parliament), still controlled by the grand coalition of SPÖ and ÖVP, refused to follow the direction of the initiatives. The FPÖ is particularly remembered for its strong and significant anti-EU orientation. In 1994, it openly opposed Austria's entry into the EU. Before the referendum, which decided in favour of Austria's EU-membership, the FPÖ was the most important factor on the side of the "No" vote (Pelinka, 1994). It was also on the losing side with regard to Austria's participation in the EMU. However, Austria joined the "Euro-zone" despite the FPÖ's opposition.

The FPÖ tried to mix a general xenophobic message with a specific anti-EU message. This became obvious when Austria – particularly during Austria's presidency of the EU-Council in 1998 – had to decide about the country's attitude towards the EU enlargement. As the applicant countries – most of them in Austria's immediate neighbourhood (four of them even bordering with Austria) – are all significantly less developed in economic terms, the anti-enlargement outlook was based on two different arguments, one rational and one irrational. The rational argument concerned the problems that the Austrian economy and, in particular, the Austrian labour market would have to face if the Central and East European countries became member states of the EU's common market. Even though most of the Austrian economists agreed that the enlargement would have a positive impact on the dynamism of the Austrian economy, the negative aspects that the impact of enlargement would have on the labour market had to be taken seriously. But as the EU (with Austria's consent) and the applicant countries agreed on a transition period of seven (or less) years, this possible negative effect seemed to be under control. Less rational was the other argument. The FPÖ mobilised itself against the membership of the Czech Republic in particular, using two justifications: first, the nuclear power plant in Te-melin in the Czech Republic and, second, the history of the expulsion of the German-speaking minority living in Czechoslovakia in 1945 (the so-called "Benes Decrees").

In its campaign against the Temelin nuclear plant the FPÖ was not alone. Many Austrians, especially the Greens, opposed the idea of ac-cepting in the EU a country that was just opening a new nuclear power plant. But only the FPÖ threatened to block the Czech Republic's access to the EU. And, given that all (or most of) the other candidate countries also had nuclear power plants – some of them, like Temelin, in the vi-cinity of Austria – there was no rational explanation of why the Czech Republic had been singled out.

In its critique on the Czech Republic's interpretation of the "ethnic cleansing" of 1945, the FPÖ was able to combine its right-wing popu-lism with the revisionist sentiments that the party nurtures due to its history. Again, there was something of an inconsistency. First, the FPÖ mobilised only against the Czech Republic – and not against Slovakia which was united with the former at the time. As a successor state of what used to be Czechoslovakia, Slovakia has the same responsibility for what the Czechoslovak government had decided in 1945. Further-more, the "Benes Decrees" were directed not only against the German-speaking minority, but also against the Hungarian-speaking minority. Finally, given that far more "Sudeten Germans" moved to Germany than to Austria, the FPÖ ran the risk of being asked the following questions: "Why does Austria (through the FPÖ's campaign) raise the issue of the 'Benes Decrees' more radically against the Czech Republic than Ger-many or Hungary do? Why is it that the FPÖ (and Austria) seems to be interested in overtaking Germany and Hungary as the advocates of a specific group of refugees whose fate must be seen in the context of Nazi Germany and its policy of aggression, occupation, and extermina-tion?"

The inconsistency of the different arguments became obvious when the FPÖ joined the government in 2000. Despite its on-going anti-EU rhetoric, the FPÖ accepted – within the coalition – the leadership of the ÖVP in all European matters. The threat to veto EU-enlargement, and, in particular, to block the Czech Republic's access to the EU was never translated into government policy. The FPÖ's anti-EU orientation, in-cluding its xenophobic and revisionist undertones, was only a factor of domestic policy. It played to the anxieties of specific sections of the

Austrian society – without being able to influence Austria's European policy in any significant way.

B. The Support for the FPÖ

The sections of society that the FPÖ represents in Austria are more or less the same as those that other right-wing populist parties represent in other European countries. It is the section of the "modernisation losers", in other words, the socially underprivileged Austrians. As already mentioned, the FPÖ, at its beginning, a small, rightist, and bourgeois party, became a proletarian party during the late 1980s and in the 1990s, which over-proportionally attracted blue collar votes.

Table 2. Blue-Collar FPÖ Voters (%)

General elections	Blue collar FPÖ vote	FPÖ votes
1983	3.0	5.0
1986	10.0	9.7
1990	21.0	16.6
1994	29.0	22.5
1995	34.0	21.9
1999	47.0	26.9
2002	16.0	10.0

Source: Plasser and Ulram (2003: 129).

The FPÖ, which had traditionally (until and including 1983) been a party that was under-represented by blue collar voters (see Table 2), became more and more attractive to the blue collar vote. In 1999, the FPÖ's share of the blue collar voters even overtook the SPÖ's share: only 35% of the blue collar vote went to the social democrats, the traditional haven of labour votes. And when the SPÖ regained its leading position of labour votes in 2002 (41% compared with the FPÖ's 16%), the attractiveness of the FPÖ to blue collar was still superior to the attractiveness of the party to the general electorate (Plasser and Ulram, 2003: 129). This fits into the general pattern of European right-wing populism. Parties such as the French *Front National* or the Italian *Alleanza Nazionale* compete successfully with the traditional leftist parties for blue collar votes. The exclusive claim of right-wing populism to protect the "modernisation losers" is, at the very least, as successful as the inclusive claim of the left is (Betz, 1994 and 2002; Helms, 1997).

The very same pattern can be seen in the gender structure of the FPÖ's electorate. As is the case with practically all right-wing populist parties, the FPÖ is predominantly male dominated (see Table 3). The FPÖ was, and still is, the party which significantly plays to male expectations more than to female. It is the less educated male voter who has been the typical FPÖ voter since the late 1980s. This gender gap is a specific characteristic of all right-wing populist parties – just as it is for the FPÖ.

Table 3. The FPÖ's "Gender Gap":
Male *vs*. Female Votes (%)

General elections	Male FPÖ Votes	Female FPÖ Votes
1986	13	7
1990	20	12
1994	29	18
1995	27	16
1999	32	21
2002	12	8

Source: Plasser and Ulram (2003: 134).

The FPÖ's predominantly male character has a very traditional aspect. It reflects specific male attitudes and male discourses which are deeply rooted in the FPÖ's traditional *milieu*; in the duelling fraternities which, of course, do not allow women as members; and in the veterans' organisations which cultivate an ambiguous memory of the Second World War. The party's male character expresses the traditional (reactionary) understanding of a clear distinction between social roles designed for men and social roles designed for women (Geden, 2004; Caramani, in this volume). The FPÖ's male character also has a less traditional side. It expresses a "gendered sub-structure" which is rather typical for right-wing organisations. By – either implicitly or explicitly – underlining social inequality between nations, ethnicities and "races", the social differences between men and women are seen as just one among other "natural" inequalities. The FPÖ does not reflect this substructure openly in an ideological or programmatical way, but it is reflected in the intra-party discourse, and fits into a general pattern (Geden, 2004: 65–120; Fuchs and Habinger, 1996; Amesberger and Halbmayr, 1998).

IV. The FPÖ as a Party with a Tradition

As the previous section has tried to show, in all significant aspects the FPÖ seems to be an average right-wing populist party – albeit the most successful among these parties. But what makes it different from all the others – with the exception of the Italian *Alleanza Nazionale* – is the fact that the FPÖ is also a party with a long tradition and an unbroken continuity, which goes back to the end of the 19th century. When some of the leaders of the VDU and some of the "major incriminated" (*Schwerbelastete*) former members of the NSDAP, who had not been allowed to re-enter politics prior to 1955, founded the FPÖ in 1956, the party's first leader was Anton Reinthaller. Reinthaller was active in the inter-war period in the small Pan-German party *Landbund* (Farmers' League) as well as in the Austrian NSDAP. Between 1938 and 1945, he had been a member of Hitler's cabinet, as a Deputy Minister (*Staatssekretär*) in the *Reichsernährungsministerium* (Ministry for Agriculture) and had also been a general of the SS.

With few exceptions, all of the FPÖ's founding fathers were former activists of the NSDAP – and some of them, like Reinthaller, had been very prominently placed in Hitler's hierarchy. From its very beginning, the FPÖ represented the section and tradition of Austrian society and politics which had also been responsible for the rise and the success of the NSDAP in Austria (Riedelsperger, 1978; Manoschek, 2002). Whereas the two other traditional Austrian parties – the ÖVP and the SPÖ – also successfully recruited former members of the NSDAP, the FPÖ was almost exclusively shaped by the background and the tradition of Austrian Nazism. More than any other organisation, the FPÖ stood for the anti-Semitic, Pan-German, xenophobic, and authoritarian tendencies of the Austrian past (Pelinka, 1998: 183–204).

However, in contrast to most of the other right-wing populist parties in Europe, the FPÖ is not a new phenomenon. Indeed, it is a combination of old and new; of *old*-fashioned anti-democratic, anti-egalitarian, ethno-nationalist (including anti-Semitic) sentiments, and *new* ("postmodern") elements of a protest movement, directed against the forces of modernisation and globalisation (Preglau, 2001; Pelinka, 2002). It is this combination of old and new elements which gives the FPÖ its common feature with the other cases of this volume. It perfectly resembles the type of right-wing populism which articulates the fears of the "modernisation losers". However, unlike other Alpine cases, the party also represents an unbroken continuity with its past, which also includes the Austrian NSADP.

Within the spectrum of European right-wing populism, the FPÖ is significantly different from the *Pim Fortuyn Movement* in the Netherlands, from the *Vlaams Blok* in Belgium, from the *Lega Nord* in Italy, and from the Danish People's Party, and even from the French *Front National*. All these parties have no institutional tradition, no identity or consistency which binds them to parties of pre-1939 Europe. The only significant party which also stands for a combination of "old" right-wing extremism and "new" right-wing populism is Italy's *Alleanza Nazionale*, which admits its unbroken tradition with Italian Fascism. Whereas Italy's *Alleanza Nazionale* can be called "post-Fascist", the FPÖ must be called "post-Nazi". And the FPÖ has stressed this tradition in a very clear way.

After the FPÖ tried to escape from this aspect of its past in the 1970s and early 1980s, the party was re-defined when Jörg Haider became its leader in 1986. He went back to the roots of the party by using apologetic rhetoric with regard to Nazism. And, simultaneously, he started to oppose Austria's post-1945 political culture in a populist way. The FPÖ used a double strategy: first, it reminded those who were interested in the party that it was still the party that welcomed an apologetic and revisionist view of Nazism; and, second, it established its credentials as a party which challenged the "haves" in the name of the "have nots" (Bailer-Galanda and Neugebauer, 1997; Scharsach, 2000). Not only is Haider on record for his many statements which can be characterised as "trivialising Nazism", but also – as was the case during the electoral campaign for the Viennese regional elections in 2001 – for falling back to an easily decipherable anti-Semitic code (Czernin, 2000; Wodak and Pelinka, 2002). Haider plays the game of double-speak and double-act, sometimes acting as a legitimate innovator, and sometimes acting as the speaker of the not yet completely forgotten tradition of Nazism.

He has become the synthesis of the FPÖ's double strategy. He can be quoted as the Austrian "Robin Hood" who fearlessly challenges the powerful in both Austria and Europe, and – since 2002, when he began his anti-American rhetoric – even in America. But he can also be cited as the advocate of all who still think "not all was bad under Hitler", that "the Germans fought Bolshevism", or that "the Jews must also be held responsible for what has happened to them". Without using exactly this kind of wording, his message is, nevertheless, clear: Hitler's employment policy was "decent", the SS fought "honourably", and a Jew is not a Jew but someone from the (American) "East-Coast".

The FPÖ symbolises the lack of a complete break with the Nazi past and the alliance of those who are nostalgic for their Nazi past with the xenophobic sentiments of an anti-EU agenda. This explains the nervous response of the other 14 EU member states when the FPÖ came to power in 2000. It is not so much what the FPÖ does in power; it is what the FPÖ stands for. And it is not just right-wing populism with its xenophobic outlook; it is not just "ordinary" Fascism which can be detected in Haider's (and others) rhetoric; it is the reminder of the most brutal and most totalitarian version of Fascism.

Conclusion: The FPÖ and the Centre–Periphery Cleavage

The FPÖ fulfils the criteria of populism as well as that of right-wing populism. But, in addition, it has added a specific flavour of post-Nazism. But does it fit into the pattern of an Alpine party, which opposes the gravity of the European centre? Can the FPÖ and its "ups and downs" be explained by using the centre–periphery model (Keating, in this volume)?

The FPÖ is both a regional and a national party. It is a regional party in so far as it often plays to the tunes of anti-centralism, especially when centralism can be blamed on "Brussels". But it is also a national party as it does not mobilise along the lines "we in the Alps". The party's ability to mobilise is to be seen more along social and cultural conflicts than along geographical conflicts: "we" includes all the "modernisation losers" in Austria; "we" does not exclude a particular region either in Austria or in Europe as such, but excludes different groups within Austria (for example, immigrants) and countries outside Austria (for example, the Czech Republic). The FPÖ's "we" is not directed against the forces of reformation beleaguering the fortress of perseverance. The FPÖ does not have specific Catholic roots, either. On the contrary, the pan-German roots of the FPÖ include a particular Lutheran, even anti-Catholic (anti-Hapsburg) resentment represented by Georg Schönerer (Pelinka, 1998: 173 ff.). The FPÖ's "we" is directed against the post-1945 Austrian élites and against the post-1945 Austrian way of consociationalism and corporatism, which reflects the exclusion of the pan-German *milieu* from post-1945 politics in Austria. And the FPÖ's "we" is especially directed against immigrants and foreigners, first and foremost, against those who come from the poor regions of Europe and outside Europe.

In this respect, the FPÖ is the product of the centre–periphery cleavage. It sees itself very much in the centre of a social order which is being challenged by Europeanisation and globalisation. It sees the end of borders, and the end of the nation-state, as a threat and a danger to the status of the society that it is defending. As the voice of the "haves" who feel jeopardised by the "have nots", the party defends a fortress in the centre of Europe, which is not so much defined by geographical terms as by social terms. As the voice of the "have nots" who feel excluded by the different corporatist, cartel-like, élitist arrangements, the party directs waves of anger against the "haves", in other words, against the social, economic, political, and cultural élites who can be blamed for all the evils that the "people" have to suffer.

It further represents the protest against the inclusiveness of catch all-parties. The FPÖ articulates the protest against the transnational inclusiveness of a European Union that has already gone beyond the limits of a confederation. By protesting against these trends of both parties and of European integration, the FPÖ has become full of contradictions. First, in its fight against the – seemingly – shapeless greys of the traditional centre-right and centre-left parties, the FPÖ has become a kind of catch-all party itself. By embracing the rhetoric of "the people", it seems to be all things to all people – a claim which obviously cannot satisfy all the ills that the party wants to heal. Second, by excluding specific nationalities, nations, and religions from Europe, it indirectly stresses an understanding of a core Europe that would be an ideal basis for a transnational federation.

CHAPTER 6

Mobilising Resentment in the Alps

The Swiss SVP, the Italian *Lega Nord*, and the Austrian FPÖ

Hans-Georg BETZ

Recent writings on the populist mobilisation of the past two decades in Western Europe and elsewhere suggest that populist movements should be taken seriously, not only because of the dangers inherent in the populist project, but also because these movements represent a "gauge by which we can measure the health of representative political systems. Where populists [...] mobilise as movements or parties, there are strong grounds for examining the functioning of representative politics and for suspecting that all may not be well" (Taggart, 2000a: 115).

Radical right-wing populist parties themselves have accorded the question of democracy an eminent position in their programmes. What this chapter argues is that, particularly in Austria, Northern Italy, and more recently in Switzerland, the populist right has made significant gains not because they have mobilised on the immigration issue, but because they have promoted themselves as the advocates and defenders of "genuine" democracy. "Alpine populism", if it exists at all, is above all a response to what its proponents consider to be a serious *degeneration of democratic institutions and democratic processes*, which needs to be remedied. In the process, these parties have made significant contributions to several important political debates which have shaped and defined the political agenda of the past two decades. At the same time, it should be quite clear that, if the populist right adopted issues such as democracy or liberal market positions, it did so primarily in order to advance its main objective: to combat and ultimately to delegitimise the established élites and thus bring about a fundamental change in regime. Radical right-wing populist parties primarily rely on the appeal to anxieties and the mobilisation of *ressentiments*. In order to advance a political project that fundamentally challenges liberal and social democratic consensus by questioning its motives and undermining its premises.

In what follows, I will first briefly analyse the political project advanced by the populist right in Austria, Northern Italy, and Switzerland, which constitutes their populist appeal. The second part of the discussion will focus on the question of ideology. Contrary to many recent observers of the populist right, I will argue that these parties have developed a strong and coherent ideology that reflects a form of exclusionary nativism. In the process, the populist right has increasingly promoted itself as the defenders of cultural identity against both immigrants and the forces of globalisation. In the final section of this chapter, I will explore whether, and to what degree, "Alpine populism" is a distinct form of radical right-wing populism.

I. The Political Project:
Against False Élites, for More Democracy

In their fight against the political and intellectual élite, the populist right has generally made explicit reference to democracy by claiming to be the only "true" democrats. This has been a central element of the populist right's challenge to the political establishment: the argument that political power in Western Europe has been usurped by a clique of professional politicians who pretend to represent and serve the ordinary citizens while, in reality, pursuing nothing but their own narrow interests. In response, in Austria, Northern Italy, and Switzerland the populist right has made it one of its most important political goals to transform the existing system fundamentally, to bring about a *Systemwechsel* (change of system) and to remove the established political, cultural, and bureaucratic élite.

In Austria, after assuming the leadership of the *Freiheitliche Partei Österreichs* (FPÖ) in 1986, Jörg Haider made the elimination of Austria's system of consociationalism (*Proporz*), which is dominated by the two major established parties, the *Sozialistische Partei Österreichs* and the *Österreichische Volkspartei* (SPÖ and ÖVP), the main political priority for his political struggle. The goal was to abolish the "*Parteienstaat*" (party state) and to replace it with a new "*Bürgerdemokratie*" (citizens democracy).[1] Like other populist leaders, Haider used strong words to describe Austria's system of interest representation which, in his view, already displayed "pre-Fascist traits" and threatened to lead to a "new absolutism".[2] In Austria, as Haider put it in 1988, what the es-

---

[1]   See the text *Vom Parteienstaat zur Bürgerdemokratie: Der Weg zur Dritten Republik*, published by FPÖ's Freiheitliche Akademie (no date). All sources in this chapter are quoted in the footnotes as well as in the bibliography.

[2]   See "Wir sind die PLO Österreichs", interview with Jörg Haider, in *Süddeutsche Zeitung* (18 October 1996: 8). See also Haider (1994: 12).

tablished political parties wanted was "total control over democracy and over the citizens" (quoted in Mölzer, 1990: 115). In this situation, the FPÖ promoted itself not only as the "driving force behind the political renewal of Austria", but also as the only political force in Austria which pursued "a strategy of system change", aiming at "completing the liberal ideas of fundamental rights through the liberation of the citizens from the political parties". This entailed above all "removing of the corporatist elements in this system and abolish privilege and corruption" while, at the same time, laying the foundations for "an open, democratic society of free citizens".[3]

Taking its cue from Anglo-Saxon neo-liberal ideology, the party extolled the virtues of individual initiative, responsibility, and entrepreneurship as a foundation for creating incentive structures for a new generation of, particularly young, Austrians who are eager to make it on their own. The FPÖ promoted a productivist enterprise culture which aimed at improving national competitiveness primarily by drastically reducing the state's ability to intervene in the economy. Haider went so far as to compare himself to Tony Blair by arguing that the FPÖ, like New Labour, wanted "a fair chance for more self-sufficient citizens to develop their real potential instead of giving state hand-outs, which can only perpetuate the poverty trap".[4] This transformation, Haider acknowledged, would entail more than a mere change of government. What he envisioned was "to bring about a cultural revolution by democratic means", which would ultimately end in the "overthrow [of] the ruling political class and the intellectual caste" (quoted in Sully, 1997: 32).

The fundamental transformation of the socio-political system was also the main political objective of the *Lega Nord* in Italy in the early 1990s. Like Haider, Umberto Bossi promoted himself as the lone fighter against an overpowering political class, which resembled a Soviet-style nomenclature, which had not only ruined the country economically and perverted it morally, but also undermined democracy in Italy. In the process, what once had been "una democrazia per i cittadini" had degenerated into "una democrazia per i partiti."[5] For Bossi, the *Lega*

---

[3] This text appears in a self-presentation of the party with the title *The Nationalrat Election in Austria: Information on 9 October 1994*, Austria Documentation, Vienna: The Federal Press Service (the quotation is from p.19); see also *Freiheitliche Thesen zur politischen Erneuerung Österreichs*, published in 1994 by FPÖ's Freiheitliches Bildungswerk, and Haider (1993).

[4] See the article Jörg Haider wrote for the *Daily Telegraph* on 22 February 2000, "Blair and Me Versus the Forces of Conservatism".

[5] The quotation is from the speech of Umberto Bossi "Intervento del Segretario Federale on. Umberto Bossi" at the *Congresso Federale Straordinario della Lega Nord* held on 14–25 October 1998 in Brescia. See http://leganord.org/a_2_discorsi_brescia98.htm.

Nord's main task was to bring about the first integral revolution in Italian history: a far-reaching transformation of the existing system which encompassed a revolution of the institutional structure of the state; an economic, social, and cultural revolution; and a revolution of the governing hierarchy and the "regime parties", as a first step towards the refoundation of the state and the transformation of Italy into a "modern, liberal, and democratic country" (quoted in Bossi and Vimercati, 1993: 14 and 143).[6]

Whereas Haider and Bossi were quite explicit about their fundamental opposition to the existing system, the *Schweizerische Volkspartei* (SVP) and its strongman, Christoph Blocher, have been comparatively moderate and subtle in tone and rhetoric. As an established participant in Switzerland's power-sharing arrangement, the SVP was in a fundamentally different position to the FPÖ and the *Lega Nord*. This did not prevent Blocher from frequently lashing out against Switzerland's "classe politique", presenting himself as the spokesman of the common people, their concerns and their worries. Under his leadership, the SVP adopted an increasingly confrontational tone while assuming the role of an active opposition to the system from within the government. Blocher's strategy was to expose and to embarrass both the government and the two centre-right parties, the Christian Democratic People's Party (CVP) and the Liberal-Radical Party (FDP) which, in his view, had abandoned their bourgeois roots by, all too often, allying themselves with the left.

Blocher's success in the 1990s derived, to a large extent, from his ability to promote himself as the defender of classic Swiss traditions and values (independence, neutrality, *Volkssouveränität*, direct democracy), all of which he saw betrayed by the political class which, in his view, had lost contact with the ordinary people. Blocher did not mince words when attacking the political class, particularly on the question of membership to the European Union (EU) which threatened to destroy the foundations of Swiss independence and popular sovereignty. In this situation, the Swiss people were called upon to "prendre garde à notre pays, préserver nos libertés garanties par la Constitution".[7] At the same time, the SVP promoted itself as the party which "fights for more democracy".[8] As Blocher put it in 2002, "democracy is finished when

---

[6] See also the blurb of this book, which consist of a conversation between Umberto Bossi and Daniele Vimercati (1993).

[7] See the discourse by Christoph Blocher "Mon discours du 1er août" (on occasion of the Swiss national holiday) held on 1 August 2003. See http://blocher.ch/fr/artikel/030801ansprache_fr.pdf.

[8] Gregor A. Rutz, on the website of the SVP: "Le PS, le PRD et le PDC détruisent notre pays!" See http://www.svp.ch/index.html?page_id=548&l=3.

citizens are no longer able to form their own opinion about political, economic, and social principles and contexts. When citizens subject themselves to the rule of professional politicians, administrators, and opinion makers, society gets divided into two castes: on top is the supposedly 'enlightened' and omniscient élite, on the bottom the supposedly simple-minded, despised citizenry. What we have then is despotism, even if the wording of the constitution and of laws still sounds nicely democratic".[9]

II. The Ideology: Freeing the Market

Radical right-wing populist parties were among the first political forces to adopt the neo-liberal creed advanced by Margaret Thatcher. Like Mrs. Thatcher, the populist right promoted an "enterprise culture", founded on the notion that the productive "be rewarded through the market for their contribution to production", whereas "the parasitic must suffer for their failure to contribute adequately (if at all) to the market (with little regard for the question of whether they are 'deserving' or otherwise)" (Jessop *et al.*, 1984: 141). The resulting heavily producer-oriented programme allowed the populist right not only to appeal to traditionally petty bourgeois values – such as individualism, merit, and free market liberalism – but also to more widespread interests, such as lower taxation, lower non-wage labour costs, end subsidies to declining and unproductive sectors, as well as budget cuts.

After left-wing parties started to adopt major parts of the neo-liberal agenda, radical right-wing populist parties, such as the French *Front National*, the Norwegian *Fremskrittspartiet*, and the *Dansk Folkeparti*, increasingly repositioned themselves ideologically, by emphasising social issues. Strategically, this was an attempt to appeal to socially weaker voter groups and, in the process, to break into the clientele traditionally represented by the social democrats. This change in electoral strategy proved to be rather successful. In the 1990s, radical right-wing populist parties attracted a growing number of blue-collar voters who were disenchanted with the austerity programmes pursued and defended by the traditional left (Pelinka, in this volume). However, not all radical right-wing populist parties shifted from market liberalism to the defence of the welfare state. In Switzerland, in particular, but to a large extent also in Austria and Northern Italy, the populist right continued to extol

---

[9] Quotation from a speech by Christoph Blocher in Swiss-German: "Chumm Bueb und lueg dis Ländli aa! Von wahren und falschen Eliten" (Come boy and look at your small country! On true and false élites). The speech was held in Albisgüetli (Zurich) on 18 January 2002. See also: http://www.blocher.ch/de/artikel02/020118albis.pdf.

the virtues of individualism and the market, albeit to a lesser extent than in the early 1990s.

In all three cases, the populist right continued to market policies designed to enlarge the free market and promote private property at the expense of the state and its bureaucracy, while at the same time allowing the people to be both free and responsible. As the FPÖ put it in its *Theses for the Political Renewal of Austria*, freedom always means responsibility: "To be responsible for oneself [*Eigenverantwortung*] is the best protection against being manipulated by others [*Fremdbestimmung*]. Nothing guarantees this better than private property." At the same time, the party argued that the more individuals took responsibility for themselves, the less there was a need for intervention on the part of the state.[10] What a prominent FPÖ strategist defined as "fundamental liberalism" was nothing less than an attempt to bring about a cultural revolution designed to break decisively with the prevailing mentality among the Austrian population. The citizens, instead of expecting the community and the state to take care of them and, in the process, sacrificing personal goals to apparent collective security, should assume and accept the responsibilities of freedom.[11] This would not only lay the foundations for the creation of an open society, but also do away with a system in which nepotism, clientelism, corruption, and the distribution of offices and privileges according to party membership were rampant (Mölzer, 1990: 173).

As Haider saw it, the precondition for this revolution was a fundamental redistribution from the state to the citizen. This entailed not only a wide-ranging programme of privatisation of state-owned enterprises, a drastic reduction of subsidies to largely unproductive enterprises in exchange for an alleviation of the tax burden of productive ones, and – last but not least – the elimination of bureaucratic hurdles and barriers impeding economic growth, but also a fundamental re-organisation of the Austrian welfare state. In Haider's view, the modern comprehensive welfare state represented a serious threat to human freedom, not only because it had given rise to a vast, self-serving, and largely unproductive bureaucracy, but also because it had led citizens to expect more and more from the state, while, at the same time, causing a drastic decline in the citizens' sense of civic duty and solidarity (Haider, 1993: 50; see also note 1 above). For him, less bureaucracy thus not only meant "less red tape for business, less 'welfare corruption', fewer union-boss privileges, as well as an end to *Proporz*", but also more citizen responsibility, solidarity and, in the end, a more equitable society (Judson, 2000: 139).

---

[10] The original German text of the FPÖ is *Freiheitliche Thesen zur politischen Erneurung Österreichs*, Vienna (no date). The quotation is taken from p.5.

[11] See note 3 above.

In the future, social welfare would have to concentrate on providing the necessary means of allowing individuals to help themselves, preventing abuse, and generally deterring people from trying to enjoy themselves in "the hammock" of the welfare state without making a contribution to the community.[12]

Like the FPÖ, the *Lega Nord* considered the fundamental transformation of Italy's economic structures central to its envisioned revolution of the Italian state. This revolution entailed nothing less than the abolition of the post-war centralist Italian state to be replaced by a "modern federal state" by democratic means. For Umberto Bossi, the federalist solution was the only way to stop the political "thieves" in Rome from perpetuating the corrupt system of *assistenzialismo* founded on the transfer of vital resources from the productive northern regions to the non-productive *Mezzogiorno* in exchange for permanent support at the polls. Once deprived of their vote-banks in the South, the political class would collapse. Corruption, clientelism, and patronage would cease, and Italy would finally become a modern European country. In order to add pressure to its demands, the *Lega* threatened on various occasions to initiate a campaign of "fiscal disobedience" against different taxes or even a comprehensive "fiscal revolt" in the North (Bossi and Vimercati, 1992: chapter 11).

Ideologically, the *Lega*'s *liberismo federalista* grew out of a rather idiosyncratic interpretation of Northern Italian identity. In the *Lega*'s view, what distinguished the North from the rest of the country was its entrepreneurial culture and productivist ethic, inherited from the enlightened administrators of the Hapsburg Empire. Unfortunately, in the post-war period, Northern virtues failed to carry the day. Instead, the political class had created an elaborate system of dependency (the mentioned *assistenzialismo*) supposedly to help the South, but, in reality, to guarantee its permanent hold on power. In the process, Italy had divided into two economic blocks: one dominated by big business, competitive only as long as it was subsidised, the (largely uncompetitive) public sector, and various groups entirely dependent on assistance; the other, composed of competitive (small and medium-sized) private enterprises, the free professions, and the few services that actually worked (Poli, 1995: 5).

The *Lega*'s proclaimed goal was to "restore dignity to the productive world and to beat the unproductive and parasitic economy, which is favoured by this system and lives on the backs of those who work, produce, and take risks" (quoted in Gold, 2003: 94). In the end, as Bossi put it, the "winning logic", i.e., the *liberismo federalista*, would prevail, not

---

[12] The quotation is from FPÖ's text *Feiheitliche Thesen*, p.10.

least because it was most in line with the demands and requirements of the small producers and their workers (Bossi and Vimercati, 1993: 209). The key to economic reform was the institutional transformation of the country into a federal state which entailed "the regionalisation of pension and welfare systems, the substitution of federal taxes with local ones, an expansion of the tax-raising powers of local bodies and, above all, the privatisation of all enterprises under direct or indirect control of the state" (Tarchi, 1998: 149).

In the early 1990s, the *Lega*'s economic vision was primarily driven by quite concrete fears that Italy might be excluded from participating in the process of further European integration (Bossi and Vimercati, 1993: 183). As Bossi put it in 1993, the *Lega*'s envisioned economic revolution was "the last opportunity for Italy to enter 'in its entirety' into Europe". This was a scarcely veiled threat that Northern producers were at a point where they might be forced to choose to go their own way, i.e., without the rest of the country (Bossi and Vimercati, 1993: 181). A few years later, the *Lega Nord* openly campaigned for secession and the creation an independent northern federal republic (Padania) in order to put an end to what the party saw as Rome's colonisation of the North.

The populist right's neo-liberalism has, at least in part, been motivated by *ressentiments* against large companies, which receive state subsidies even when their managers have proven to be incompetent while, as Christoph Blocher has charged, small businesses, small firms, and even medium-sized enterprises would never receive such help.[13] In response, the populist right-wing parties have generally promoted themselves as the champions of the *Mittelstand*, considered to be the productive backbone of the economy, which accounts for much of a country's prosperity and social welfare (Haider, 1997: 167). To quote a SVP politician: "The larger the *Mittelstand* in a society, the better off that society".[14] The populist right has generally aimed at putting an end to the privileged relationship between the state and big industry while, at the same time, giving top priority to the interests and goals of small and medium-sized enterprises in order to improve their competitive edge (Bossi and Vimercati, 1993: 192–93). At the same time, liberalism has served as a handy weapon against the political class, whose biased policies the populist right hold to be responsible for the growing economic problems of the past twenty years. Strategically, the focus on the *Mittelstand* has been a conscious attempt to appeal to a segment of the political marketplace deemed to be particularly disenchanted with the policies of the established parties.

---

[13] See note 9 above.

[14] The quotation is taken from Gérard Nicod, "Ruiniert der Staat die Schweiz?" See http://www.svp.ch/?page_id=411&I=2.

III. Questions of Identity: The Own People First

A. Anti-Immigration Positions

In the late 1980s and early 1990s, successful radical right-wing populist parties, such as the FPÖ and *Lega Nord*, focussed primarily on economic issues in their attempt to undermine the political establishment and bring about a regime change. In contrast, immigration played only a relatively minor role in most cases, if it played any role at all. By the end of the 1990s, this situation had dramatically changed. By then, immigration had become the central issue for virtually all parties on the populist right. In Austria and Northern Italy, it took the populist right until the early 1990s to adopt immigration as a salient political issue.

In Northern Italy, the situation was particularly complex. Initially, the *Lega* directed its attacks on immigrants almost exclusively against the large number of Southern Italians from the *Mezzogiorno*, who had moved to the North during the years of the Italian economic miracle in order to find jobs in the factories and, increasingly, in the public sector. For the *Lega*, the influx of Southerners constituted nothing less than a "colonisation of the North", made worse by the fact that the Southerners had brought with them a mentality of clientelism and patronage, which were alien to the North. The result had been growing discrimination against Northerners with respect to public housing and getting jobs in the public administration. The *Lega*'s expressed goal was to put an end to "Southern hegemony (egemonia meridionale)" defined as the "power to loot the North" (Biorcio, 1997: 135–36).

It was not until the early 1990s that the *Lega Nord* shifted its focus onto the "invasion of negroes and Arabs" (Vimercati: 1990: 88). At the same time, however, the *Lega* launched a campaign designed to counter charges of xenophobia and racism. The tenor of the campaign was that the *Lega* had nothing against immigrants, as long as they were prepared to adapt and particularly to adopt the Northern work ethic. In his 1993 programmatic book, *La Rivoluzione*, Bossi devoted only a few lines to the question of immigration, which stated that the *Lega* was opposed to mass immigration and the "indiscriminate influx" of foreigners from non-EU countries into Italy and Europe. The reason for this position was not "racial prejudice" but the desire to avoid the "uprooting" (*sradicamento*) of people from their land and from the traditions of their parents. Migration was the wrong solution to the problems of the developing world. The focus should be on "capital mobility" rather than the moving of people (Bossi and Vimercati, 1993: 196–97).

The early 1990s also saw the FPÖ adopt the migration question as a central issue in its political assault on the Austrian system, largely in response to the strong influx of immigrants from Central and Eastern Europe following the fall of the Iron Curtain. In the process, the FPÖ transformed the "foreigner question" in a highly emotionalised fashion into a central issue in the national political debate, which culminated in 1993, when the party started to collect signatures for a national petition (popular initiative) on immigration, entitled "Austria First". As Eva Walkolbinger has pointed out, the party's vigorous effort to occupy the immigration issue was motivated, not least, by the expectation that a campaign designed to evoke fear of foreigners would appeal particularly to lower-class voters who were generally very susceptible to xenophobic politics of resentment (Wakolbinger, 1995: 15; Sully, 1997: 77–78). Although the petition drive significantly fell short of the party's goal, it firmly established the FPÖ as an uncompromising champion of a hard-line position on immigration.

Like its counterparts in Austria and Northern Italy, the Swiss SVP was a relatively latecomer on the immigration issue.[15] Although Blocher voiced his concern about the growing number of problems associated with asylum seekers demanding immediate political action as early as 1989, it was not until the late 1990s, that the party made *Ausländer-politik* (politics towards foreigners) a main theme of its political campaigns. The goal was to mobilise popular *ressentiments*, particularly against the growing number of refugees entering the country. The anti-immigrant campaign reached its first climax in the weeks before the national election of 1999, with SVP posters depicting a foreign-looking, bearded man tearing up the Swiss national flag. In the election, the SVP became the largest party in Switzerland, not least because it managed to attract former supporters of far right splinter parties, such as the *Auto-partei*.

Buoyed by its dramatic gains in the election, the SVP intensified its anti-immigrants campaign with the launching of a popular initiative against the "abuse of the right to asylum" in late 2000. In this campaign, the SVP demanded, among other things, a significant reduction in the social services granted to asylum seekers as well as the introduction of the so-called "third country rule", which would have meant that refugees who entered Switzerland from a safe country would no longer have been eligible for asylum in Switzerland. Although all the other major parties were strongly opposed to the initiative, which they considered overly restrictive, it was rejected by only a slim majority of those participating in the vote. Despite the negative outcome, the close result was a victory for the SVP (Hirter and Linder, 2003). In response, the party made

---

[15] With the speech "Sofortmassnahmen im Asylwesen", an interpellation by Christoph Blocher in the Swiss *Nationalrat* (lower house) on 15 March 1989. See http://www.parlament.ch/afs/data/d/gesch/1989/ d_gesch_19890391_002.htm.

Ausländerpolitik the leading issue in its campaign for the national parliamentary election of 2003, accusing the *"Multi-Kulti-Politik"* of the three other major parties of being responsible for the growing "alienation" in the Swiss population.[16]

For the populist right, the immigration issue has served as an important weapon in the fight against the élite. Umberto Bossi put it, perhaps, most succinctly when he stated in an interview: "The people don't want immigration [...] it's the political class, it's the entrepreneurs who want it".[17] In Austria, the FPÖ prefaced a pamphlet explaining the party's proposed solutions to Austria's "foreigner problems" with the suggestion that the political class had wrongfully imposed multi-culturalism on Austrian society. Jörg Haider went even further, asserting that one major reason for the political establishment's hostility toward his party was the fact that Haider had forced the Austrian political class to adopt a different (i.e., more restrictive) *Ausländerpolitik*.[18]

The strategy of the populist right has been to present itself as the only political force that dares to stand up to this "powerful lobby" which is accused of having used the weapon of political correctness to silence and criminalise any divergent opinion. For the *Lega Nord*, this represented an attempt to create a "new inquisition" designed to impose the extra-European immigration on European peoples forcibly, while *a priori* criminalising all the people and organisations who resist this. In the populist right's view, the increase in xenophobia and racism in recent years is a direct result of the demands and behaviour of the pro-immigration lobby. It is these *buonisti* and *Gutmenschen* (i.e., people with good intentions) who are the true racists working "toward one sole goal: to change the world as they see fit, while, at the same time, filling their pockets".[19]

In their campaign for a dramatic change in immigration policy, the populist right has, to a large extent, relied on relatively simple, seemingly logical and common-sense arguments. Thus, the SVP has suggested that recent rises in the crime rates were intricately connected to Switzerland's "wrong asylum policy", which did nothing to discourage

---

[16] See Yves Bichsel text, "Früchte der Verharmlosungspolitik", written for the SVP press services (No.33, 18 August 2003).

[17] Interview with Giancarlo Bosetti, "Bossi, sarà lui, non il popolo, a non volere gli immigrati", in *Il Nuovo*, 15 September 2001. See http://www.ilnuovo.it/ nuovo/foglia/0,1007,74953,00.html.

[18] FPÖ quoting Irenäus Eibl-Eibesfeldt, *Österreich zuerst: Volksbegehren: 12 gute Gründe Punkt für Punkt* (no date); see also Haider (1993: 244).

[19] Umberto Bossi quoted in "Immigrati, Bossi contro la Chiesa: 'La Finanza dai vescovoni'", *La Repubblica*, 9 September 2002. See www.Repubblica.it/online/ politica/immigrazionedue/ bossi/bossi.html.

the growing number of bogus refugees intent on exploiting the country's hospitality.[20] As the SVP-Zurich argued in Zurich in 1998, most new migrants were uneducated, lacked qualifications, and were only on rare occasions willing to work. Immigrants thus represented "above all, a burden on [Switzerland's] economic and social systems".[21] The *Lega Nord* took great pleasure in pointing out that, while one heard almost daily that Italy needed immigrants to work in the factories, "only 31% of regular immigrants actually worked and paid contributions". Without having to do anything, immigrants could claim "all benefits and, moreover, free of charge".[22] As the president of the SVP in Basle put it: "With its open barn-door politics toward foreigners, Basle's parliament has for years significantly contributed to increase the city's attraction for hammock tourists [*Hängemattentouristen*] and those who thirst after social help [*Sozialhilfebegierige*]."[23]

With regard to concrete measures and demands, the radical right's *Ausländerpolitik* is, to a large degree, derived from their common sense position. Generally, the populist right has advocated the position that immigration policy should give priority to *Integration vor Zuwanderung* (integration before immigration), as the FPÖ has put it. Again, the implied reasoning was straightforward: given the fact that Western Europe had already taken in too many foreigners who had so far failed – or been unwilling – to adapt the culture, customs, and norms of their host countries, it made little sense to allow more immigrants into Western Europe, only to exacerbate an already intolerable situation (Haider, 1993: 96).

Many of the other demands and policy proposals advanced by the populist right to fend off the "rising tide of mass immigration" follow directly from this proposition – from the call on a complete stop to immigration to be lifted only when the situation on the housing market is alleviated and unemployment is drastically reduced (FPÖ), and the demand that immigrants be only allowed to enter the country if they can prove that they already have a guaranteed job and adequate housing (*Lega Nord*), to the demand made by all right-wing populist parties that both illegal immigrants and foreign residents convicted of a serious crime be immediately expelled from the country in order to put an end to the abuse of the right to asylum.

[20] SVP, *Wahlplattform 2003 bis 2007*. Berne: Generalsekretariat SVP, 2003, p.10.

[21] SVP, *Das Konzept für eine Züricher Ausländerpolitik*. Zurich, 1998.

[22] Lega Nord, *Elezioni 2001: Ragionamenti per la campagna elettorale*, April 2001, p.24; *Ragionare sull'immigrazione*, p.10.

[23] See "Votum von Angelika Zanolari zum Anzug betreffend eine neue Asylpolitik gehalten an der Grossratssitzung vom 09./16.04.2003." See http://www.svp-basel.ch/zanolari54.html.

True to their populist strategy, the three parties have generally structured their positions on immigration in such a way as to appeal to popular *ressentiments* targeted against the established political parties and the cultural élite. Thus, the SVP, a few weeks before the most recent national election of 2003, produced a poster that depicted a grumpy man with distinct African features and a ring through his nose under the caption "We Swiss are increasingly the negroes."[24] The poster was designed to reflect what many Swiss citizens had come to feel during the past several years: that they were increasingly being disadvantaged and treated both unfairly and with disrespect while simultaneously becoming poorer and poorer. The "ruling political élite" turns a blind eye, instead of reversing these trends.[25]

The populist right's success has, in large part, derived from a discourse designed to generate and then ride a wave of "justified outrage" over real and imagined abuses and ressentiments against those held responsible. One of the main strategies pursued by the populist right has been to transform this sense of outrage into a revolt of the "silent majority", ordinary, hard-working, tax-paying citizens, whose attitudes and views were shaped and informed not by political correctness but by a healthy common sense, but who, as a result, were ignored, if not outrightly treated with contempt, by the ruling élite. The radical populist right promotes its project as a politics "out of self-defence" (to borrow a prominent *Vlaams Blok* slogan), or, as the SVP in Basle has put it, "Damit wir Schweizer auch noch etwas zu sagen haben!!!" (So that we, the Swiss, continue to have a say).

B. Defending Cultural Identity

In 1998, the Zurich branch of the SVP issued a position paper on immigration. Like other right-wing populist parties, the SVP had made the defence of values and cultural identity against multi-culturalism and the influx of foreigners, particularly refugees, a cornerstone of its campaign against the political left. For the SVP, multi-culturalism was a dangerous experiment which threatened to bring about nothing less than

---

[24] The poster was commented on by Vincent Feval, "L'UDC parle des 'nègres'", in *Le Matin*, 27 July 2003. The term "Neger", in this context, has a double meaning (see also next note).

[25] Discourse by Toni Brunner, "Rede zum Wahlauftakt", 14 August 2003, Ennetbühl (www.svp-stgallen.ch/Presse/TEXTARCHIV/Wahlen03/030814RedeTBrunner.htm). The French translation on the website of the SVP of the canton of Vaud added the following note from the translator: "Le terme de nègre signifie ici la personne dont on abuse, dont on se moque, en l'occurrence, les Suisses que l'on exploite, donc qui passent toujours pour des imbéciles. Cette expression n'a strictement aucune connotation raciste, mais elle avait été présentée comme telle par les habituels bien-pensants adversaires de l'UDC" (http://www.udc-vaud.ch/a_lire/a_lire.htm#2).

"the demise of culture".[26] In response, the Zurich SVP demanded that foreigners intent on staying integrate themselves completely and unconditionally into Swiss society. But the party went even further, charging "certain immigrant groups" with "cultural intolerance", which made living together with them on a multi-cultural basis simply unthinkable. The party was not loath to spell out which groups it meant:

> Islam is increasingly becoming the main obstacle to integration. And yet, the proportion of immigrants from Islamic countries is continuously on the rise. In Europe, we fought for centuries for liberal and democratic values, for the separation of state and church, and gender equality. It is a particular irony of history that the same left-wing and liberal forces that led this fight are today the most eager to advocate generous immigration policies – policies that threaten the basic occidental values.[27]

The argument was clear: Muslims were both incapable and unwilling to integrate themselves into Swiss society, i.e., to respect its laws, customs, and habits, and, as a result, represented a lethal threat to the survival of Swiss culture. As the title of a review article in *Schweizerzeit*, a weekly edited by a prominent SVP national councillor, put it: "Islam in liberal Europe: Christian-occidental culture before its self-liquidation?"[28]

The SVP case offers a clear demonstration of the extent to which the preservation of European cultural identity, reflected in the strict rejection of multi-culturalism, and Islam, in particular, has become central to a new type of ethno-cultural nativism in contemporary Western Europe. These attacks on Islam reflect not only the growing demographic concerns and the diffuse fears of displacement, but also the growing alarm about the installation of a religion, which is seen as alien and increasingly hostile.

Jörg Haider had already warned in the early 1990s that the "social order of Islam is fundamentally opposed to our Western values"; that human rights and democracy were incompatible with Islam, as were women's rights, and that in Islam the individual and his/her free will counted for nothing, "faith and *jihad* – holy war – for everything". Starting in the late 1990s, and particularly after 11 September 2001, the campaign against Islam intensified even more. With it, Islamophobia became central to radical right-wing cultural nativism, reflected in the often repeated charge that certain immigrant groups hold values that are

---

26 See Thomas Meier, "Irrweg 'Multikulturelle Gesellschaft'", *Schweizerzeit*, 3 March 2000.

27 SPV Zürich, "Das Konzept für eine Zürcher Ausländerpolitik". See http://www.svp-stadt-zuerich.ch/seiten/auslaenderkonzept.asp.

28 Matthias von Eysz, "Der Islam im liberalen Europa: Christlich-abendländische Kultur vor der Selbsauflösung?" *Schweizerzeit*, 13 July 2001.

fundamentally incompatible with both the political culture and the democratic traditions and institutions of the host country.

The *Lega Nord* made similar points in the process adopting the language of differentialist nativism in order to launch a frontal assault on multi-culturalism and globalisation. The party's cultural nativist turn started in the late 1990s (see Chiantera-Stutte, in this volume). It was affirmed by the party's leader, Umberto Bossi, in 2000. According to Bossi, the party stood for "the diversity of the peoples, starting from our own peoples, and from their right for freedom".[29] Two years earlier, a section of the party had diffused a paper which laid down its position on immigration, "Identity and Multi-Racial Society", which was later diffused via the party's web site. The authors claimed for themselves the "sacrosanct right of our people to maintain and defend their ethno-cultural and religious identity"[30] and the right "not to be reduced to a minority in their own home". For the authors, immigration and multi-culturalism were part of a larger process of globalisation (*mondialismo*) designed "to destroy the peoples" in order to construct an "anglophone and totalitarian Global Village on the ruins of the peoples". From the party's perspective, immigration threatened to transform European countries into colonies by means of what the authors called "a form of demographic imperialism" designed to turn "our nations demographically, culturally, and politically into an appendix of countries that do not belong to the European continent". These trends could only be reversed if Europe shifted its strategic objective and concentrated on finding ways of getting the people "to revolt against this new authoritarian ideology, which seeks to annihilate all Europeans".[31]

In this context, it was hardly surprising that the *Lega* increasingly focused on Islam. Bossi had written as early as 1993 that "Islam on the one side, and colonisation by America on the other, put the great European culture in danger [...] [T]he battle for the cultural identity of the continent coincides today with the battle for the protection of the culture of the little people, ambushed by massification and by ideological or religious fanaticism" (Bossi and Vimercati, 1993: 205–06). In the late 1990s, the *Lega*'s position on Islam turned into a comprehensive *Kulturkampf* inspired by Huntington's notion of the clash of civilizations (Guolo, 2000: 890). In the process, the *Lega* developed a comprehensive conspiracy theory built around an increasingly strident anti-

---

[29] Umberto Bossi, Pontida speech, 2000. See
      http://www.prov-varese.leganord.org/doc/bossipontida00.htm.
[30] All following quotations are from Enti Locali Padani Federali, "Padania, identità, e
      società multirazziale", 1998. See www.leganord.org/documenti/elpf/padania_
      identità.pdf.
[31] Guido Colombo, "In difesa dell' Europa", *La Padania*, 31 January 1999.

Americanism. Thus, the party maintained that the Italians had a choice between a "mondialist American multi-racial society" and a "Padanian (or Italian) and European society based on its peoples." America meant a individualistic-type of capitalism without guaranteed pensions or minimal health care, which would destroy small enterprises and lead to mass unemployment while allowing America to regain the economic position which it had lost through the creation of the European Union in 1993.[32]

The *Lega*'s anti-American tone gained particular stridency during the Kosovo crisis. During the Nato intervention against Yugoslavia, the *Lega* adopted the ideas of an obscure French expert on Islam, Alexandre del Valle.[33] Del Valle stated that the Nato war against Yugo-slavia was essentially designed by the United States "to compromise the construction of an independent and strong Europe" in order to prevent it from challenging the United States economically. U.S. foreign policy aimed at bringing about a "clash of civilisation" by pitting the Europe-ans against the Muslim world. At the same time, Islam itself presented a fundamental threat, hanging like a sword of Damocles over Europe.[34] The *Lega*'s motives for opposing the Nato intervention in Kosovo were obvious. For Bossi and many in his party, the Albanian minority in Kosovo had gradually reduced the Serb majority to a minority and pushed it out of the province, mainly on a demographic basis. Thus, Kosovo was a prime illustration of what might happen if Europe failed to halt the "Islamic invasion."[35]

In line with these arguments, the *Lega* started in the late 1990s to promote itself with growing urgency as the defender of Western values, of a Christian Europe, and of the Catholic faith against the "new coloni-alism" under the banner of Islam.[36] With this strategy, the *Lega* gained new visibility, especially after it had started to embark on a crusade against the construction of mosques in Northern Italy. The most spec-tacular incidence was a demonstration against the planned construction of a mosque in the town of Lodi in late 2000, which turned into a major

---

[32] Lega Nord leaflet "Anche tu! Dal 20 Febbraio firma per il referendum 'Contro l'invasione di immigrati clandestini'." Milan, 1989.

[33] Alexandre del Valle, "La stratégie américaine en Eurasie", see http://utenti.tripod.it/ ArchivEurasia/delvalle_sae.html. *Idem*, "Genèse et actualité de la 'stratégie' pro-islamiste des États-Unis", see http://members.es.tripod.de/msrsobrarbe/valle.htm.

[34] Alexandre del Valle, "La poussée islamiste dans les Balkans: la responsabilité améri-caine et occidentale", see http://www.geo-islam.org/content.php3?articleId=23.

[35] Stefano Piazzo, "No all'impero mondiale", *La Padania*, 29 April 1999.

[36] "Siamo davanti a nuovo colonialismo: un tempo fu opera degli occidentali, ora sono i mussulmani a farlo a casa nostra", quoted in "Sull'Islam le bugie della sinistra", *La Padania*, 17 October 2000.

anti-Islamic manifestation with slogans such as "Europe is Christian and must remain so", and "[t]he shadow of the minaret will never darken our *campanile*".[37] For the *Lega*, the aim was simple: to stop the "Islamic invasion." In line with these propositions, the *Lega* introduced a motion in late 2002 that would have made it mandatory to display the crucifix in all public buildings and offices, from schools and universities to prisons and railways stations. The *Lega* argued that the crucifix was an identitarian symbol and an emblem of civilisation and Christian culture and, as such, was an essential part of Italy's historical and cultural patrimony, "independent of any specific religious confession".[38]

In Switzerland, too, the SVP affirmed that "our culture, tradition, and religion must always remain the basis of our society". Like the *Lega Nord*, the party maintained that "a crucifix belongs in every class room". Non-Christian religions had a right to be lived and practiced, but only as long as they did not "disturb our daily life, neither in the class room nor on the job".[39] Angelika Zanolari, president of the SVP in the canton of Basle, made it quite clear who the SVP meant. In an intervention in the Basle parliament, a few weeks after 11 September 2001, Zanolari stated in support of her negative vote on according foreigners the right to vote in local elections: "Before the outbreak of the war between the West (i.e., "us") and fundamentalist Islam, which is already in power in some countries (Iran) and which might grab power in others (Pakistan is already a nuclear power), it is in our interest both to prevent the influx of more Trojan horses and to prevent those who are already here from participating in the political decision-making process".[40]

Even the FPÖ, which had traditionally harboured strong animosities towards the Catholic Church, made sure to include, in its new 1998 party programme, a passage in which it referred to Christianity, together with the world of antiquity, as the most important spiritual foundations of European civilisation. Furthermore, the party not only insisted that the "preservation" of these foundations required a "Christianity which

---

[37] Claudio Morgoglione, "Lodi, la Lega alla guerra santa", *La Repubblica*, 15 October 2000; Gianluca Savoini, "Basta all'invasione islamica", *La Padania*, 15 October 2000.

[38] Paolo Bassi, "Il Crocifisso torni nei luoghi pubblici", *La Padania*, 18 September 2003; Giulio Ferrari, "Il Crocifisso non si tocca", *La Padania*, 19 September 2002; "Crocifissi contro l'Islam: la Lega li vuole ovunque", *La Repubblica*, 18 September 2002.

[39] "Wer muss sich hier integrieren?" *SVP-Hackbrett*, June 2002. See http://www.svp-stadt-luzern.ch/hackbrett-12.htm.

[40] "Wollen wir einen Taliban als Regierungsrat?" See http://www.onlinereports.ch/ZanolariStatement.htm.

defends its values", but promised that, in this enterprise, the Christian churches could count on the FPÖ as "spiritual partners".[41]

IV. "Alpine Populism": Small Producers in Revolt

The evidence presented so far suggests that the radical populist right in Austria, Northern Italy, and Switzerland has progressively developed a rather complex ideology, which appeals to a range of different themes. Undoubtedly, in all three cases, the radical populist right has owed much of its initial success to its relentless attacks against the prevailing – open or hidden – "consociational" power-sharing arrangements, such as the integration of the major political parties in a formal system of bargained conflict settlement (*Konkordanz* in Switzerland), or their inclusion in government via the formation of grand coalitions (and the resulting *Proporz* system in Austria), or their informal involvement in the decision-making process (*consociativismo* in Italy). From the radical populist right's point of view, these arrangements not only led to a gradual blurring of ideological differences, rendering the notion of opposition increasingly meaningless, but also to the formation of a political class, which progressively lost touch with the interests and concerns of ordinary people. In response, Haider, Blocher, and Bossi initially promoted themselves as political outsiders who dared to say outloud what ordinary people only dared to think while, at the same time, relentlessly exposing the clientelistic machinations and political ineptitude of the political class.

This, however, is only part of the story. In all three cases, the success of radical right-wing populist parties has also depended on their ability to articulate and promote a new politics of identity, both national and individual. In the process, these parties have been crucial in shaping a new multi-dimensional political cleavage, which brings together cultural and material concerns. Hanspeter Kriesi has forcefully argued this point with respect to the case of Switzerland. In his view, the SVP articulates the concerns of "the traditional, rustic and inward-looking (parochial, internal market-oriented) Switzerland", of those who "believe in the myth of the 'special case' [*Sonderfall*] and who wish to continue the 'solitary route' [*Alleingang*] in foreign policy" (Kriesi, 1999a).

Blocher has been particularly apt in fusing material worries and cultural concerns into a political programme ("threats" as Caramani calls them in his chapter), which has allowed him to promote himself as the defender of Swiss interests and values, determined to resist the pressures from Brussels and elsewhere. Blocher's political programme reflects a certain mentality, characteristic of "Alpine populism" in general, which

---

[41] FPÖ, *Das Programm der Freiheitlichen Partei Österreichs*, Vienna, 1998, p.13.

is not found in other radical right-wing populist parties or, at least, not to the same extent or with the same intensity. Central to this mentality is a strong sense of – individual and community – self-reliance coupled with an equally strong sense of moral superiority which finds expression in the appeal to traditional virtues, such as decency, honesty and, as Marco Tarchi has written with respect to the *Lega Nord*, "work and sweat" (Tarchi, 2003). At the same time, the radical populist right has claimed that decency and hard work no longer pay off or, as the SVP put it a few weeks before the most recent election, that those who are honest and work hard are increasingly becoming the "idiot[s] of the nation".

The radical right-wing populist discourse in Austria, Northern Italy, and Switzerland has, to a large degree, focused on the groups and institutions that allegedly threaten the ethos and material well-being of these regions – refugees, those living on welfare, the established political and cultural élite, big transnational business and finance and, last but not least, "Brussels". The radical populist right's attacks against Brussels are especially revealing about the particular nature of populist mobilisation in the Alpine region and the motives behind it. Its opposition to the EU is based on at least two lines of argumentation.

On the one hand, there is the claim that the EU represents a non-democratic, highly centralised, and centralistic super-state. This is a point not only advanced by Christoph Blocher but also by Jörg Haider and, in particular, Umberto Bossi who has characterised the European institutions as an élitist, anti-democratic and, thus, unreachable technocracy which, because of its power to pass norms and laws written by a stateless bureaucratic machine, represents a "threat to liberty". On the other hand, there is the claim that European integration is nothing more than a last attempt on the part of big government and big business to preserve their monopoly at the expense of small and medium-sized companies, which represent the economic backbone of the Alpine region, and are increasingly the most innovative, productive, and competitive enterprises. Or, as Haider has put it, the original ideas behind European integration have increasingly fallen victim to the growing number of lobbyists who are primarily interested in curtailing competition, if not eliminating it altogether (Haider, 1997: 216).

What differentiates Alpine populism from radical right-wing populist parties and movements in other advanced capitalist democracies is neither the appeal to *ressentiments* against the political class nor the promotion of a new form of nativism or the politics of exclusion (following the slogan of our "own people first"). Both are constituent elements of contemporary radical right-wing ideology, from Western Europe to New Zealand (Betz and Johnson, forthcoming). What makes Alpine populism distinct is its *pronounced "producerist" bent, together with an equally pronounced emphasis on the entrepreneurial virtues* characteristic of the *Mittelstand*. As Haider has put it, the "*Mittelstand* is the foundation of the country's prosperity and level of social security" (Haider, 1997: 67). Similar statements have been the staple of both the *Lega Nord* and the SVP (which promotes itself among other things as *die Mittelstand-spartei*).

Politically, this means the promotion of policies that restore competition by drastically reducing the dominant position of big business on the one hand, and that strengthen the competitive position of small and medium-sized enterprises on the other. This explains why the parties in Austria, Northern Italy, and Switzerland have generally continued to promote modified versions of neo-liberalism (such as Haider's notion of a "fair market economy"), whereas elsewhere the radical populist right has largely abandoned the neo-liberal rhetoric of the 1980s. Radical right-wing populism in the Alpine region still reflects, to a considerable extent, the *ressentiments* of small (and medium-sized) producers in revolt, even if the gains of these parties from the early 1990s has meant an expansion of their electoral bases well beyond their core constituencies.

CHAPTER 7

Once Again the Deviant Case?

Why the *Christlich-Soziale Union* Only Partially Fulfils the Image of an "Alpine Populist Party"

Claudius WAGEMANN

I. The CSU: A Deviant Case of the German Party System

The *Christlich-Soziale Union* (CSU) is a very specific element in the German party system, as it only stands in Bavaria, whereas its sister party, the *Christlich-Demokratische Union* (CDU), puts up candidates everywhere else except Bavaria. Although Bavaria has only 15% of the German population, the five per cent hurdle necessary to be allowed to participate in the allocation of seats in the German *Bundestag* has never posed a problem for the CSU in nationwide elections.[1] The CSU is now the third largest party in the national parliament after the *Sozialdemokratische Partei Deutschlands* (SPD) and the CDU, in spite of its regional concentration. In Bavarian *Land* elections, the CSU regularly achieves a high proportion of the vote which is unique in German post-war history: more than 50% of the seats in the Bavarian *Landtag* since 1966 (peaking at 62.1% in the 1974 election). It has been in power in Bavaria since 1946 (with only a three-year break in 1954 to 1957). In 2003, the CSU was the first party in Germany to win a two-thirds majority of the seats in a *Land* parliament.

The literature treats the "phenomenon" of the CSU in a variety of ways.[2] When the CSU is not completely overlooked (as it frequently happens in textbooks), a cultural approach has often been used to explain its success, offering the simple conclusion that Bavarian politics is different from German politics in general, because Bavaria is different from Germany (see Falter, 1982; Mintzel, 1987a; Falter, 1988; Mintzel,

---

[1] Even if the CSU had not passed the five per cent hurdle, the directly elected members would have ensured its presence in the *Bundestag*.

[2] For an overview, see Mintzel (1993) or, in a shorter version, Mintzel (1999: 18 ff.).

1999: 28 ff. and 260 ff.). This, however, overlooks the fact that all German *Länder* are somehow distinct both from each other and from Germany as a whole (Mintzel, 1999: 260 ff.). Furthermore, such studies tend to concentrate exclusively on the CSU, and disregard the fact that the success of one party is, necessarily, always connected to the failure of the other parties.

The sociologist Alf Mintzel, trying to overcome these shortcomings, describes the history of the CSU as being rooted in the historical, institutional, and social structural context, from which he derives the factors which account for the success of the CSU.[3] In this chapter, a similar approach will be used. First, I will briefly sketch the history of the CSU. Second, I will set out the reasons for its success. Third, I discuss whether and, if so, how the characteristics of an "Alpine populist party" apply to the CSU. Finally, I will link the argument to the CSU's position with regard to European integration.

II. Conquering Bavaria:
The Rise and Continuing Success of the CSU

The literature on the Bavarian party system distinguishes two phases in the rise of the CSU, namely, early political competition between the CSU and the *Bayernpartei* (BP), and, successively, political competition with the Bavarian SPD.[4]

Having won an absolute majority in the first *Land* elections in 1946, the CSU's lead was strongly challenged in 1950, when its share of the vote fell to 27.4%, and the BP gained 17.9%. This led to severe internal fighting about the future direction of the party. One proposed strategy was to defeat the BP by borrowing its programme. This would have meant a clear strengthening of Bavarian identity (even claiming the maximum independence possible for Bavaria short of questioning the Federal Republic as a whole), but also stronger emphasis of a Christian nature. Other CSU leaders favoured the opposite strategy, namely, presenting the CSU as being clearly distinct from the BP and accepting the integration of Bavaria into the Federal Republic. This conflict was only resolved when the CSU unexpectedly became an opposition party at the

---

[3]   For a summary see Mintzel (1995) and for a more extensive explication see Mintzel (1999).

[4]   For a more detailed description, see Mintzel (1995, 1999). Most of the information given here draws on Mintzel (1999: 43 ff). Some data is taken from Thränhardt (1987: 230). Most data for the period after 1995 is based on the author's own calculations.

1954 elections.[5] The CSU used this interval to re-present itself as a more moderate protector of Bavarian interests than the BP (Mintzel, 1993: 90; 1999: 46; see also Henzler, 1995a: 139 ff.). The strategy worked well, and the BP did not win any seats in the Bavarian *Landtag* in 1962, and received less than one per cent of votes from 1974 onwards, and has only limited local importance today.

Subsequent to the electoral conquest of Bavaria, the competition which followed between the CSU and the SPD was rather different. Whereas the CSU's victory over the BP mainly resulted in an increase of votes for the CSU and a significant loss for the BP, such a massive exchange of votes was not observed in the competition with the SPD. Indeed, until the most recent elections in 2003, the level of votes for the SPD had not changed very much throughout Bavarian post-war history: it won its best result in 1966 (35.8%) and its worst soon after in 1974 (26.0%). In the 1980s and 1990s, the results were regularly a little lower than 30%, but were nonetheless fairly stable. Thus, until recently, political competition between the CSU and the SPD did not bring about an erosion of the SPD votes.[6]

Instead, the new electoral result was that the CSU was successful across all the Bavarian cultural sub-regions. Mintzel distinguishes three principal Bavarian cultural areas: Old Bavaria, Swabia, and Franconia. A Protestant corridor, largely covering the eastern areas of Middle and Upper Franconia, can be seen to constitute a fourth cultural region (Mintzel, 1999: 34 ff.). In fact, until the late 1960s, the regions in which the CSU was most successful electorally were Swabia and Old Bavaria, but not Franconia – which was mainly dominated by the SPD (excepting Lower Franconia). Since the 1970s, however, the CSU has won over 50% majorities also in Franconia and, as a consequence, the traditional Bavarian sub-regions have lost their political distinctiveness (Koch, 1994: 272). This also means that the CSU has lost votes in its traditionally strong regions which were not, however, notably high (Mintzel, 1999: 46). Consequently, the CSU became the first party in Bavarian history to be a truly all-Bavarian party (*ibid.*: 44), giving an additional meaning to the word "union" in the party name.[7] At the same time, the

---

[5] Although the CSU won most of the seats in the Bavarian *Landtag*, the SPD formed a coalition with the *Freie Demokratische Partei* (FDP), the Refugees' Party, and the BP. Not surprisingly, this heterogeneous coalition broke up in 1957.

[6] The 2003 result was 19.6%, a new negative record for the SPD (a fall of 9.1% compared to the 1998 elections). However, this defeat was only a snapshot of the political situation at federal level. It did not mark a further step in the Bavarian victory of the CSU over the SPD. Furthermore, all opinion polls correctly foresaw an enormous victory for the CSU, making it impossible for the SPD to run a meaningful campaign.

[7] In Upper Palatinate and Lower Franconia, the CSU has continuously achieved over 50% of the vote since 1958; in Lower Bavaria and Swabia since 1962; in Upper Ba-

CSU developed its own organised local groups all over Bavaria (*ibid.*: 55, 63). The SPD, in contrast, is still heterogeneously represented in the Bavarian regions, with an especially weak local party organisation in Swabia (*ibid.*: 184).[8]

Whereas the CSU had largely consolidated its hegemonic position in (nearly) all parts of Bavaria by the 1970s, the early 1990s saw a number of problems which seemed to threaten this position. First, the charismatic long-term leader of the CSU and Bavarian prime minister, Franz-Josef Strauß, died in 1988. Neither Theo Waigel, the new party leader, nor Max Streibl, the new Bavarian prime minister, seemed adequate successors, although the *caesura* was not as disruptive as was expected (Mintzel, 1999: 164). Second, the right-wing *Republikaner* (initially a splinter group of the CSU) surprisingly won 14.6% of the Bavarian vote in the European elections of 1989 (peaking over 20% in some Upper Bavarian areas). Third, Germany was re-unified in 1990, became bigger, and thus the CSU's national political influence was proportionally reduced.[9] Fourth, these changes were accompanied by a series of political scandals, which involved leading CSU officials and caused prime minister Max Streibl to resign (Jung and Rieger, 1995: 233). The new prime minister, Edmund Stoiber, managed to overcome these problems in less than a year, and continued the CSU's electoral success from 1994 onward. In 1998, he also challenged the party leadership and was the joint CDU and CSU candidate for the chancellorship, but did not obtain electoral success outside Bavaria.[10] The 2003 *Landtagswahlen* gave the CSU the historic result of 60.7% (its second best), and the CSU won all Ba-

---

varia and Upper Franconia since 1970 (except for 1998 in Upper Franconia); and in Middle Franconia from 1974 to 1982 and again in the 2003 elections (Mintzel, 1995: 221, and http://www.statistik.bayern.de). The average variation of the CSU results in the Bavarian regions in the 1950s and 1960s was 6–7%, around 5% in the 1970s, 3–4% in the 1980s, and below three per cent in the 1990s (Mintzel 1999: 53). The average variation in 2003 (2.4%) was again lower than in 1998 (2.8%).

[8] However, although the CSU nowadays wins a nearly equal share of the vote in all Bavarian sub-regions, a closer look to the statistics reveals weak points in the large cities (rural–urban cleavage). Except for very brief periods, the political history of both Munich and Nürnberg is characterised by SPD dominance.

[9] In the light of both the *Republikaners'* success in 1989 and the political scandals of the early 1990s, leading CSU officials were worried before the European elections in 1994 that their share of the vote might not be sufficient to gain any seats: they suspected that it might be difficult for the CSU to surmount the nationwide five per cent hurdle in an enlarged Germany. This also triggered discussions about a possible extension of the CSU to the new *Länder*, and the resolution to create an East German sister party of the CSU, the DSU (on the failure of this project, see Fahrenholz, 1994: 17; Jesse, 1996: 32; Mintzel, 1993: 114; 1999: 107 ff.; Niclauß, 1995: 88).

[10] For a comparison of CDU and CSU results, see Hartenstein and Müller-Hilmer (2002: 19); Hilmer (2003: 207–18); Roth and Jung (2002: 10).

varian constituencies for the first time. Today, the party seems more consolidated than ever before (Jesse, 1996: 35; Niclauß, 1995: 89 ff.).

III. The CSU Today: The Bavarian Hegemonic Party

Clearly, this success story raises the question of how the CSU has been able to reach and maintain its uncontested success. The main reason offered is the unique position of the CSU as a regional party (Jung and Rieger 1995: 234; Mintzel 1995: 236; Renz and Rieger 1999: 89 ff.), reflecting substantial (or policy-oriented), process (or politics-oriented), and structural (or polity-oriented) factors. What follows in this section develops these three aspects.

A. Policy-Oriented (Substantial) Factors

Undoubtedly, a federal system provides a very suitable context for comparisons between regions. If a region is more successful than other regions, and if a single party has been governing this region for a long time (and has not been governing another, less successful region), then, this success can be easily attributed to that party. Consequently, the CSU (above all, its current leader Edmund Stoiber) continuously points to the fact that, with regard to the most important policy issues, Bavaria is the leading *Land* in Germany. Indeed, most statistics confirm that the Bavarian economy is prospering; unemployment rates are among the lowest in Germany (with lower rates only in Baden-Württemberg); and the regional budget is mainly in good condition. In education, one of the most important areas of competence for the *Länder*, the Bavarian school-leavers exams are the most highly considered. A recent comparative study of schoolchildren's education level ("PISA E") clearly showed that the results obtained in Bavaria were far better than in any other *Land*. Similarly, statistics for internal security (the second field of *Länder* competence after education) also confirm Bavaria's leading position. In environmental issues, this position is however less uncontested, although, here again, in certain respects (for example, the use of sustainable energy) Bavaria is among the leading group of *Länder*.[11]

However, these are not the only policy successes pursued by the CSU. Every once in a while, the CSU very successfully emphasises policy issues which are perceived as being rather ridiculous outside of Bavaria, but provoke serious and emotional discussions within Bavaria.

---

[11] Unlike Baden-Württemberg, Bavaria did not start with a high level of economic prosperity after the Second World War. It was among the poorest *Länder* which received subsidies under the federal system of transfer, but nowadays it is part of the rich group of *Länder* which gives money (Sutherland, 2001a: 32, footnote 34). In other words, the Bavarian economy grew enormously during the CSU hegemony.

Clearly, it is easier for a Bavarian party to lead such discussions than it would be for parties which represent a German-wide electorate.

For instance, in August 1995, the German Federal Supreme Court decided that, if a request were made, crucifixes in Bavarian classrooms would have to be removed (*Kruzifixurteil*). The CSU called this decision anti-Bavarian and centralist, and managed to mobilise the Bavarian electorate against the measure (for more details see Jesse, 1996: 34; Mintzel, 1999: 85 ff.).[12] Another example is the *Biergartenrevolution* (beer garden revolution). Here, a Bavarian court instructed beer garden owners to close at a comparatively early hour. Temporally, this nearly coincided with the *Kruzifixurteil*. In the beer garden case, the CSU fought (successfully) against this measure, which seemed to be disrespect towards inherited Bavarian traditions. Unlike the *Kruzifixurteil* episode, the CSU was supported in the *Biergartenrevolution* by all the other important Bavarian parties (one of the largest demonstrations ever to take place in Bavaria was organised), but public perception was that the CSU, alone, had "saved" the beer gardens.

B. Politics-Oriented (Process) Factors

As can be seen Bavaria and "Bavarianness" are important policy issues for the CSU. Its strategy moves between a serious presentation of data and a rather populist responsiveness to emotional attitudes in the population (which, clearly, can also be created by their politicisation alone). Thus, it is not surprising that Bavarian identity is more important for CSU than for any other party. This is enhanced by the fact that the circumstances in Bavaria (advantageous figures, societal basis) allow such identity politics, and because the CSU, as a regional party, can fully exploit local identity.

"Bavarianness" is achieved through the use of symbols. The Bavarian symbols of the lion and the rhombus are also the official party symbols of the CSU (Mintzel, 1999: 81); white and blue, the colours of the Bavarian flag, are also the colours of the party. Moreover, slogans for election campaigns and party posters increasingly refer to the CSU as the sole guardian of Bavarian identity (Toman-Banke, 1996; Hanns-Seidel-Stiftung e.V., 1995; see also Mintzel, 1999: 81), and are even written in Bavarian dialect. Thus, components of the Bavarian image are converted into components of the CSU's image. This results in the identification of the CSU with Bavaria and *vice versa*. As a result, the CSU

---

[12] Clearly, the court decision could not be overruled. The CSU created a legal framework which formally reflected the court decision, but which did not change the situation substantially.

becomes a kind of a state party.[13] As a consequence, the CSU presents its political competitors as less Bavarian (Pauli-Balleis, 1987: 320), above all in its own newspaper, the *Bayernkurier* (which is the only exclusively party-owned newspaper in Germany). Thus, the CSU by making use of Bavarian symbols underlines that the Bavarian SPD is not Bavarian at all, and therefore should not be elected to decide upon Bavarian matters (Wagemann, 2000: 77, 126).

As a reaction to this, the SPD, the FDP, and the Greens regularly seek to display a more "Bavarian" image, but without great success.[14] It has also been shown that the Bavarian SPD is not rooted in Bavarian society and does not have a Bavarian image (for example, Hesse and Ellwein, 1997: 208; Mintzel, 1987b: 86 ff.; or, most telling, the empirical study by Patzelt, 1991), despite calling itself the *"Bayern SPD"*. The SPD's attempt to combine its party traditions with Bavarian identity in the 1970s by using the slogan *"Das andere Bayern"* ("the different Bavaria") failed: most Bavarians did not want to have a different Bavaria (Mintzel 1999: 119). In view of this failure, it comes as no surprise that it is part of the CSU's strategy to ignore other parties, as if they did not exist (Renz and Rieger, 1999: 82). For example, unlike their federal equivalents, neither the Bavarian SPD as a party nor even the most highly profiled Bavarian SPD politicians, are discussed (even negatively) in the *Bayernkurier* (Wagemann, 2000). Another aspect of this strategy is to attack federal politicians (for the time being, mainly Chancellor Schröder) for not caring about Bavaria. This happened even during the years of right-wing governments (for the importance of this double role of the CSU, see Jesse, 1996: 32 f.; Leersch, 1992: 27; and Mintzel, 1993: 104).

In summary, the CSU's strategies clearly make use of Bavarian identity and place the CSU somewhere between a highly responsive and a populist party. Erwin Huber, today chief of staff of the office of the Bavarian prime minister, once called the CSU's largely uncontested opinion leadership a *"Lufthoheit über den Stammtischen"*, unsatisfactor-

---

[13] This Bavarian-concentrated strategy has only been applied since the 1970s (Pauli-Balleis, 1987: 248, 324). When the CSU competed with the *Bayernpartei* after the Second World War, it would have been the wrong strategy to simply "copy" the *Bayernpartei* by also promoting Bavarian identity. Instead, most election campaigns were pronouncedly anti-socialist. However, when it came to the competition with the SPD, the Bavaria-oriented strategy turned out to be fruitful. See Mintzel (1987b: 85; 1990b: 830 ff.); Pauli-Balleis (1987: 321 ff.); Sutherland (2001a: 18). For the similar, but not equal, strategies of the North Rhine-Westphalian SPD, see Schneider (1997: 422).

[14] Mintzel demonstrates this with the example of the Ash Wednesday speeches (Mintzel, 1999: 83), but he sarcastically doubts if the strategy of imitating the CSU could be successful (*ibid.*: 85, 120).

ily translated as "air sovereignty over the tables reserved for the regulars" (Hefty, 1995: 419). His formula nicely describes how deeply the CSU is rooted in the Bavarian society and traditions.

C. Polity-Oriented (Structural) Factors

As mentioned above, it took a while before CSU votes achieved similar levels in all Bavarian regions. In Bavaria, there are seven administrative districts (*Regierungsbezirke*) between the level of the *Lander* and the city regions (*Landkreise*), which are equipped with their own parliaments and responsible for highly specialised issues (such as psychiatric hospitals, professional schools, cultural projects, etc.). Although the deputies and their political role are little known publicly, people very often identify themselves with their *Regierungsbezirk* region.

The CSU adopted the same administrative structure for its party organisation. In addition to the *Regierungsbezirk* structure, there are further party sub-units for the three big cities (Munich, Nürnberg/Fürth, and Augsburg) so that the CSU is organised in ten party districts with an approximately similar population (the small Augsburg party district is an exception). This arrangement not only allows effective party organisation, but also enables the CSU to respond to regional needs, particularities, and identities.[15] Above all, maintaining its own sub-units for the big cities was a clever move: the CSU can present itself as an urban party without necessarily upsetting its rural electorate. Furthermore, crises like the recent one within the Munich CSU section can be resolved more easily.

The Bavarian SPD adopted this organisational principle only very late, in 1991, after massive pressure from the newly elected party leader Renate Schmidt. Previously, its party organisation did not aim to overcome disparities in electoral support (Mintzel, 1987b: 86; Mintzel, 1999: 34, 125; Poguntke, 1997: 266). Although the SPD's party organisation nowadays follows administrative and identity borders, the old territorial cleavages in its party support seem to have remained (Mintzel, 1995: 239; Hausleiter, 1994: 179; see also Koch, 1994).

In addition, formal and informal connections between the CSU and societal groups must be mentioned. Overlapping memberships of the CSU and the *Vereine* (associations) have led to a deep embeddedness of the CSU in Bavarian society, which helps close translation of social reality and information about important (local) issues into the party

---

[15] Even for the choice of the members of government the CSU adopted the strategy to represent all *Regierungsbezirke* in fair proportions (see Jung and Rieger, 1995: 247; Sutherland, 2001a: 19). For the variety of Bavarian "identities" which can be found in the different *Regierungsbezirke*, see Mintzel (1999: 27).

organisation. Very often, this connection builds on overlapping membership in the *Vereine* and the working groups of the CSU (such as the *Junge Union* organisation of party members under 35 years of age, or the *Frauenunion* or women's organisation) (Mintzel, 1995: 233 ff.). A similar effect can be observed in relations between the CSU and the (Catholic) Church.[16] Their collaboration has been called a trinity of the state, the party, and the Church, and clearly interlocking participation in the CSU and (mass and local) media also plays a certain role in the party's success.

Another structural aspect is the representation of the CSU in the *Bundestag* at federal level. Following an arrangement between the CDU and CSU, CSU members of parliament are part of a joint CDU/CSU parliamentary group, headed by a CDU leader with a CSU member as first deputy. The joint CDU/CSU parliamentary group is organised in 16 *Landesgruppen*, one for each *Land*. Naturally, the Bavarian *Landesgruppe* corresponds to the whole group of CSU members of parliament. The media refer to this group (rather incorrectly) as the "*CSU-Landesgruppe*" ("Bavarian *Landesgruppe*" would be the correct term – yet another instance of equating Bavaria and the CSU) and to its leader (again incorrectly) as the *CSU-Landesgruppenchef*. This special constellation has been strategically very useful both in power games between CDU and CSU, and when it comes to the representation of Bavarian interests at federal level.[17]

Thus, overall the electoral success of the CSU can principally be traced back to its special situation as *the* Bavarian party. Clearly, the enlargement of the geographical scope of such a successful model was tempting. Not only did German re-unification provoke such discussions (see footnote 9 above), but so did the federal elections of 1976, which could have been won by CDU and CSU if they had presented separate lists. However, a number of empirical analyses (most prominently, Falter and Schumann, 1991 and 1992) made it clear that the enlargement of the CSU and, as a consequence the creation of a Bavarian sub-unit of the CDU (Mintzel, 1977: 406 ff. for more detail) would clearly worsen the position of the CSU. Today, such a discussion seems to have come to an end.

---

[16] The CSU also tries to have good relations with the Protestant Churches (Mintzel, 1999: 55). See also Mintzel (1987b: 88), similarly Mintzel (1999: 85 ff.); Renz and Rieger (1999: 84).

[17] See the insights and analyses of Mintzel (1989), summarised in Mintzel (1993: 108 and 1999: 92 ff.); for the specific role of the *CSU-Landesgruppe*, see also Oberreuter (1995: 330 ff.) and Schmid (1990: 258).

IV. The CSU as an "Alpine Populist Party": A Slightly Differentiated View

Whereas there is no doubt about the CSU being a Bavarian party whose success can be traced back to its regional identity and its deep embeddedness in Bavarian society, the extent to which it is possible to call the CSU an "Alpine populist party" will be now discussed. Here, I will start with geographical aspects, move on to elements regarding Alpine political culture, and, finally, discuss the extent to which CSU strategies can be called "populist".

A. Geography

The concept of "Alpine populism" describes political behaviour in a certain geographic area, namely, the transnational Alpine region. However, a definition of this zone cannot be limited to mountain areas only. The Alps, and most of the matters and problems connected to them (infrastructure, communication, transport), also affect a good part of the geographical hinterland of the mountains (in German the *Voralpenland*, the foothills of the Alps, or the *prealpi* in Italian). Important economic aspects such as agriculture and tourism also have an impact on the *Voralpenland*.

Taking a closer look at Bavaria, however, it is doubtful whether the whole territory can be described as *Voralpenland*. Definitely, large areas of Swabia, Upper Bavaria, Lower Bavaria, and Upper Palatine are either mountain areas or *Voralpenland*. But Nürnberg can hardly be said to be located close to the Alps. Nor is Munich an Alpine city (compared to cities such as Innsbruck in Tyrol), although its surrounding countryside is clearly Alpine. Munich, in particular, is also where the SPD has traditionally been the strongest in Bavaria and where it has held the mayorship for a long time. This compares to other cities on the fringes of the Alps, in which populist Alpine parties do not receive much support: Milan, Turin, and Venice in the case of the *Lega Nord* (Chiantera-Stutte, in this volume), Geneva, Basle, Bern, and Zurich (albeit to a lesser extent) in the case of the Swiss SVP (Betz, in this volume), and Vienna, before the 1990s, in the case of the Austrian FPÖ (Pelinka, in this volume).

It can also be observed that Bavaria is not at all culturally uniform in terms of life style in the different regions (see Mintzel, 1999: 27); above all the Alpine culture cannot be claimed to encompass all its parts. Whereas the political landscape has been homogenised, this did not happen culturally (see the catchword of "cultural variety in Bavarian unity", quoted in Mintzel, 1999: 77). This view of Bavaria as a politically homogeneous and culturally heterogeneous area does not support the idea that there is a correlation between the Alpineness of a region/city and the level of electoral success for the CSU, as the latter does well across most of Bavaria. Even if this were not the case, the correlation between "Alpineness" and success of the CSU does not apply to Lower Franconia, where the main city is Würzburg (close to Frankfurt), which is located more to the north than Baden-Württemberg and Saarland). In this area, the CSU obtains one of its best results, but it can hardly be called an Alpine region. This means that the adjective "Alpine" is difficult in its geographical use when connected to the CSU, but certainly entails an urban–rural dimension.

B. Political Culture

The characteristic features of the Alpine political culture can be described along three dimensions:[18]

- A goal-oriented aspect, expressed in the importance of traditional values (religious and anti-modern values, as opposed to secularised attitudes) and the importance of nature and the (social and economic) importance of agriculture;
- The importance of group identities and their relationship with concepts such as *Volk*, *Gemeinschaft*, and *Heimat*;
- Scepticism towards party politics and a general anti-state attitude.

As far as the goal-oriented aspect is concerned, the CSU undoubtedly emphasises the importance of traditional values. Institutionally, this can be seen in the various links between the Church(es) and the *Vereine* on the one hand, and the CSU on the other. Its party platform includes many Church-related issues, from religious education in schools to the highly contested issue of crucifixes in classrooms (see above). Other recently controversially discussed issues such as abortion or homosexual marriage have shown that the CSU's positions are very close to (if not identical with) those of the Churches (see also Renz and Rieger, 1999: 79). Similarly, at the local level, the CSU also supports all kinds of associations which are engaged in the preservation of the local and regional culture (for the importance of this kind of civil society in Bavaria, see Mintzel, 1999: 76). However, these programmatical links with the Churches and other associations do not overlap perfectly. Recently, the CSU and the Churches have had notable disagreements on issues such as genetically manipulated food, the integration of foreigners, and the war in Iraq. It can be speculated as to whether or not these disagree-

---

[18] For more details, see Caramani's chapter in this volume in which ideas presented in a co-authored paper at the ECPR Joint Sessions in 2003 are developed (Caramani and Wagemann, 2003).

ments are unique to specific policy issues, or whether these developments show an increasing decoupling of the CSU from the Church(es).

Whereas the adherence of the CSU to traditional values is indeed notable, the CSU, on the other hand, cannot be described as an anti-modern party. The catchword that the CSU combines "Laptop and *Lederhosen* (leather trousers)" illustrates the double strategy of the CSU very clearly: although it follows traditional policies on the one hand ("*Lederhosen*"), it also emphatically promotes the development of new technologies ("Laptop").[19]

The importance of nature is reflected in the continuous attempts by the CSU, from the early 1970s onwards, to develop an ecological profile. And indeed, "green" issues in Bavaria are not just linked to the Green Party (Mintzel, 1987b: 86; Mintzel, 1999: 81). However, the CSU represents a different kind of "Greenness" than that of the Greens. The CSU emphasises, above all, the preservation of the landscape, the maintenance of an agricultural structure, and the protection of the *Heimat* (Sutherland, 2001a: 17). It comes as no surprise that the CSU also maintains close personal links with agricultural organisations, that some of its leading politicians were farmers before going into politics, and that farmers give enormous electoral support to the CSU. This confirms the rural–urban character of "Alpineness" in Bavaria mentioned earlier. Thus, the CSU is a true representative of the goals embodied in an Alpine political culture, albeit with the reservation regarding the description of the CSU as an anti-modern party. Other Bavarian parties do not or (in the case of very minor parties such as the *Bayernpartei* or the *Ökologisch Demokratische Partei*) only partially pursue these goals.

As for the question of group identity, this must be considered in the light of the German past: words such as *Volk*, *Nation*, and *Vaterland* have a clear national socialist legacy. In a recent study, it has been argued that the CSU replaced the term *Nation* with the term *Heimat* for this reason. Moreover, the use of *Nation* or *Volk* in political discourse became even more obsolete because of Germany's division (Sutherland, 2001a: 17–24; see also Pelinka and Pallaver, both in this volume, for comparisons).

Its hegemonic position (not only electoral success, but also in opinion leadership) has enabled the CSU to define the concept of a Bavarian *Heimat* and make use of it in its campaigns. The concept goes back to the notion that the CSU regards itself (and is regarded) as the sole

---

[19] This characterisation dates to a speech by the former German president Herzog. Other slogans illustrating the combination of modernity and traditionalism in the CSU are "crucifix and capital" and "High tech and the Virgin Mary" (Mintzel, 1999: 11, 79).

guardian of Bavarian identity against outside influence (see the discussion above). Thus, the CSU avoids the term *Nation* but uses the term *Heimat* in a nationalist way. *Nation* and *Volk* are found in the rhetoric of the CSU but are connected to the idea of citizens' responsibility to the state, and thus the emotional connotation is neutralised. The emotive term is *"Heimat"*. This pattern makes it clear that the dimension of identity in an Alpine political culture is, indeed, a strategy of the CSU, although the legacies of the German past have caused the CSU to adopt a different concept of "levels of affinity" (Sutherland, 2001a: 21–26).

With regard to attitudes towards political institutions and personnel, the CSU experiences a conflict: it would be easy for the CSU to exploit the scepticism that is present in Alpine political culture towards political institutions, politicians, and bureaucracy at both federal and European level. This potential is enhanced by the old cultural conflict between the Prussians (and their capital Berlin) and the Bavarians. However, such a strategy would be risky for the CSU. First, the CSU cannot refer to Bavarian politicians as "us" and to federal or European politicians as "the others", as it also participates in federal and European policy-making. Second, the CSU itself is continuously exposed to critique because of clientelism and nepotism in Bavaria ("Bavarian *Filz*"). If the CSU criticised the political class as a whole, it would immediately draw attention to its own performance in Bavaria. In this way, being part of the political *élite* at federal level, and being the only powerful political *élite* in Bavaria, the CSU cannot fully build on negative attitudes towards political life.

As can be seen from this discussion, the CSU clearly builds its strategies on most, but not all, of the elements of an Alpine political culture. However, the general idea of an external *threat* which is central to the description of the Alpine political culture (Caramani, in this volume) is also important for the CSU's strategies. This touches upon populist strategies.

C. Populism

It is not just the close connection between Alpine political culture and its representation through a political party which renders the CSU an "Alpine populist" political party. The populist elements are (1) a general attitude of protest, (2) a distinct voting behaviour, and (3) a strong idea of political leadership.

In the CSU case, a *protest* element cannot be observed. Research into electoral behaviour makes it clear that the CSU is not a protest party. Furthermore, its election results are simply too high to allow it to be a protest or opposition party. As explained above, the double role of the CSU as the guardian of Bavarian or Alpine interests on the one hand,

and its deep integration into governing both in Bavaria and at federal level on the other, are not suited to protest activities. Instead, a CSU voter is more likely to support the existing political system (including the *Filz*) than to try to overcome it. Protest voting in Bavaria actually means voting for the SPD, the Greens, or an occasional splinter party.[20] Indeed, CSU *voters* do not equate with the "losers of modernity" (Betz 1998a: 52) as conceptualised for Alpine populism. Certainly, the "losers of modernity" are a part of the CSU electorate but, to an ever larger extent, the CSU reaches industrialists and local intellectual *élites*. Moreover, young voters increasingly opt for the CSU.

The notion of *strong ideas of leadership* can only be partially applied to the CSU. Throughout its history the CSU has always been identified with its leading politicians. This, however, is not very different from other *Volksparteien*, such as the CDU (leaders such as Adenauer, Erhard, and Kohl) or the SPD (Schumacher and Brandt). In any case, Franz-Josef Strauß, party leader from 1961 to his death in 1988, and Bavarian prime minister from 1978 onwards, is undoubtedly the figure with whom the CSU is most identified (Jesse, 1997: 67; Krieger, 1995: 193). Even more than 15 years after his death, CSU politicians continuously refer to him, and the "FJS" *post mortem* remains the father figure of the CSU (Jesse, 1996: 34). His death left a gap which was not easy to fill. Neither Max Streibl as the Bavarian prime minister (for a different opinion, see Leersch, 1992: 21) nor Theo Waigel as party leader, were charismatic enough to take over the "myth" created by Strauß. Edmund Stoiber, Streibl's successor since 1993 and Waigel's successor since 1998, is not as charismatic, either. Nonetheless, Stoiber has developed a reputation which makes him appear as a strong leadership figure without, however, rivalling the charisma of Franz-Josef Strauß (Hilmer, 2003: 193; for similar arguments, see the empirical evidence in Renz and Rieger, 1999: 92). Thus, there is a strong idea of leadership in the CSU but, at least after Strauß's death, this has not meant that the CSU as a party can be fully identified with the figure of its leader.

D. A Plea for a Slightly Differentiated View

Overall, therefore, it is difficult to call the CSU a populist party, as a variety of studies have recently shown (for an overview see Mintzel, 1999: 261 ff.). Based on the previous discussion, the CSU can be categorised as an "Alpine populist party" only to a limited extent. First, geographically, it can be characterised as Bavarian, but not as an Alpine

---

[20] One of the few examples in which protest can be observed is the above-mentioned *Kruzifixurteil*, when CSU politicians recommended resistance to the decision of the Federal German Supreme Court (Mintzel, 1999: 86 ff.).

party. Second, with regard to Alpine political culture, the CSU represents most of, but not all, the elements of such a political culture, as far as its position as the dominating Bavarian government party permits. Third, in terms of populism, the CSU does contain some populist elements but, compared to other "Alpine populist" parties, it falls short of the definition.

Thus, categorisation of the CSU as an "Alpine populist party" is difficult. The reason for this is the context in which the CSU operates: it both participates in the arrangements of the political system of the Federal Republic of Germany and dominates politics in Bavaria. Thus, rather than an "Alpine populist party", it is an "Alpine party in government", whose leaders have sought to embody the political culture of the area into their party platform and strategies, without necessarily relying exclusively on populist elements. In this respect, it strongly resembles the *Sudtiroler Volkspartei*, the dominant party in the South Tyrol/Alto Adige (Pallaver, in this volume) [21]

V. The CSU and Europe: "Yes, But"

Parties in the Alpine area are usually quite sceptical about European integration, as is emphasised throughout this volume. In this last section, I will discuss the CSU's attitudes towards European integration, which do not entirely conform to the concept of an "Alpine populist party".

The current party platform (established in December 1993) opens with a kind of preamble entitled *Orientierung im Wandel* (orientation in changing times) which notes that the CSU presents itself as a solid unchangeable force for tradition. After the first words on the party's fundamental and solid principles (*Die CSU kann auf bewährten Grundsätzen aufbauen*) and on its success story in Bavaria and Germany, the third section is devoted to the new challenges for Germany and the world. Under the sub-heading "unity of Europe in partnership", the building of a European common market and European political union are immediately linked to the new issues of German national identity, the federal structure of Germany, and the threat to traditional societal structures. This triple challenge is the best description of the attitude of the CSU towards European integration.

In following parts of the 1993 programme different "levels of affinity" (cited in Sutherland, 2001a: 26) are defined: firstly, towards Bavaria

---

[21] This is also linked to the issues which Yannis Papadopoulos discusses in his contribution in this volume. However, unlike in other cases, the CSU is not embedded in a consociational political system. Instead, the different aspects and cleavages of the Bavarian society are incorporated in the CSU as a hegemonic party, as is the case of the *Südtiroler Volkspartei*.

(the beloved *Heimat*), secondly, towards Germany (responsibility), and thirdly, towards Europe (partial scepticism).[22] The presentation of the party profile starts with a sub-section entitled "The CSU is a Bavarian party", moves on to "The CSU is the party of German responsibility", and finally states that "The CSU is the Europe-party of federal order, national identity, and regional variety". Similarly, the brochure which was used for the 2004 European election campaign was entitled: "Think European, live Bavarian" and underlines the necessity "for a strong Bavaria in Europe". In the more detailed part of the party programme Europe is only mentioned as the 18th out of the 20 topics. Although the CSU underlines its clear commitment to deep economic and political integration (positive effects are not only seen for the economy, in so far as the EU is an important international player in a global security order, but also reducing criminality and introducing a common asylum policy),[23] the same three issues are again addressed as in the other parts of the party programme: most importantly, the role of regions in Europe, and those of national identity and traditional societal structures (with a focus on minority rights).

In conclusion, this overview illustrates, first, that European integration is not the most central issue for the CSU and, second, that the discussion of European integration is focused around the three main issues of global security, economic growth and, above all, the role of regions in Europe.

A. The Role of Regions in Europe

The CSU programme highlights that Bavaria is the oldest state (*nota bene*) in Europe,[24] and suggests that this allows the CSU to claim competence in European integration affairs. This leads to a plea (1) for a federal Europe; (2) for clear dominance of the subsidiarity principle (not *vis-à-vis* the nation-states but *vis-à-vis* the regions); and (3) for a strengthened role for regions in the European polity. In other words, European integration is accepted and supported, but should be as limited as possible in its scope. It is most interesting that the CSU party programme is not aimed at defending the German nation-state from influences from "Brussels", but aimed at defending Bavaria from them.

This insistence on greater influence for the regions serves the interests of the CSU in a twofold way. First, with regard to *responsiveness to*

---

[22] This also refers to the famous (and often used) quotation by Franz Josef Strauss: "Bavaria is our home, Germany is our fatherland, Europe is our future".

[23] This was a very politicised issue in Germany at the time of writing the party programme (Jung and Rieger, 1995: 240; Wagemann, 2000: 45 ff.).

[24] In the 2004 European election campaign, it was underlined that the Bavarian population is larger than 18 out of the 25 EU member states.

the people's wishes, the CSU can present itself (again) as the best guardian of Bavarian interests. Second, it is also of *strategic importance* (Mintzel, 1993: 116 ff.): if the regions gain a stronger role in Europe, then the position of (dominant) regional parties would also be strengthened. As the CSU, for the most part *is* Bavaria, the logical conclusion is that the influence of the CSU at European level can only be guaranteed if the influence of Bavaria (or of regions in general) increases. If so, the CSU could act as the uncontested representative of a territorial unit which is larger than Denmark, the Netherlands, and Belgium, and hardly smaller than Ireland (Mintzel, 1992: 262).

B. National Identity

As for the protection of national identity, the most well-known recent issue is the discussion about the introduction of the Euro as a common European currency in the late 1990s. Important elements within the CSU (but certainly not the whole of the CSU) were deeply sceptical about the European Monetary Union (EMU) (Mintzel, 1999: 17; Renz and Rieger, 1999: 81). In addition, the CSU did not fully agree with the European perspectives of the Kohl government (Mintzel, 1999: 281). To some leading politicians, the criteria for joining EMU seemed to be too soft. Here, again, there are two main reasons that justify this position:

- First, when it comes to *responsiveness to the people's wishes*, German public opinion has never been as much in favour of the Euro as other countries have. By the late 1990s, the *Deutschmark* had reached such a symbolic value, through its stability and low inflation achievements, that the common currency was not popular. It is to be suspected that this was especially the case in the well protected Alpine and Bavarian political culture. Thus, the scepticism promoted by the Bavarian hegemonic party can also be interpreted as an attempt to respond positively to the people's worries (Mintzel, 1999: 110; Renz and Rieger, 1999: 81).

- Second, as far as *strategic considerations* are concerned, the internal situation of the CSU is significant: discussions about the EMU culminated in a conflict between the Bavarian prime minister Edmund Stoiber (who was not in favour of the Euro) and party leader Theo Waigel (who was in favour of the Euro as he was involved in its introduction, being the Federal Minister of Finance). Displeasure about the common currency within the German population offered an ideal strategic advantage for Stoiber to win the internal conflict against Waigel, but also provided a chance for the *Land*-level politician Stoiber not to suffer from bad opinion polls which would affect the federal government (Renz and Rieger, 1999: 81). Clearly, the drawback was that the CSU presented itself as suffering from deep disagreements (Mintzel, 1999: 111). Furthermore, the initiative was not greatly appreciated by export-dependent Bavarian industry (Fahrenholz, 1994: 19).

A similar strategy can be currently observed with regard to a referendum on the European draft constitution which is favoured by CSU leader Stoiber. Although this claim is merely symbolic, it nevertheless corresponds to the dissatisfaction of the people with the "democracy deficit" of the EU, given that a nation-wide referendum is not foreseen under the German Basic Law.

C. Maintenance of the Traditional Societal Structures

The recent process of drafting a European constitution also offers an example of the CSU's attempts to maintain traditional societal structures in Europe. The CSU has always been in favour of explicitly mentioning Europe's Christian roots. Furthermore, the Christian roots are also one of the most important arguments against the accession of Turkey to the EU. There are frequent threats by CSU politicians to challenge the possible accession of Turkey in coming election campaigns. Needless to say, the CSU is explicitly against the admittance of Turkey.

Whereas these three points mainly characterise the attitudes of the CSU towards European integration, it must also be noted that European integration is not an important issue for the political communication of the CSU (Wagemann, 2000: 49 ff.). Again, the CSU is too deeply integrated in the German policy-making arrangements to allow itself to make a pronounced critique of European integration, let alone reject it (in response to attitudes among the electorate). It is not opposed to the idea of European integration (Jesse, 1996: 35). Instead, its strategy is to criticise selected aspects of European integration and, above all, to try to enhance the role of the regions in Europe with regard to the maintenance of national (political and societal) structures.

Conclusion: The CSU, a Deviant Case of an "Alpine Populist Party"

At the beginning of this chapter, I argued that the CSU reflects a regional Bavarian identity with regard to policy issues, its party strategies, and its organisational structure. Both the CSU as a political party and Bavaria as a political unit are largely identified with each other and overlap. The CSU both represents and fully exploits Bavarian political culture.

When it comes to the identification of an "Alpine political culture", most of the characteristic elements can be identified in the CSU. However, the CSU is not a fundamental opposition protest party like the other parties with strong Alpine regional identities discussed in this volume, as it is the dominant political force in Bavaria. This special role also has to be considered when it comes to the discussion of the CSU's attitudes towards European integration. Although some elements within the CSU are, in the main, sceptical about European integration (as is its electorate), the party itself takes a reserved attitude which cannot be said to express a wish for a general decline in European integration. Consequently, it is not easily possible to attribute the same label to the CSU as can be attributed to similar parties in the same geographical region. Rather than being an "Alpine populist party", the CSU is an almost unique "regional party in government" (similar, perhaps, only to the *Südtiroler Volkspartei*) which is only partially related to the Alpine political culture.

CHAPTER 8

The *Südtiroler Volkspartei*
and Its Ethno-Populism

Günther PALLAVER

Introduction

A. Populism and Democracy

Based on historical analyses of populist movements, current discourse analysis, and analyses of organisational structures of such movements, Yves Mény and Yves Surel, co-authors of *Par le Peuple, Pour le Peuple* (2000), have succeeded in filtering out several general and distinctive principles of right-wing populism. Although the term "populism" is imprecise and multi-dimensional, we can establish that it maintains its hold in relatively similar contexts which are characterised by imbalances as regards political-institutional or socio-economic adaptations. Thus, according to Mény and Surel, populism is, in a certain sense, an indication of a disintegration (Mény and Surel, 2001: 169).

There are two complementary and key elements for the analysis. First, there is the conviction that a people's intrinsic virtues justify "the people" as the exclusive source of the community's legitimacy in terms of its social and political organisation. Second, "the people" is also seen as the source of the legitimation processes which ensure that both the group and its structural ties will endure. Basing themselves on this assumption, Mény and Surel show that such a conviction affects the perception of the current representative political systems. This alleged superiority is based on the construction of the community itself, together with a number of historical, social, and normative factors which, in turn, render it as an "imagined community" (Mény and Surel, 2001: 279–80).

Let me start with the assumption that, by means of this two-fold approach, it is possible to characterise populism and determine its limits. First, establish a delimitation of the term "people" (*Volk*) as a source and legitimisation of power and, second, establish a delimitation of the term "community" (*Gemeinschaft*) as a functional framework to define "the people". In its conceptual multi-facedness, the term "people" lends itself to inspiring confusion (Canovan, 1981: 285–86; Mény and Surel, 2001: 167–207; Taggart, 2000a). The concept is also well-suited for legitimising any conceivable concrete form of power. Yet, there are two clear ways of defining "the people": first, as an historical (and current) antithesis to the only, self-contained, alternative and self-justifying ideology of power – namely, the doctrine of the divine right of kings in all its variations; and, second, as a conception of inclusion and thus as well as of exclusion; in other words, the question of who belongs to "the people" is defined politically, which also makes it possible to withdraw it politically as well (Pelinka, 1996: 234). Such inclusion and exclusion, by recourse to the term "people", also refers to the major issues of nationalism.

Since politics in democracies must be justified by reference to the people, and since populism constantly refers to the people, populism claims its right to be accepted as a democratic ideology. Nonetheless, two features differentiate populism from classical liberal democracies. First, it is simply taken for granted that "the people" is homogenous and autonomous. Second, the population claims that there is a homogenous and autonomous *bloc* of people which exists in inherent opposition to the (illegitimate) power of the privileged élites (Ernst, 1987: 23). Populism thus distinguishes itself not only in terms of the definition of "the people", but also – and above all – in terms of the function and the role attributed to the people for the political system's frictionless operation.

The people are seen as the legitimising pillar of the political system which, according to the accusations of populists, is essentially ignored by the respective representatives. In this light, populists consider that they have an obligation to draw attention to this deplorable state of affairs and to grant to the people, once again, their rightful place in a renewed and "healthy" society (Mény and Surel, 2001: 170). And, since populists reject – or at least criticise – the element of representation, they also reject and criticise constitutionalism, in other words, self-containment and the harnessing of the popular will.

B. *Ethnos* versus *Demos*

Before investigating the *Südtiroler Volkspartei* (South Tyrolean People's Party) as a case-study in terms of what ethno-populism consists of and how it is expressed, a clarification of the term "ethnos" *vis-à-vis* the term "people" is necessary. In the social sciences, *ethnos* or an ethnic group is traditionally defined as a large group that has developed a sense of community and solidarity. This definition presupposes the belief that people are (at least fictitiously) of common descent. Ethnic minorities perceive themselves as large clans, and they are bound by a show of solidarity within the clans and kinship groups. As a rule – though there are exceptions – members have a common language. Other distinctions, such as religion, might also be commonly held.

Ethnicity is constituted by (common) ideas which "raise some element of unity to the specifics of collective solidarity" (Altermatt, 1996: 48). *Ethnos* tends to correspond to the concept of community (*Gemeinschaft*), whereas society (*Gesellschaft*) tends to become a concept of *demos*. The latter is the politically significant dimension of "the people" as an expression for the aggregate of those citizens who rule over themselves. *Demos*, not *ethnos*, is acknowledged as the bearer of the political will (Leggewie, 1994: 61). The change of perspectives from the entity of "the people" to that of *"ethnos"* is more than a mere semantic distinction; it also has consequences on the political actors who are criticised by populism, on the function of this criticism, and on the goal which is aimed at and connected to this criticism. I will attempt to analyse this change in order to show that recourse to the concept of the ethnic minority as a community of destiny (*Schicksalsgemeinschaft*) is not only employed to maximise votes, but also has led – in South Tyrol – to a curbing of fundamental rights.

To do this, the following analysis starts with a brief presentation of the South Tyrolean People's Party, which illustrates the historical conditions that led to the construction of the South Tyrol's "community of destiny". The chapter then moves on to explain how the tension between "us" and "the others", as well as political culture in general, has been employed to serve a specific function, and which inclusive and exclusive criteria have been applied. Finally, the chapter investigates the consequences for the political system, and the role that the European integration process plays therein.

I. The Success Story of the South Tyrolean People's Party

South Tyrol was annexed by Italy at the end of the First World War following the collapse of the Hapsburg monarchy. Attempts to return to Austria after the Second World War failed, and South Tyrol has remained a part of Italy until the present day. As a result of the "Paris Agreement", concluded in 1946 between Italy and Austria, Italy renounced full sovereignty over one part of its territory, Austria renounced the re-incorporation of the South Tyrol, and South Tyrol renounced *de facto* to the right to self-determination (Pallaver, 2003b).

The Paris Agreement, which is bound by international law, guarantees full equality of rights among the various language groups (see Table 4) and grants the German-speaking (though not explicitly the

Günther Pallaver

Ladin-speaking) South Tyroleans a number of special measures to safeguard their ethnic character and their cultural and economic development. It also contains elements for the protection of minorities, both as individuals and as groups, and constitutes the basis for territorial autonomy (Hilpold, 2001: 159 ff.). In many ways, South Tyrol today serves as a model-case for how minority issues may be resolved peacefully (Marko, 2001; Toniatti, 2001).

**Table 4. Population Development in South Tyrol 1991–2001
According to Linguistic Groups (%)**

Year	Italians	Germans	Ladins
1991	27.65	67.99	4.36
2001	26.47	69.15	4.37

Source: Landesinstitut für Statistik (2002: 109).

On 8 May 1945, the *Südtiroler Volkspartei* was founded in order to, first and foremost, achieve self-determination, and, subsequently, autonomy (Holzer, 1991; Lill, 1991; Holzer and Schwegler, 1998; Minárik, 1999; Pallaver, 2001a). Since then, the *Südtiroler Volkspartei* has been extremely successful as a political party as can be seen from Table 5. From 1948 onwards, the party has won the absolute majority of votes and seats in provincial elections. At the same time, it has always provided the absolute majority of representatives in the provincial government as well as an uninterrupted succession of provincial governors (see Table 6). At the start of the 2003–08 legislative period, 21 of the 35 delegates in the provincial parliament were representatives of the *Südtiroler Volkspartei*, and the party dominates the provincial government with the provincial governor and eight out of the ten provincial councillors. At present, all of the three German-speaking South Tyrolean parliamentary representatives and three senators in Rome come from the *Südtiroler Volkspartei*, and the party has a representative in the EU parliament as well. It provides 105 out of a total of 116 mayors in South Tyrol and in 45 municipalities the *Südtiroler Volkspartei* alone makes up the municipal council representatives. All the important functions in the central institutions of the public and private sectors are controlled by the *Südtiroler Volkspartei*. Indirectly, the party also controls all of the relevant media in the province. Because of this dominance in a region, it is possible to draw a parallel with the *Christlich-Soziale Union* in Bavaria (Wagemann, in this volume).

190

Table 5. *Südtiroler Volkspartei* **Election Results
in the Provincial Elections: 1948–2003 (%)**

Year	Votes	Year	Votes
1948	67.6	1978	61.2
1952	64.7	1983	59.4
1956	64.4	1988	60.4
1960	63.8	1993	52.0
1964	61.3	1998	56.6
1968	60.7	2003	55.6
1973	56.4		

Source: Data from the *Südtirol Handbuch* (22)2003; and *Dolomiten*
28 October 2003.

The party's success is related to the general historical framework, to the politics of ethnic tensions, the penetration of social sub-systems, the politics of incentives, and the ethnic monopoly of representation towards the outside (Pallaver, 2001b). Since 1945, the *Südtiroler Volkspartei* has formed the centre of political power in South Tyrol. The *Südtiroler Volkspartei* is an "ethnic catch-all party". According to the party statute, the *Südtiroler Volkspartei* represents the interests of German and Ladin-speaking South Tyroleans, not those of the Italians. This restriction to German and Ladin-speaking South Tyroleans shows the central ethnic cleavage within the party system of South Tyrol. This means that the political camps are distinguished ethnically, and that the *Südtiroler Volkspartei*, together with some other German-speaking parties, does not compete with the Italian-speaking parties. Thus, in South Tyrol, one can speak of two (German/Italian), or, to be precise, three (if Ladin is counted) political arenas divided along an ethnic cleavage.

Under these circumstances, the competitive situation in the South Tyrolean party system could be described as "segmented competition". This means that there is an admitted intra-ethnic competition – that is, within the single ethnic arenas – but no inter-ethnic competition. Competition between parties occurs within, but not between, ethnic arenas. Among the South Tyrol's political parties, only the Greens claim to be – and *de facto* are – an inter-ethnic party.

By classifying the South Tyrolean parties along ethnic line it can be seen that, for many years, the *Südtiroler Volkspartei* has been the only German-speaking party represented in the provincial council. In the eleven legislative periods from 1948 to 1988, there were five occasions in which the *Südtiroler Volkspartei* was the only German-speaking party in the provincial council. From 1948 to 1960, it could claim to be the only representative of the German- and, with some limitations, the Ladin-speaking population. The first German-speaking rival, the *Tiroler Heimpartei* (2.4% of the votes) did not enter the political arena until the 1964 provincial council elections. All the German-speaking opposition parties which have, until now, been represented in the provincial council have not been able to obtain more than 12% of the vote (10.8 in 1993 and 8% in 1998). If the German-speaking voters of the Greens and of the others (*Pace e diritti/Partito democratico della sinistra, Lista rosa*) are added to these ethnic parties, then about 17% is reached (in 2003). Until the 2003 elections to the provincial council, it had always been under 10%. Thus, the *Südtiroler Volkspartei* today represents about 80% of the German-speaking population in the provincial council.

Table 6. Linguistic Affiliation of the Members of the South Tyrol Provincial Council: 2003 and 1998 Elections (35 Members)

Parties	2003			1998			Variation
	Germans	Ladins	Italians	Germans	Ladins	Italians*	2003-1998
Südtiroler Volkspartei	20	1	–	21	–	–	0
Alleanza nazionale	–	–	3	–	–	3	0
Grüne-DPS	3	–	–	1	–	1	+1
Union für Südtirol	2	–	–	2	–	–	0
Die Frei-heitlichen	2	–	–	1	–	–	+1
Pace e diritti	–	–	1	–	–	1	0
Unione autono-mista	–	–	1	–	–	2	-1
Forza Italia	–	–	1	–	–	1	0
Unitalia	–	–	1.0	–	–	1.0	0
Ladins	–	–	–	–	1.0	–	-1.0
(%)	77.1	2.9	20.0	71.4	2.9	25.7	N.a.
Percentage of the population (2001 census)	69.2	4.4	26.5	68.0	4.4	27.6	N.a.

Notes: (*) One of the representatives of the Italian *Unione Autonomista* belonged to the party list *Popolari–Alto Adige domani*; the other to *Il centro–UDA*.
Legend: N.a. = not applicable.
Source: Data from the ATZ, 28 October 2003.

As a result, one can speak of the *Südtiroler Volkspartei* as being not just the predominant party, but as also being a democratically hegemonic one (Sartori, 1976 and 1982) insofar as it has, from its beginning, always obtained the absolute majority in votes and seats. Furthermore, it has also dominated South Tyrol's socio-political system. It obtains its absolute majorities under conditions of political competition and membership. For years, there have been around 70,000 *Südtiroler Volkspartei* members, which roughly corresponds to a 40% degree of organisational participation (Pallaver, 2004). Thus, the party does not so much resemble an ethno-regional party as a non-ethnic, national party. This is revealed in several ways: for example, it is not organised within the European organisation of regional parties, but is istead organised in international party organisations, such as the European Democratic Union and the European People's Party, where it has observer status (Johannsson, 2002: 51 80).

II. Longing for Community as a Resource of Ethno-Politics

The *Südtiroler Volkspartei* has been – and certainly still is – a very successful party, and there are many reasons which account for this. One of them is the longing for community (*Gemeinschaft*). A number of recent studies (Wakenhut, 1999; Gallenmüller, Martini, and Wakenhut, 2000; Baur, 2000) indicate that the people of South Tyrol are frequently oriented towards an ideal of social life in their own group, which can be described more as a community than as a society. This appears to be the result of the basic ethnic structure of the South Tyrolean society if we assume that *ethnos* is a category which, like *Gemeinschaft*, conceives the (constructed) uniformity of descent, tradition, and spiritual disposition as a basis of belonging (Baur *et al.*, 1998: 230). This constructed unity sharply disassociates others from the community, and determines who belongs and who does not.

Thus, *Gemeinschaft* describes a form of socialisation established in pre-modernity. The sociologist Ferdinand Tönnies characterises *Gemeinschaft* as a special attachment of a small, identifiable group of people – as opposed to *Gesellschaft*, an anonymous mass – in which he distinguishes four discriminatory characteristics: familiarity and foreignness; sympathy and antipathy; trust and distrust; commitment/attachment in contrast to interdependence and lacking of attachment (Tönnies, 1969: 86–95).

In post-modern society (*Gesellschaft*), social science has diagnosed a paradoxical connection between an objectively increasing sense of dependence on the one hand, and a subjectively decreasing sense of attachment on the other. This means that, although we see society developing towards increasing integration and differentiation, there is also a rising sense of isolation among individual members. We are thus confronted with a process in which an advancing rationalisation is connected to a type of regression. In South Tyrol, this regression has been made the basis of politics by virtually all political groups, and especially by the German-speaking ones. It is not the dialectics between *Gesellschaft* and *Gemeinschaft* which establish the political terms of the co-existence of the various language groups on a common territory, but rather the ethnic *Gemeinschaft*. From the beginning, political tendencies have been fostered to return to a backward-looking idyll. However, compared to other multi-ethnic societies, these tendencies also reveal attitudes of ethnic isolation in the idylls of *Gemeinschaft*, which may lead to extremes, as the Bosnian example clearly illustrates (Baur *et al.*, 1998: 236).

In this context, Ulrich Beck has spoken of the "risk society" (Beck, 1986), noting that the guarantees for collective and individual security, God, nature, truth, science, technology, morality, love, etc., have been transformed into "risky freedoms" by a logic of development inherent in modernity. The *Südtiroler Volkspartei* has promoted its politics based on the ambivalence between *Gemeinschaft* and *Gesellschaft*. In their own mind, the *Südtiroler Volkspartei* represents the "ethnic" interests of German-speaking and Ladin-speaking South Tyroleans, whereby, among the German-speaking population, the party falls back on a traditional (self-)understanding of the ethnic group: a community of descent.

The principle of *Gemeinschaft* was also the force behind the establishment of the *Südtiroler Volkspartei* on 8 May 1945. As already stated, the primary goal of this fledgling party was to realise the right to self-determination. Its secondary goal was to obtain autonomy for the South Tyrol (Gatterer, 1968: 867). Although, in 1945, the South Tyrolean society was very deeply divided between the *Optanten* – who, because of the Hitler-Mussolini Pact, opted to emigrate to the German Reich in 1939 – and the so-called *Dableiber*, who expressed their desire to remain in South Tyrol (Stuhlpfarrer, 1985), the rifts separating these two groups were healed right from the start. The ideological fracture between supporters and opponents of National Socialism was eclipsed by the *Südtiroler Volkspartei*'s "ethnic politics". This ethno-national and inter-class model was hardly new. It goes back to the late 18th century, when a special ethnic Tyrolean affiliation was elevated to the sacred. It occurred in 1797, when the Tyrol allied with the "Most Sacred Heart of Jesus", as a defence against the achievements of the French Revolution, an alliance which has been renewed every year up to the present day. This ethno-centrism also has its origins in the national mobilisation after

1860–61, and particularly after 1867, when conflicts between nationalities arose in peripheral zones of the German-speaking areas of the Austrian Monarchy.

Just as in 1945, the development and consolidation of the cleavages in the Tyrolean party system, above all the merger of the conservative parties, was characterised by an essentially defensive strategy. Prior to the First World War, this defensive line supported a position against the recognition of autonomy for Trentino-Alto-Adige as well as against the rising working class movement. However, the political mobilisation, which resembled a special class conflict, was eclipsed by national conflicts. The model of a (German) national collective movement, which the *Südtiroler Volkspartei* had given birth to in 1945, had first been seen before the First World War in 1905 with the founding of the *Tiroler Volksbund* (Tyrolean People's League). All the German-speaking parties, with the exception of the Social Democrats, worked together in the *Tiroler Volksbund* and supported its aim of inner-national colonisation. This co-operation was clearly expressed in close and personal connections between the leading representatives of the bourgeois-conservative parties and the leading circles of the Tyrolean People's League (*Volksbund*). German nationalism cemented all ideological conflicts – i.e., beyond any political conflicts (Holzer, 1991).

After the Italian annexation of South Tyrol, the *Deutscher Verband* (DV, German Association) was able to built upon this model of a national-civic cartel when the *Tiroler Volkspartei* (Tyrolean People's Party) and the German liberals merged in October 1919. The DV was the new base for the co-operative work of all the German-speaking parties. Just like the one prior to 1914, this new bourgeois alliance immediately positioned itself against the Social Democrats, but it was also clearly positioned against Italians. What had earlier been the alliance's struggle against Trentino-Alto Adige's efforts to obtain autonomy had, after the annexation of the South Tyrol to Italy, become an anti-Italian defence strategy.

Fascist de-nationalisation policies led to regional patriotism and a strong ethnic sub-culture. Indeed, the foundations of the "South Tyrolean Nation" were laid in the interval between the world wars. The threat to the German-speaking minority by the de-nationalisation policies – as well as the excessive symbolism of all things German caused by this, as well as by National Socialism – ushered in the ethnic group's gradual identification with the territory. Thus, Fascism and National Socialism shaped South Tyrol and South Tyroleans into a community of destiny (*Schicksalsgemeinschaft*). Italian policies after 1945, which were not particularly in favour of minority rights, perpetuated the South Tyrolean perception of being a constantly threatened minority. Although other parties could only attempt to control a specific territory (Biorcio, 1997: 110), the *Südtiroler Volkspartei* from 1945 onwards has, at least in a figurative sense, been able to take and keep possession of this territory.

III. The Policy of Ethnic Tension: "Us" and the "Others"

The *Südtiroler Volkspartei* was very successful first in the struggle for the survival of the German and Ladin linguistic groups, then in the struggle for verification, and also in the development of minority rights and autonomy. The policy of "ethnic defensive action" and its use for the protection of minorities and autonomy touches upon the model of "community" and its opposites, "us and them". The idea of community should express that the conflict of interests which exists within the peoples' group is secondary to the highest goal, namely, the preservation of the peoples' group, and that the unity of the group is the premise for a successful policy.

This pressure on the unity of the national group has meant the sacrifice of internal political pluralism. After the election of the provincial council in 1948, the *Südtiroler Sozialdemokraten* (the South Tyrolean Social Democrats), the only German-speaking party besides the *Südtiroler Volkspartei*, practically dissolved. From this point on, the breakthrough of the ethnic and political identification which everyone had hoped for from the start was successful. In the absence of other parties which could credibly represent the interests of the South Tyroleans, the peoples' group and the party became one. This "fetishism of unity" more or less resulted in the failure of all the relevant German opposition parties which had emerged after their separation from the *Südtiroler Volkspartei*.

The strategy of presenting the South Tyrolean People's Party as the party of the South Tyrolean people was designed to protect its power. Political dissent was branded as a betrayal of one's own people (Holzer, 1991: 75). Loyalty to the party was presented as flowing from loyalty to the people. The semantic nature of this equation was expressed very clearly in a 1964 party statute: "The *Südtiroler Volkspartei* is the political union of all South Tyroleans faithful to the homeland". Whoever rejects this loyalty to the *Südtiroler Volkspartei* is considered unfaithful to the homeland and is therefore excluded from it. The term 'homeland' is used as a synonym for community. A party conference speech cannot be given, nor an official occasion take place, without mention of the homeland, its preservation and verification, and the risk of losing it again. The Fascist period is recalled the most, a time when the homeland as a synonym for the ethnic minority was abandoned to assimilation.

The term "people in need" was also used in the post-war period as a call to political unity.[1]

The same characteristic shape could also be found in the last-adopted party agenda of 1993, which stated that:

> The *Südtiroler Volkspartei* is the collective party of German and Ladin South Tyroleans from all social classes, which declares its belief in the democratic sense of responsibility for freedom, the people and the homeland. Its political aim is the safeguarding and promotion of the German and Ladin-speaking group and consolidating their majority in their hereditary homeland (*Südtiroler Volkspartei*, 1993).

The claim to unity (the collective party of the German- and Ladin-speaking South Tyroleans of all social classes) is present in the term community (people and homeland), and alongside the ethnical claim, the political claim to unity can also be found in the party manifesto.

Although the *Südtiroler Volkspartei* has always stood in the tradition of a Christian-Democratic and conservative party. Moreover, it is a collective catch-all party "also open to social-democrats who do not represent the dogma of class struggle, as well as for liberals who represent the value of the democratic order of society" (Lill, 1991: 165–85). This identification of the party with the entire minority, or to put it another way, the identity of the party and community, is commonplace in political discussion and has been in every election campaign from 1945 to the present day. To maintain this, the opposing pair of "us" and "the others" (the Italians) has been used, not only ethnically, but also ideologically. The myth of the union of the community was used to counter all political dissent, as the classification of "others" has been one of the most successful strategies, along with pointing out the dangers of a division of the people, in order to hold up the symbiosis between inter-classism and the myth of the people. Furthermore, in the 1996 parliamentary elections, the *Südtiroler Volkspartei*'s slogan was: "To be as one in Edelweiss,[2] strong in our Tyrolean conviction, united as a people's group" (Brugger, 1996).[3]

---

[1]   The speech given by party chairman Siegfried Brugger at the 2001 Party Congress evokes this as well: "A person needs a homeland. We South Tyroleans know only too well what a homeland is: it is the love of our land, the feeling of safety and security; it is familiarity and friendship" (Brugger, 2001: 2).

[2]   The edelweiss (an Alpine flower) is the *Südtiroler Volkspartei* party symbol.

[3]   Party chairman Brugger in his 1999 Party Congress speech: "The whole province of South Tyrol is behind the *Südtiroler Volkspartei*!" (Brugger, 1999: 12). Or, in his Party Congress speech of 2000: "The fact is that, over the last few years, we have behaved much more as a unit, as a family" (Brugger, 2000: 5). Similarly, in his 2001 Party Congress speech: "As a party of the middle, the *Südtiroler Volkspartei* was and is an independent power on all levels and works from the self-conception, that with

To maintain its political hegemony, the *Südtiroler Volkspartei* deliberately placed the opposing pair of "us" (the Germans) and the "others" (the Italians) together, and this was expressed in the policy of ethnic tension. It needed the concept of the enemy from outside for its internal cohesion. Ethnic tensions are the bond, the cement which holds the people's party together. Should this bond fail, then, the *Südtiroler Volkspartei* would collapse in a crisis of legitimisation as an ethnic collective movement. As a consequence, ethnic conflicts are the elixir of life for the *Südtiroler Volkspartei*. These have to be permanently kept on the boil but not allowed to escalate so that autonomous success is brought into question again. It is a political balance between ethnic escalation and inter-ethnic normalisation, between a policy with awareness of the Fascists' policy of de-nationalisation and one with awareness of a unified and multi-cultural Europe.

These lines of tension are present in the "foreign policy" between Rome and Bozen/Bolzano, which finds expression in a permanent tug-of-war over competence, and in the accusation that autonomous rights are being eroded. Since the conclusive implementation of the packet of measures and the end of the running disagreement at the UN between Austria and Italy over South Tyrol (1992), these tendencies have, however, moved away from Rome towards Brussels. Reduction in autonomy is feared more as coming from the European Union (EU) than from the Italian institutions. In South Tyrol itself, this relationship of tension is expressed in the debate about political symbols and in the ethnic struggle over allocation, which has lowered the ethnic proportional representation.

A central pre-requisite for the permanence of ethnic tensions lies in a complete as possible separation of the linguistic groups (Baur, 2000; Pallaver, 2001a, 2001b, and 2003b). This is commonly articulated in the ethnic separation of the institutions and is continued in everyday practice (Bettelheim and Benedikter, 1982). There is a separate school and further-education system, separate departments of culture, ethnically-divided arts and leisure centres, associations, and social housing, and there are ethnically-divided media and information systems and separate religious festivals. The allocation of resources also occurs along ethnic lines. The strategy of the lasting ethnic mobilisation has its basis in two essential guidelines. First, the upholding of an ethno-political society with as many separate structures as possible, which creates a distance between the linguistic groups. Second, the ethnic conflict between the linguistic groups which is upheld through continuous demands for ex-

the South-Tyrolean Party, one can define *the* party for the whole of the South Tyrol" (Brugger, 2001: 9).

pansion or restriction on the boundaries of the territorial autonomy (Baur *et al.*, 1998: 247–48).

IV. Political Culture in the Service of an Ethnic Defensive Action

Separation from "what lies outside" has always been based on a political culture with strong roots throughout the Alpine area. It is a culture based on a specific family structure which has evolved over time and is connected with historical variables such as religion, (agrarian) economic structures, and ideology.

A. Religion

Since the time of the Reformation, (South) Tyrol has been regarded as a stronghold of Catholicism. And even if the process of secularisation has led to a substantial erosion of religious bonds today, the *Südtiroler Volkspartei* still holds to religious symbolism. Thus, in 1993, it clearly professed Christian principles in its party programme (*Südtiroler Volkspartei*, 1993). Earlier, in 1984, it had also defended them during the negotiations of the amendment to the 1929 *Concordato* between Italy and the Vatican. Whereas compulsory-school pupils in the rest of Italy have a right to religious instruction and may enrol in such a class, in the South Tyrol, children are automatically enrolled in religious classes and can only be excused from it by revoking their enrolment.

The Sacred Heart of Jesus Festival between the region of Tyrol and the Sacred Heart of Jesus is an exclusive alliance and one that is celebrated annually. This festivity dates back to 1796, at the time of the wars against Napoleon. It is a great orchestration which is politically projected into the present. A large number of Catholic associations represent organisations which are informally under the *Südtiroler Volkspartei*'s influence, and they have the traditional advantage of being recruitment places for its political personnel. Even though religion is now often considered merely as ritual and as part of everyday popular culture, the *Südtiroler Volkspartei* consistently places fundamental Catholic moral concepts at the centre of its politics: for example, the traditional family arrangement, work ethics, and the defence of local communities. When one speaks at times of the "Holy Tyrol" (*Heiliges Land Tirol*) today, the underlying sense is the submission to the authority of a social order willed by God and to the recognition of timeless principles.

Religion is strongly bonded with the traditional "folk culture", whose primary values can be seen as an expression of the genuine Tyrolean identity: traditional values, loyalty to the homeland, religious faith, and the legacy of the fathers, the unity of the Tyrolean people, and the defence against external influences[4] are only a few of the "virtues" which purportedly represent a true (South) Tyrolean. Appeals by *Südtiroler Volkspartei* spokespersons against the (material) "selling out of the homeland" to tourists and foreigners may be regarded as one example among many of "the defence of the territory". History, which in the South Tyrol can be described as an auxiliary science in the service of political needs, has been used as a special instrument for cementing the imagery of collective identity.[5] It is often employed as an answer to socially-caused identity crises. The people's own past is idealised and glorified; the ethno-centric protectors of the homeland (*Heimatschützer*) persecute whatever is foreign, and they ward off everything bad and negative – which they do not want to admit as actually part of them (Baur *et al.*, 1998: 40). The attitude that "all which is foreign should be kept at a distance" turns against Rome, immigrants and (Southern) Italians.

B. Ruralism

However, the *Südtiroler Volkspartei* does not leave it at merely political symbolism; it also deliberately promotes that very social category which represents the foundation of this ideology, when it states about the peasantry: "Rural agriculture in South Tyrol is a basic pre-requisite for economic well-being and quality of life, for the preservation of the rural area, and for the cultural and recreational landscape" (*Südtiroler Volkspartei*, 2003). Looking at the economic subsidies handed out by the South Tyrolean provincial government, which is dominated by the *Südtiroler Volkspartei*, one is struck by the *Südtiroler Volkspartei*'s clear ideological reins. Agriculture and forestry, for example, among all other branches of the economy, receive strong preferential treatment, even though they make up only 13% of total employment in the province (data for the year 2000) (Istat, 2003: 196). And, to a considerable extent, this treatment has led to the reinforcing of the *Südtiroler Volkspartei*'s conservative hegemony. Although the transition from the primary to the secondary sector has changed the objective affiliation to social class, it has not changed the subjective perception of belonging to the farming class. Thus, South Tyrol is often presented as an area which is characterised by agriculture and peasantry, despite the fact that those

---

[4]   Tyroleans have always rejected all political currents originating from abroad: liberalism just as socialism. The one political ideology arising outside of the Tyrol and which has not been rejected was National Socialism.

[5]   Critical historical sciences could only – and gradually – take root since the 1980s, and it has developed almost exclusively outside the *Südtiroler Volkspartei*'s sphere of influence.

employed in this sector actually represent a minority within the province's wage or working population.

Ideologically and financially, the *Südtiroler Volkspartei* promotes the construction of just such a reality. As late as 1996, the financial support for agriculture amounted to 44.6% of the total. Between 1972 and 1981, their average was even higher, at 66.5% (Holzer, 1991: 157). Provincial payments to agricultural enterprises increased by 22% between 1998 and 2000 (Istat, 2003: 458), even though payments have slightly decreased recently. The total amount still remains disproportionately high compared to the sectors of handicrafts, industry, and tourism (Giovanetti, 2000).

As regards industrialisation, the *Südtiroler Volkspartei* – for historical and political reasons – has always taken a negative position. Starting from the mid-1930s, Italian Fascism with its policies of mass immigration of Italian workers into the newly built industrial plants, attempted to create a demographic turnaround, an Italian majority in the province. These Fascist policies led to the antagonism between the Italian industrial proletariat and the German peasantry, which was also encouraged politically. The resulting tension remained perceptible well into the 1990s. It was also one of the reasons for the establishment of a "German" labour union federation in 1964, which, based on the Austrian model, was oriented towards social partnership, as opposed to "Italian" unions (based on differing political currents).

The successful defence of the unique political and cultural sphere of influence which the *Südtiroler Volkspartei* achieved over time was also possible because the process of changing the social stratification, from a largely agrarian-based society – in 1951, some 70% of the German-speaking population worked in agriculture (Atz, 1991) – into a largely service-based economy, took place directly, without any detours, through enhanced industrialisation. Similar structures in the primary and tertiary sector, such as family businesses and small enterprises, a low degree of union organisation, a relatively high percentage of self-employed workers, and so on (Holzer, 1991: 102), fostered the penetration of a conservative ethno-centric party into this section of society. The attempt to harmonise contrasting interests within the party and within the German-speaking community succeeded in establishing different mechanisms to regulate conflicts between the party and the respective interest groups, which were largely strong (financial) associations.

What stands out about such associations in South Tyrol is the mono-ethnic orientation of most of these interest groups, as well as their (in part) civil-law character. Formally, the South Tyrolean interest groups have rather limited possibilities of influencing decision-making in economic and social policies. The right of associations to have a say and make decisions on the province's various committees and advisory boards falls under the "weak" forms of associative participation in the political process. The associations may merely offer advice, provide evaluations, make proposals, and raise them at hearings. Although politicians, trade unionists, business representatives and the media often speak in South Tyrol of "social partnership" and "social partners", there is no pronounced system of an institutionalised neo-corporative representation or interest mediation. The term "social partner" is used with an ideologically appealing intent to postulate the conviction of a peaceful resolution of economic conflicts of interest.

Thus, the exertion of influence on the part of the economic and social associations takes place mainly on an informal level, through deliberate personal networking between the *Südtiroler Volkspartei* and the associations, as well as through the inclusion of associations in the *Südtiroler Volkspartei* advisory bodies (Piras, 1998).

C. Political Participation

The constructed, backward-oriented harmony within the South Tyrolean community is manifested also in how German-speaking youth understand democracy. For them, political participation is less central than the delegation of decisions to the professional politicians of one's own linguistic group. In a survey taken in South Tyrolean high schools and vocational schools in 1998, only 19% of those interviewed expressed any great interest in politics; 73% expressed limited interest; and 18% no interest at all (Messner, 1998).[6] These youths claimed that they hardly talked about politics when among themselves. For them, democracy means, above all, freedom of expression and the right to vote. In this context, 77% said they were against lowering the legal voting age. In addition, 20% of those interviewed expressed the opinion that a "healthy dictatorship" would be better than democracy under certain circumstances. Furthermore, these youth have quite traditional priorities regarding (a range of) values: in the first place, health (67%), followed by family (60%), and friendship (49%). Surprisingly, only a few mentioned economic well-being (6%), or religion (3%) (Alto Adige, 1999: 3). As concerns their relationship with the various linguistic groups, the ethnic consciousness of South Tyrolean youth mirrors society-at-large quite closely. The majority perceive the ethnic borders as impermeable, and they submit to ethnic divisions (Gallenmüller-Roschmann, 1999: 121–22).

---

[6]   In 2001, the rate for the North Tyrol – that is, the Austrian half of Tyrol – was 31%; in Austria as a whole in 1996, it was 35% (Claus *et al.*, 2001: 31).

V. Inclusion/Exclusion and Its Consequences

This submission is due *inter alia* to the legal framework of the South Tyrolean autonomy which is based on the principle of ethnic separation. South Tyrol's provincial constitution, the statute of autonomy, reveals a dual legality. On the one hand, it grants territorial autonomy and, on the other, it contains a series of rights to protect the ethnic minorities living in this area. The primary basis of the protection of minorities is individual human dignity (Verdross and Simma, 1984). The starting point for protection rules favouring minorities is the ban on discrimination and the principle of equality. However, due to structural disadvantages, these rules do not prove sufficient, and further positive action measures are needed (Woelk, 2002: 117–37). Parallel to individual human rights, collective rights which recognise the protection of minorities are provided for, in the sense that there is a right of the minority *as a whole* and not only of each individual member. The group, not the individual, possesses the rights (Kymlicka, 1995).

The question of who can exercise these minority rights leads to the problem of deciding who belongs to an ethnic group. Ethnically-drawn boundaries occur according to very different needs, though fundamentally there are two main possibilities: to be *included or excluded*. If we take the ethnic auto-definition used by those affected, then the boundaries are pulled inwards; but they can also be pulled outwards in the sense of an ethnic hetero-definition. To put it another way, whether one can vote or not is connected with this inward or outward pull, the question of attribution or acquisition. The "subjective criteria" stands opposite the "objective criteria" (Reiterer, 1996: 74–76; 2000). Furthermore, although the discussion about the South Tyrolean identity is still active,[7] belonging to the ethnic minorities has always led to heated debate, as occurred in the 1960s and 1970s in particular. Lawyers moved back and forth between the *jus sanguinis* and the *jus soli* from the third generation onwards and made efforts to use the language, ways of life, history, traditions and cultural heritage, self-awareness, feelings, manners, needs, religion or points of view as the symbols of a Tyrolean heritage (Ermacora, 1984: 216–19).

The autonomy statute introduced the subjective principle, that is, the principle of declaration. All citizens, who are residents at the time of the population census in South Tyrol, have to declare themselves as belong-

---

[7] The party chairman of the *Südtiroler Volkspartei* Brugger said about the identity of the South Tyroleans at the 2000 party congress: "We need no new type of South Tyroleans, who are a mish-mash, with a little bit German, a little Ladin, a little Italian. That is a political approach which is old-fashioned and has been superseded" (Brugger, 2000: 3).

ing to one of the three linguistic groups officially recognised in the autonomy statute: German, Italian, or Ladin. The 1971 census had allowed the language spoken in the home to be listed anonymously, but in 1981, a resident had to declare him- or herself as belonging to one of the three linguistic groups (Poggeschi, 2001: 653–85). Admittedly that did not mean that the problem of ethnic identity and the question of who is a member of the ethnic group had long since been solved. However, it did offer a means to allocate resources according to objective criteria. Such a declaration is binding for ten years and cannot be altered during this time (Zeller, 1991).

It was only after a series of cases and adjudications at the Italian supreme court of justice that those who did not wish to declare themselves as belonging to one of the three linguistic groups recognised in the statute of autonomy were able to choose a category termed "others". This gave not only those who were multi-lingual – about 13% of the population (Baur *et al.*, 1998: 35) – but also Italian citizens with a mother tongue other than German, Italian or Ladin, and immigrants (3.5%) the opportunity to declare themselves as not belonging to one of the official linguistic groups. However, in order not to lose a series of subjective rights, the "others" too had to classify themselves as belonging to one of the three official linguistic groups. Only thereby could they claim their statutory rights which were bound up with membership of one of the three official linguistic groups.[8] Those who do not declare which linguistic group they belong to, dive up de facto their minority rights and thereby also the social rights connected with them.

With the establishment of ethnic membership (starting from age 14) there is always a periodic return to ethnic mass-mobilisation, as the numerical size of the population group is the key for the allocation of resources. Official positions among the linguistic groups were granted according to the results of the population census and a whole series of material resources are allocated, especially in the area of social services. These ranged from the support of sports associations, to the awarding of scholarships to students, and the allocation of council housing. The fight for each "German", "Italian", and "Ladin" soul during the population census is a recurring process of ethnic mobilisation and a planned struggle for allocation (Langer, 1988). It has the effect of strengthening the identity of the "winners" and weakening the "losers". Long before the chosen time of declaration to one linguistic group, the "us" have already been placed against the "others" as the *Südtiroler Volkspartei* is unre-

---

[8]   As the smallest linguistic group, the Ladins cannot claim certain rights at all, even when they comply with the rules, as the rules themselves are discriminatory. For example, they cannot be elected president of the provincial council nor be an administrative judge.

lenting in calling on its own community in order to maintain and expand ethnic power.

It is not just about social but also about political rights. Whoever refuses to declare their linguistic group is not only excluded from every public trade-competition, but also from passive voting rights at local and provincial level. Furthermore, according to the statute of autonomy, the active right to vote is tied to a four-year residency in the region of Trentino-Alto Adige. Truly these political rights are now no longer part of the protection of an ethnic minority. The recourse to the protection of the ethnic group means that subjective rights have been refused, and there is no legitimisation apparent for this – apart from an ethnic one.

The denial of individual, social, and political rights is the logical consequence with which the political élite, i.e., the *Südtiroler Volkspartei*, moved the principle of the community to being the fore of attention. The principle of the protection of minorities was placed at the centre thereby making the group to be protected the focus of attention. Therefore, everything is done to prevent deviations within the relationship of the group members as, for example, the obligation to declare oneself as a member of, or at least associated to, a linguistic group; otherwise, the individual rights which themselves are the product of group rights are relinquished. Those who turn their back on their own group will be punished and have to accept a series of (material and political) disadvantages.

If the first level concerns the collective rights of the minority, a second level deals with territorial autonomy, which concerns all citizens living within this territory. This level is irrespective of the three linguistic groups officially recognised in the statute, or whether they are immigrants, bi-lingual integrated citizens, or others (Lampis, 1999). In the first case, the protection of both the minority as a group and of material equality (in the sense of righting wrongs) is foremost. In the second case, the individual rights unconnected with ethnicity, such as formal equality, are foremost.

The historical starting-point of the statute of autonomy was the collective protection of minorities. The statute of autonomy had formed this concept into a barely flexible legal model in the legal institutions. This model legitimised the deviation from formal principles of equality, of which ethnic proportional representation is an example. The relationship of tension between individual and collective rights was also virulent in a time when there were fewer social preconditions for the deviation from a formal principle of equality. Thus, as long as a declaration of membership to a linguistic group was required, primarily to enable the realisation of ethnic proportional representation, then this measure in the sense of righting an enduring wrong was justified. In this case, deviations from the formal favouring of the material principle of equality were legitimate. If, however, a balance among the linguistic groups is achieved and the disadvantages of an ethnic minority are removed, then collective protective measures which restrict individual rights on an atypical scale are less justified.

VI. Europe as an Ally Against the Nation-State

Right from its very beginning, the *Südtiroler Volkspartei* has been a strong advocate of the process of European integration, in other words, long before the emerging regionalism against centralism in the 1970s. This advocacy had a political, a territorial, and an economic dimension to it. It was in European institutions that the *Südtiroler Volkspartei* perceived its allies against the Italian nation-state. The stronger the process of European integration, the fewer the opportunities the government of Rome would have to influence the South Tyrolean autonomy. In addition, the border with Austria would become increasingly permeable. The latter took place with Austria's joining the EU in 1995, as well as with the Schengen Agreement. Already prior to that, the establishment of the term "Europe of Regions" and the Maastricht Treaty of 1991 had been heartily welcomed by the *Südtiroler Volkspartei*.

In the 1993 party manifesto, it was stated that:

The *Südtiroler Volkspartei* does not want a Europe of states, levelling out and central bureaucracy, but rather a Europe of regions as manageable unities [...] One of the main goals is [...] the formation of a multi-lingual federalist European region Tyrol within the boundaries of the European federalist system.

In an article on the principles of the *Südtiroler Volkspartei* about the future of the European Union written in 2002, it was emphasised that the *Südtiroler Volkspartei* was "convinced of the need for the expansion of Europe and will actively work with and do its part to realise the collective European aims and ideals". The reference here is to the protection of minorities, a Europe of Regions, the protection of the Alpine area, the promotion of cultural diversity, and cross-border co-operation (*Südtiroler Volkspartei*, 1993).

By the end of the 1980s, *Südtiroler Volkspartei* policies aimed at creating a cross-border "European region Tyrol". In accordance with *old regionalism* (Keating, in this volume), this project was initially conceived of as only between the (North) Tyrol and the South Tyrol. Through a cross-border European region, the re-unification of the Tyrol should have taken place through the European backdoor. Only when this path turned out to be politically hopeless was the province of Trentino included in the programme (Pallaver, 2003b). The *Südtiroler Volks-*

partei also participated in the debates on regionalism movements in the 1980s which focused on the discussion of economic competitiveness, which would remain independent from the territorial domestic structures of the respective nation-state. It is thanks to the INTERREG programmes and other EU subsidies for the improvement of economic infrastructures that South Tyrol belongs to one of the ten richest regions of Europe today.

Due to the importance that the *Südtiroler Volkspartei* accorded to both the European Community and the EU, the *Südtiroler Volkspartei* continuously strived to be represented in the European Parliament. From 1979 onwards, it succeeded in becoming one of the four ethno-regional parties to send a representative to the EU parliament at each European election (Caciagli, 2003: 188). At the European Parliament, the *Südtiroler Volkspartei* behaves less like a minority party and somewhat more as a supra-regional party, which goes beyond federal level. This is a manifestation of the fact that the *Südtiroler Volkspartei* does not have the European umbrella organisations of regional parties as its point of reference, but has the Group of European People's Party, instead (Johannsson and Zervakis, 2002: 206). Here, it cultivates a particularly close relationship to the Bavarian CSU (Wagemann, in this volume).

However, in recent years the *Südtiroler Volkspartei* no longer views the process of European integration in an exclusively positive light. It represents a conservative concept for the protection of minorities which emphasises group protection rather than fundamental individual rights. Since Italy, like all other member states, is ceasing to be the main reference point for minority issues, certain limitations according to the South Tyrolean autonomy (personal rights and freedoms, linguistic regulations, ethnic quotas) increasingly fall under its own scrutiny, and are, in part, openly challenged in the light of EU citizenship.

Conclusion

The ethno-populism of the *Südtiroler Volkspartei* rests on the mystification of the ethnic minority as a "community of destiny". As a democratic-hegemonic party, the *Südtiroler Volkspartei* is the "incarnation" of this community. The development of the community goes back to the 19th century, became enunciated through the policy of Fascism (the assimilation) and National Socialism (the Hitler-Mussolini pact), was carried out by the long implementation of the requirements of the definition of autonomy (1948–72), and was reinforced by the post-war democratic Italian governments. The relationship of tension between "us" and "the others", which is based on a traditional political culture, has been used functionally and maintained through a permanent ethnic mass-mobilisation to establish which inclusion and exclusion criteria are applied and what consequences will follow for the enjoyment of human rights. Focusing on the community and on the collective rights of minorities has led to a situation in which those who do not subordinate themselves to the community logic cannot enjoy social and political rights. This system has recently encountered criticism and reservations on the part of the EU.

As we can now see in Figure 3, an analysis of the *Südtiroler Volkspartei*'s ethno-populism has also revealed deviations from some of the central characteristics of populism. While the criticism of populism is directed at the political representatives, the privileged or, in general, at "those above" whose policies do not correspond with the supposedly "true will of the people", ethno-populism in South Tyrol is not so much directed against its own leadership, which has always been strong and undisputed, as against "the others". The "others" includes all those who do not belong to their ethnic group. The rules of inclusion/exclusion are determined by the ethnic group itself, and are constructed in such a manner that massive pressure is placed on the members of the community. Within ethno-populism, the function of excluding the others goes together with the (idealised) aim, to be able to rule without the others.

Figure 3. Differences between Populism and Ethno-Populism

Dimensions	Populism	Ethno-Populism
Basis	People	Ethnos
Enemy	Those above	The other
Function	Exclusion of the enemy	Exclusion of the other
Final aim	"True" people in power	Rule without the others

On the one hand, this implies the absence of (occasionally constructed) threats which endanger the ethnic minority and reduce the opportunities for the self-realisation of the own ethnic group. On the other hand, it means the predominance of the *Südtiroler Volkspartei* within a political system. Within the self-staging of the *Südtiroler Volkspartei*, the wielding of this power is coupled with a party which knows the supposed "true" needs and interests of the ethnic minority, and, thus, takes these into account in its policies. The aim of populism is "true people's power", in which a fictitious identity between the governing and the governed prevails. Without doubt, this is not the normative understanding of democracy, but is, in its stead, the sense of a mystical will of the people.

CHAPTER 9

Multi-Level Populism and Centre–Periphery Cleavage in Switzerland

The Case of the *Lega dei Ticinesi*

Oscar MAZZOLENI[1]

Ever since its foundation in 1991, the *Lega dei Ticinesi* has been a significant feature of Swiss politics, particularly in Ticino, the Italian speaking canton located at the south of the Alps. Today, the *Lega dei Ticinesi* is the only Swiss party to reflect a political centre–periphery cleavage, while promoting a dominant anti-establishment rhetoric. Over the last ten years, it has achieved significant electoral success. At its height, during the second half of the 1990s, the party could count on polling around 20% of the vote at cantonal level. Today, after the decline registered in the cantonal and federal elections of 2003, the *Lega dei Ticinesi* retains a share of around 8–10%.

Until now, scholars have investigated the origins and the historical antecedents of the *Lega dei Ticinesi* (Knüsel and Hottinger, 1994; Mazzoleni, 1995), its relationship with the political system in the canton Ticino (Mazzoleni, 1999) and its analogies and differences with regard to Christoph Blocher's Swiss People's Party (*Schweizerische Volkspartei*) (Mazzoleni, 2003a and 2003b; Betz, in this volume). However, the analysis of the *Lega dei Ticinesi*'s rhetoric has yet to go beyond an essentially descriptive approach. It has been observed that it expresses a "populist" rhetoric on various levels, from the national level through the regional and the local levels (Bohrer, 1993: 47 ff.). However, this rhetoric has not been analysed in terms of the opportunities offered by the cultural, economic, and political-institutional context.

This chapter is divided into three sections. In the first section, after a brief theoretical framework, I intend to illustrate the contents of the rhetoric of the *Lega dei Ticinesi*, stressing the diverse institutional, po-

---

[1]   The author is indebted to Andrea Ghiringhelli, Maurizio Masulin, Pascal Sciarini, and Elio Venturelli for comments on previous drafts.

litical, and territorial levels involved. In the second section, I will show the particular cultural, socio-economic, and political conditions of the canton Ticino, where the *Lega dei Ticinesi* has successfully developed and propagated its rhetoric. Finally, I will attempt to show why suitable political conditions for the development of a populist party capable of creating a centre–periphery cleavage do not currently exist elsewhere in Switzerland.

I. Populism and Cleavages

At first sight, it is by no means easy to combine theoretical analytical approaches which use concepts such as "populism" and "cleavages" in the study of political parties. In the first case, what dominates is a flexible "form" from the point of view of the ideological content, which is capable of adapting itself both to diverse contents and to changing contexts (see, for example, Taguieff, 2001). In the second case, the definition of 'cleavage', developed in a rich vein of political sciences studies, especially from Lipset and Rokkan (1967a) onwards, focuses on the specific contents and, above all, the duration of these divisions.

Recently, a number of authors have observed how the rise of the so-called contemporary European populist parties is associated with the dissolution of traditional cleavages, which are affected by the internal crisis afflicting party systems (Kitschelt, 1995; Mény and Surel, 2000: 223 ff.). This implies that it is possible to distinguish two analytical approaches in the use of these concepts. If, in general, cleavages reflect the social, cultural, and economic conditions at the time of the emergence of a party's configuration, party populism (politicians' populism, as defined by Canovan, 1981) instead hinges on the level of the political rhetoric. Despite the recognised polysemy of the concept, the populist rhetoric of the contemporary political parties in Europe may, in general, be defined as a combination of an exaltation of the virtues of the people (understood as an homogeneous entity), a systematic *critique* of the élites and the establishment, both of which are accused of betraying the people's ideals and interests (Mény and Surel, 2000), and a critical attitude towards representative democracy (Taggart, 2000a; see also Papadopoulos, in this volume).

At the same time, populist rhetoric is capable of adapting itself to different contents. As a consequence, right-wing and populist parties in Europe may possess a "winning formula" which is ephemeral and contingent primarily in relation to economic issues (Betz, 2001). There has been little reflection on how this flexible "winning formula" is linked to the multiplicity of the territorial and political-institutional levels (local, regional, national, European), in which the neo-populist parties interpret the social-structural and cultural cleavages. As a consequence of the sub-disciplinary specialisation in the current political science, the territorial and institutional frame of reference often remains one-dimensional. Some scholars turn their attention to the national parties (such as the FPÖ in Austria, the *Front National* in France, and the *Schweizerische Volkspartei* in Switzerland). Others look to the peripheral regional or local parties instead (De Winter and Türsan, 1998). The parties of the first group would defend the nation in its entirety; the second, the periphery under threat. The first would see their spatial frame of reference as the nation; the second, the region or local territories.

In fact, the action and rhetorical spaces of theses parties do not always correspond to the territorial limits of their organisation bases. The more institutional opportunities there are, the more the action and the claims become not only regional, but also national or supra-national. This question becomes central where the relationships between the institutional levels (sub-national, national, supra-national) is changing, for example, in the context of supra-national integration. As Keating's chapter in this volume argues, the European integration process has produced new opportunities for the regional parties, which are placing their demands beyond the state border. But the pressure of European integration could also open up new opportunities for an emerging regional populist party which claims the national integrity as a condition for regional interests.

In general, in a multi-level opportunity space, a centre–periphery cleavage may take on different meanings, depending upon how the political actor combines the use of the regional, national, and transnational institutions, and connects it with other parties within or outside the national context. These opportunities vary not only according to the degree of autonomy, but also according to the political weight of each institutional level (more important in a federalist context). In such a configuration, the rhetorical components, especially the anti-establishment *critique*, constitute a stock of ideological resources that regional populist parties can adapt with regard to the different institutional opportunities and the visibility of the "targets" or " enemies".

II. The *Lega dei Ticinesi*:
Between Rhetoric and Opportunity

The *Lega dei Ticinesi* is a good example of a regionalist party that exploits, outside the EU, the multi-dimensional opportunities of its political and institutional context. During its evolution from 1991 onwards, the claimant rhetoric of the *Lega dei Ticinesi* continually oscillated between the international, national, regional, and local levels. For this party, the "people" are those of the canton Ticino, as well as of Switzerland and of the Lugano region (economically and financially the main city in the canton). Similarly, the political and administrative élites are respectively those of the federal capital (Berne), the administrative capital of the canton, Ticino (Bellinzona), and Europe (Brussels), depending on the interlocutors and the symbolic relevance of the chosen targets or enemies. From the point of view of its rhetoric, the *Lega dei Ticinesi* cannot be said to be a purely regionalist, localist or nationalist party, but is simultaneously regionalist, localist, and nationalist.

The multi-level rhetoric of the *Lega dei Ticinesi* is made possible by a number of factors. In general, it is favoured by the Swiss federalist structure and the construction of the Swiss national state. Modern Switzerland has some of the most de-centralised institutional structures in the world and a weak central state (Lijphart, 1999; Badie and Birnbaum, 1979), both of which have allowed the acknowledgement and survival of sub-national, cantonal, and communal identities. The construction of the Swiss national identity did not cancel out the ancient cantonal or regional allegiances, but re-modelled and integrated them within a fundamentally non-conflictual co-existence, at least from the 1940s onwards. Despite the recent changes towards an electoral "nationalisation" (Caramani, 2004), the significant autonomy of the sub-national political, cultural, and institutional entities still entails a centrality of the cantonal level in the electoral mobilisations in Switzerland. At the same time, we observe a strong differentiation of the cantonal party systems, a significant autonomy of the cantonal party sections with regard to the weak national confederations and the variety of electoral legislation, and an heterogeneous political weight for direct democracy (Kriesi, 1998a; Ladner and Brandle, 2001; Vatter, 2002). In this sense, if, at federal level, the political parties play a relatively marginal role in the decision-making processes, it is more difficult to claim the same at cantonal level, and not just because of the lack of systematic studies in this field. We may, actually, suppose that both the weight of the diverse cantonal parties and their role in the decision-making processes depend on the specific characteristics of the cantonal political system.

In the same way, if the Swiss federalist system encourages the plurality of the political spaces and the institutional references, the emergence of the *Lega dei Ticinesi* is, above all, associated with the particular position of Ticino in the Swiss context, the specific construction of the Swiss identity in this canton, the weakening of the traditional social cleavages, and the crisis affecting the traditional parties of Ticino.

A. The Anti-Establishment Critique: People versus Élites

Together with other parties in the Alpine region (see Betz, in this volume), the *Lega dei Ticinesi* tried to present itself as the advocate of "genuine" democracy. The emergence of the phenomenon of the *Lega* in the canton Ticino is frequently interpreted as the expression of an anti-party revolt (for example, Rusconi, 1994). Its anti-establishment *critique* has, above all, been expressed as a protest against cantonal partyism and the "big families", political corruption, and the inefficiency of the bureaucracy.

This kind of *critique* aimed at the *cantonal* élites was an essential part of the *Lega dei Ticinesi* politics between 1991 and 1995, that is, until one of its representatives was elected to the cantonal government and it began to intensify its political alliances (Mazzoleni, 1999). Over the last few years, while public demonstrations have been definitively abandoned, even the *Lega dei Ticinesi*'s free weekly newspaper, *Il Mattino della Domenica*, has lowered its voice. Protest against the *national* élites have instead been a constant in the history of the *Lega dei Ticinesi* and is manifest both in its rhetoric and organised action, making a substantial contribution to its visibility at national level. To a greater extent than at cantonal level, the *Lega dei Ticinesi* has made use of the instruments of direct federal democracy (initiatives and referenda). With regard to foreign policy in particular, it has denounced the Swiss "political class" and the federal bureaucrats, accused of selling-out Switzerland or paying little attention to the interests of the canton Ticino. It has regularly targeted the federal institutions of Berne, especially the government and the federal administration, as well as the management of the Swiss national bank.

In general, during the 1990s, the *Lega dei Ticinesi* was thus able to exploit the declining trust in the political élites, the institutions and the political parties. It was able to cultivate an anti-party resentment that was particularly widespread in the canton Ticino during this period. According to the Selects post-electoral inquiries conducted in 1995 and 1999 on the occasion of the federal elections, the percentage of citizens expressing anti-party opinions[2] was significantly greater in the canton Ticino than in Switzerland as a whole, as well as in other cantons (for example, Zurich and Geneva). Moreover, these opinions were more widespread among the electors of the *Lega dei Ticinesi* than those of the other Ticino parties and the non-voters (Mazzoleni and Wernli, 2002: 139). Furthermore, to a greater extent than in Switzerland as a

---

[2] The interviewees were asked whether they considered parties to be "necessary" to the Swiss political system or not.

whole, these opinions proved to be positively correlated to the degree of dissatisfaction with the performance of the parties themselves in Ticino.

It is possible to see the breadth of the disappointment generated by the cantonal consociational system and the frustrated expectations produced by the traditional parties in these results. At federal level and in many cantons, especially in those where the use of direct democracy proved to be more accessible and straightforward, the parties played a limited role in the making of public opinion and the decision-making processes.[3] According to historians, Swiss cantonal parties are, in general, considered to be the children of direct democracy, as crystallisations of the referendum committees in the second half of the 19th century (Gruner, 1969). However, this was not the case for the two parties of Ticino founded between 1830 and 1840, the Liberal Radical Party (LRP) and the Conservative Party (now the Popular Democratic Party, PDP). These party organisations were created prior to the advent of universal male suffrage and the introduction of the instruments of direct democracy. As a matter of fact, the accessibility and use of cantonal direct democracy was, and still is, one of the lowest ever in cantonal comparison, in which these same parties have dominated the cantonal political scene for the past 170 years, demonstrating an exceptional longevity not only in international comparison, but also in the Swiss context. Today, they are still the first and second most important parties in terms of votes, and have been governing together since 1922, when proportional representation (via direct popular suffrage) for the election of the cantonal government was definitely institutionalised.[4]

The governmental role of these parties in a consociationalist system accompanied the consolidation of the structures of the cantonal state (the first constitution dates back to 1803), contributed to the building of the nation, and played an essential role during the post-war years of economic growth in the mediation of interests and in the distribution of public resources (Bianchi, 1989; Ghiringhelli, 1987; 1988; Mazzoleni, 2001; Vitali, 1996). Moreover, for several decades, this form of conso-

---

[3] In general, it cannot be said that cantonal direct democracy weakens political parties. However, in the cantons in which the instruments of direct democracy are most widely used, the party system is more fragmented and unstable (Ladner and Brändle, 1999).

[4] It is important to note that Ticino's proportionalism in the cantonal executive election is not a response of the traditional élites to the challenges launched via direct democracy, as would appear to be the case in other cantons, but the result of an "external" imposition by the federal council which, towards the end of the 19th century, obliged the canton Ticino to introduce a proportional system in order to sedate the exceptional violence of the conflict between the two traditional parties. Gruner has spoken of Ticino's *Sonderfall* (1969: 68). With the exception of Zug, a majority system is applied in all the other Swiss cantons.

ciationalism demonstrated an elevated capacity of integration (supported by the proportional system), bringing in all the challenges in the party system, particularly with the Socialist Party in the 1920s and the Independent Socialist Party (PSA) in the 1980s. Nevertheless, the logic of consociationalism also increased the internal opacity of the governmental system, the confusion in the perception of political actors and the expansion of a generic anti-party attitude (Papadopoulos, in this volume). Given this institutional specificity, it is not surprising that the populist rhetoric of the *Lega dei Ticinesi* has successfully been able to play on the negative image of the traditional parties, when an unexpected economic downturn was damaging their capacity to answer their social demands.

B. *"Cantonal-Nationalism": Ticino* **versus** *"Bern" and the German-Swiss Majority*

Regionalism, or rather "cantonalism", is a central component of the *Lega dei Ticinesi*'s rhetoric. This party may define itself, above all, as a regionalist or "peripheral nationalist" party, in the sense that it is active in a sub-territorial national division, seeks to represent a minority with culturally distinct characteristics, and expresses a programmatic policy that claims increased power on behalf of this territorial collectivity (De Winter and Gomez-Reino Cachafeiro, 2002: 500). It is not demanding the independence of Ticino from the Swiss Confederation, but it is asking for a more de-centralised federalism, in which the federal capital Berne has less power. Above all, it is demanding greater fiscal autonomy for the canton.

Nonetheless, it opposes the presumed cultural and economic "colonisation" of the canton Ticino by German-speaking Switzerland. It denounces the economic concentration and the dependence of Ticino's economy on the transalpine economic centres and asks for the Swiss-German companies which are active in the canton to pay taxes in Ticino. With these critiques and demands, the *Lega dei Ticinesi* interprets the hardships and uncertainties that emerged with the crisis of the 1990s in a regionalist key, characterising Ticino as a canton which was discriminated against in the federal context.

In the construction of the relationships between the centre and the periphery, this canton may in a European context be considered an example of the "victorious periphery" (Rokkan, 1999: 185 ff.) in administrative, linguistic, and territorial terms. It represents the "third" Switzerland, the Italian-speaking minority. Individuals speaking Italian as their first language represent around seven per cent of the Swiss population: four per cent (around sixty per cent of all the Italian-speaking persons) reside in Ticino, in which Italian is the only official cantonal language.

Thus, the survival of the Italian linguistic identity is not just a consequence of Swiss federalism or the recognition of indigenous cultural
minorities.

In Switzerland itself, the canton Ticino constitutes an exception from
the point of view of the relationship between linguistic cleavage and
cantonal borders. In no other Swiss canton is there the same degree of
overlap between linguistic space and cantonal borders. The two largest
Swiss linguistic communities (German and French) are distributed in
25 cantons. With the exception of small and fragmented areas of the
canton of Grisons, Italian-speaking Switzerland coincides with the canton Ticino. Cantonal identity is further reinforced by the relative geo-
morphological insularity of Ticino's territory. Furthermore, as the only
canton to the south of the Alps, Ticino was physically isolated from the
rest of Switzerland, at least until 1980 and the opening of the
St. Gotthard motorway tunnel. Confirming this "structural" insularity, a
survey conducted in the mid-1990s shows that the sense of cantonal
identity was significantly higher in Ticino than in the French-speaking
and Swiss-German cantons (Kriesi *et al.*, 1996: 56).

Historically, the relative linguistic and geo-morphological insularity
of the canton Ticino has been accompanied by a status of economic
peripherality. Until the 1940s, Ticino was a canton of emigration, with
an economy based on subsistence agriculture. Processes of industrialisation were very late in developing in Ticino compared to the more advanced cantons in Switzerland, as well being as sporadic and relatively
ineffective. Between the 1950s and 1970s, the focus of the economy of
Ticino rapidly shifted from agriculture to the tertiary sector, with an
increasing percentage of citizens employed in banks, insurance companies and public administration. The "Glorious Thirties" were marked by
the development of the financial market (Lugano became Switzerland's
third financial centre), tourism and, in recent years, by the opening of a
university. Impressive post-war economic development did not, however, succeed in bridging the gap between incomes in Ticino and the
other more developed parts or in reducing the dependence of the economy of Ticino on the Swiss-German financial and commercial trusts
(Toppi, 1998; 2003).

According to Rokkan, the social state, through the establishment of
social rights for the weak and marginalised, contributed to the construction of a sense of "togetherness", which emphasises the territorial and
national identity (Rokkan, 1999: 265). In the traditionally poor canton
Ticino, the economic welfare of the post-war period, the fruit of economic growth, and the development of the cantonal and federal welfare
state, reached a stage in which the consolidation of the national identity
was still a recent experience and largely signified "protection" and

"common solidarity" against warring Europe. More so than elsewhere, national identity and the model of Swiss welfare ("sure, we are the richest of the world") have been interwoven in Ticino. To a greater extent than in other parts of Switzerland, to be Swiss was, for the citizens of the canton Ticino, synonymous with economic welfare. Integration in terms of identity and economic status not only resulted in the partial and momentary neutralisation of the effects of the canton's economic peripherality and a specific translation of the national "myths" of Swiss "insularity" and "exceptionality" (Froidevaux, 1997), but also in an enduring increase in expectations with regard to the Confederation.

Expectations of security and welfare contrasted with the new conditions that resulted from the socio-economic transformations of the 1980s and 1990s. With the stagnation of public spending during the 1980s, there were already warning signs of the "fiscal crisis" of the cantonal state (Rossi, 1984). The permeability of the socio-economic boundary began to increase and change, particularly with regard to Lombardy. In these decades, this Italian region became one of the main economic locomotives of Europe but, in comparison to Ticino, it was also distinguished by lower average wages.

Above all, the 1990s were characterised by the explosion of an unprecedented economic crisis and recession (not since the 1930s do we find similar conditions in Ticino), which highlighted the intrinsic fragility of the degree of welfare attained. Moreover, in response to the crisis, the Confederation introduced a series of neo-liberal reforms which aimed at increasing the competitiveness of the Swiss economic market, thereby acknowledging numerous reforms promoted by the European Union (EU), including the deregulation and the privatisation of the public areas traditionally integrated with policies of regional development (Mach, 1998). These reforms subsequently became some of the favourite targets of the *Lega dei Ticinesi*. The *Lega* exploits the image of a discriminated canton, the so-called syndrome of Swiss-German "domination." It tries to reinterpret the "tradition" of the economic and linguistic claims that characterised the history of the canton from the mid-19th century.[5] Before the advent of the *Lega dei Ticinesi*, these claims had been shared during the 20th century, in a moderate way, by all the government parties in Ticino (Marcacci, 2003; Bianchi, 1989).

In summary, with regard to the claims of the *Lega dei Ticinesi* that Bellinzona and, above all, Berne, exploited the socio-economic uncertainties besetting the canton Ticino in the 1990s, we can talk of a politi-

---

[5] It is also important to remember that, before the foundation of the "Republic and Canton Ticino" in 1803, for three centuries the regions of Ticino were subject to the administrative power (though not a colony) of many German-speaking cantons.

cal capitalisation of a relative deprivation in the form of a "chauvinism of welfare" (Kitschelt, 1995). This defence of the Swiss economic *Sonderfall* tries to capitalise on the resentment not only against the applicant refugees, but also against the cantonal and federal élites. We can also observe this "chauvinism" in the opposition to EU and in the defence of the Luganese economic centre.

C. "National-Nationalism": The Swiss versus "Brussels" and Ticino versus Lombardy

Today, although not a member of the EU, Switzerland's relationship with Europe has been one of the most important issues in the Swiss political field since the early 1990s. In contrast with the Swiss legacy, which is based on strong political independence in international affairs, the Swiss foreign policy has changed greatly since the collapse of the Berlin Wall, in favour of increasing international co-operation and integration. But this new foreign policy, elaborated by the Swiss government and the main parties, has often divided Swiss public opinion in recent years.

In this context, the *Lega dei Ticinesi* played a leading political role in opposing the process of European integration. For the *Lega*, the defence of the so-called Swiss *Sonderfall* – the exceptionality of its founding principles (neutrality, federalism, and direct democracy) and the singularity of its economic success in the second post-war period – manifests itself in strong opposition to European integration. Its protest against both EU bureaucrats and the Swiss government started with the campaign against the Treaty on the European Economic Space (EES) in 1992, subsequently continued in terms of foreign policy with the opposition to any adherence whatsoever to supra-national organisations.[6] There is a clear affinity with other Swiss "national" parties, such as the Freedom Party, the Swiss Democrats and Christoph Blocher's *Schweizerische Volkspartei* (Betz, in this volume), with which the *Lega dei Ticinesi* established alliances, either for elections or on the launching of its support of referenda and popular initiatives on the subjects of European integration and immigration. At the same time, its opposition to European integration is not only in contrast with almost all the regionalist parties that were active in the EU countries in 1990s, but is also partly in contrast with the Blocher's *Schweizerische Volkspartei*, which accepts

---

[6] After a very hard and polarised referendum campaign, the majority of the Swiss electorate and the cantons refused to support the official policy.

many economic aspects of integration (for example, the first set of the bilateral agreements with EU accepted in 2000).[7]

As the Selects post-electoral surveys of 1995 and of 1999 show, the opposition to European integration was significantly greater among the *Lega dei Ticinesi*'s electorate than in those of the other main parties in Ticino. Furthermore, in contrast with those same parties, the non-acceptance of the criticism aimed at Switzerland during the 1990s for the ambiguous role it played during the Second World War is significantly and positively correlated with the *Lega dei Ticinesi*'s popularity.[8] The opposition to European integration expressed by the national-populist parties, particularly, those situated in German-speaking Switzerland (the *Schweizerische Volkspartei*, the Freedom party, and the Swiss Democratic Party), has essentially been based on the defence of independence, direct democracy and Swiss federalism, as well as on the critique of the supposed technocratic European centralism. Besides these aspects, the *Lega dei Ticinesi* also encompasses uncertainties about its relations with neighbouring Italy. The opposition to Europe expresses a potential centre–periphery cleavage in which the centre is not just Berne or Brussels, but also Lombardy and Milan.

The *Lega dei Ticinesi* has not openly declared that it is "anti-Italian" or "anti-Lombard", but did actually borrow certain "anti-political" stereotypes from the neighbouring *Lega Nord*, such as "organisational Italian disorder", Roman "centralism", and "bureaucratic obtusity" (Chiantera-Stutte, in this volume). In the early 1990s in connection with corruption scandals in Italy, the *Lega dei Ticinesi* used symbols that echoed the condemnation of the party system by Bossi's *Lega Nord*. Moreover, the use of a certain anti-Italian feeling is expressed on an economic level as an accusation of the allegedly "unfair" competition practised by Lombardy on the economy of Ticino and the threats to its financial market. On the occasion of the unsucessful campaign against Switzerland's entry into the EES, the principal leader of the *Lega dei Ticinesi*, Giuliano Bignasca, criticised the opening of the border with Italy, insisting on the supposed risks of an increase in "crime, mafia operations, and [...] immigration" (Rusconi, 1994: 166).[9]

---

[7]   It would seem that, despite the different approaches and emphasis, a significant number European regionalist parties tend to see the supra-national space as an alternative to the power of the central states today (Caciagli, 2003: 191–94; Keating, in this volume).

[8]   At national level, it was primarily the electorate of the *Schweizerische Volkspartei* that tended to express this attitude (Kriesi, 2002).

[9]   More recently, the *Lega dei Ticinesi* was first in line when the cantonal parliament proposed to write Swiss banking secrecy into the federal constitution, following the legislative attempts of the Berlusconi government to promote the return of the Italian

In supporting the maintenance of the twin keystones of insularity and welfare, the *Lega dei Ticinesi* is not only opposed to European integration, but also to Ticino's ambivalent relationship with its Italian neighbour. Historically, the linguistic ties (not due to a common identity, as much as to the widespread use of the Ticino dialect) have been flanked by a different political experience that helped the diffusion of mistrust and stereotypes. The long and tormented construction of a national identity came about via the reinforcement of the political barrier with Italy, and the full consolidation of this national and cantonal identity came with the confrontation of internal irredentist strands, with the pressures of the Italian Fascist regime (which pursued a policy of annexation for Ticino), and through the politics of the national defence during the Second World War.

In the second post-war period, the substantial differences that existed in the respective political systems and political cultures (neutrality *vs.* Atlantic Alliance, absence/presence of a strong communist party, stability/instability of government, etc.) contributed to the consolidation of the political barrier with Italy. On the socio-economic level, at least from the 1950s onwards, the border became a resource, and a guarantee of autonomy and later of welfare for the canton Ticino. The arrival of immigrants, cross-border commuters, and huge financial flows from Italy were considerable sources of wealth and development for Ticino. At the same time, the Swiss and cantonal laws, particularly the custom laws, protected the region of Ticino from the pressure of the Italian economy.

The *Lega dei Ticinesi* came onto the stage at a moment of in-depth definition of the relations of Ticino with Italy. The late 1980s and early 1990s marked a strong discontinuity from the geopolitical and economic points of view (the relaxation of the policy of trade controls and European integration). The increased permeability of the border with Italy called into question certainties that had been consolidated over time. The process of European integration involved a new liberalisation of access to the markets of Ticino, and, with protectionism now a thing of the past, this bred fears that the canton would be marginalised. Today, Ticino risks direct competition with Lombardy, a region that in the last 30 years has become one of the leading economic powers in Europe. This growing permeability introduces pressure and creates potential apprehension on the part of the *petite bourgeoisie* and the working

---

capital that had been illegally exported abroad, in particular to Swiss banks. In other words, to a greater extent than the other parties, the *Lega dei Ticinesi*'s rhetoric has exploited fears that Ticino could become the economic periphery not only of the Switzerland, but also of neighbouring Lombardy.

people of the Ticino.[10] While the cantonal government and the other principal parties intended to take on the European economic challenge by officially embracing the path of European integration, the *Lega dei Ticinesi* developed a Euro-sceptic rhetoric which appealed not only to the fear of immigration from afar, but also of immigration from nearby.

D. Lugano's Localism versus Bellinzona

Parallel to these dimensions, a local dimension is involved in the rhetoric and the political action of the *Lega dei Ticinesi*, although, on the whole, it plays a minor role with regard to the preceding dimensions. While the condemnation of the "partitocracy" has been weakening along with the process of institutional integration, the importance in the *Lega dei Ticinesi*'s rhetoric and actions for the defence of the economic position of Lugano have grown instead, especially after the party's principal leader Giuliano Bignasca was elected to the communal executive council in 2000. It is also worth noting that all the main leaders and founders of the *Lega dei Ticinesi* are from Lugano and its environs.

On more than one occasion, the *Lega dei Ticinesi* has taken up positions in defence of the city and the region of Lugano against Bellinzona, the capital of the canton, as the centre of the public administration and the symbol of cantonal political power. The defence of Lugano as the leading economic (and financial) force of the canton has been expressed in the form of opposition to the mechanisms of redistribution in favour of the economically weaker zones of the canton. The *Lega dei Ticinesi*'s anti-fiscal policy is also to be seen in this context, in contrast with what happens at the level of the federal claims (which include a critique of the dismantling of public enterprises), but remain in tune with the neo-liberal wing of the Radical Liberal Party of Lugano with which it has formed numerous opportunistic alliances, at both local and cantonal levels.

The *Lega*'s rhetoric has been able to drive between Lugano and Bellinzona, reinterpreting a "new" centre–periphery cleavage in the context of the traditional divisions. First, in the 1980s and 1990s, it is possible to observe a decrease in the rural–urban cleavage and the emergence of a potential new economic cleavage between Lugano and the rest of the canton. The electoral erosion of the Popular Democratic Party (PDP), the second largest cantonal party, from the highpoints of the 1970s reflects the weakening of the importance of the political cleavage that existed between town and countryside in the 1970s. This party, which

---

[10] In contrast with the border regions around Geneva and Basle, the wage's differences between residents and Italian cross-border commuters in Ticino are particularly marked (Flückiger and Falter, 2000). In 2002, around 30,000 Italian workers went to work in Ticino (which has a resident population of around 300,000).

was decisive in the construction of the party system during the 19th century, was always stronger and better represented in the valleys and in the most rural regions of the canton. Today, however, the proportion of Ticino's citizens making their living from agriculture has been reduced to less than five per cent.

Social modernisation, the exodus from the valleys towards the urban centres, the development of intensive internal geographical mobility and the processes of peri-urbanisation have, in many ways, homologated the cultural space of the canton Ticino, which is today defined by many geographers and territorial planners as "a diffused city" (Carloni, 2003). This new configuration has witnessed the growing economic and political importance of Lugano and the surrounding area which, in the 1990s, showed a dynamism in its development and a good deal of adaptation to the crisis of those years that was clearly superior to the rest of Ticino.

Second, the importance of the religious cleavage in Ticino has diminished, after dominating throughout the 19th and much of the 20th century. Alongside the rural–urban cleavage, the religious cleavage was once embodied by the PDP. But, in the cantonal election preceding the advent of the *Lega dei Ticinesi*, the PDP lost one of its two seats in the cantonal "power-sharing" government for the first time since the 1920s. In the wake of the secularisation and the cultural changes that took place in the 1970s and 1980s, it is possible to observe a partial melting of the cleavage that had dominated for more than hundred years, from the 1830s at least, when the Catholic (Conservative) Party formed in opposition to the Liberal Radical Party.

Third, the *Lega dei Ticinesi* came onto the stage at the beginning of a dispute which was generated when the most significant of Ticino's opposition parties joined the government in the 1970s and 1980s. The Independent Socialist Party (*Partito Socialista Autonomo*, PSA) profited from the defeat of the PDP in 1987 and won a seat in cantonal executive. It had been born on the crest of the 1968 wave of change, in opposition to the traditional Socialist Party, which had been represented in the cantonal government for many decades. At the beginning, it made criticism of the party system one of the mainstays of its agenda, but its winning of a government seat involved its integration into the consociationalism system.

Generally, the electoral success of a party derives from a combination of factors that include not only the social, economic, and cultural conditions at the time of its emergence, and thus the cleavages, but also the capacity of the party to capitalise electorally on the latent social questions at party system level. In any case, the aspects that defined the principal conditions of emergence and nourished those of the *Lega dei Ticinesi*'s success are also largely reflected in terms of the composition of the party's electorate in the 1990s. Since 1991, its electorate has resided, above all, in the districts around the two main centres of the canton, Locarno and Lugano, to the exclusion of Bellinzona. Furthermore, according to the surveys conducted between 1995 and 1999, the *Lega dei Ticinesi*'s electorate presents a high proportion of those without confession, those with greater mistrust of the political parties and institutions, young people under 30, salaried workers, artisans, small businessmen, and sectors with low levels of education.

The *Lega* rarely pronounces itself on religious or ecclesiastical matters, to which it maintains an ambivalent attitude, seeking instead to take up the "legacy" of the PSA in terms of anti-party protest. However, the electorate of the PSA, was situated on the (extreme) political left of the left–right axis, and was made up of people with a medium-high educational level. In contrast, the voters of the *Lega* are composed not only of the lower middle classes, but are also, in general, located in the centre-right strand. Moreover, it has a smaller "right wing" voter component than the electorate of the Liberal Radical Party (Mazzoleni, 1995; 2003a; Mazzoleni and Wernli, 2002: 126–27; 139).

III. The Centre–Periphery Cleavage in Switzerland

The *Lega dei Ticinesi* was thus able to move simultaneously on multiple levels, exploiting its compound identity (local, cantonal, national) and political agenda (condemnation of the cantonal, national and European élites), and taking advantage of the opportunities offered by the context of Ticino. But where is the case of the *Lega dei Ticinesi* in Switzerland to be placed? The *Lega* is the sole political force to have mobilised – successfully – a centre–periphery cleavage during the 1990s to the present day. Does this, perhaps, mean that the conditions for the emergence of a party which defends the interests of the "periphery" do not exist elsewhere in Switzerland?

On the structural level, there are a number of factors or "threats" which suggest that several conditions for a possible centre–periphery cleavage in Switzerland – as in the Alpine region as a whole (Caramani and Mény, in this volume) – have been reinforced in recent years: these include the socio-economic crisis of the 1990s, the acceleration of the processes of globalisation and European integration, the diffusion of neo-liberal politics, the increased economic concentration around the main centres of the German-speaking Switzerland, the increased disparity in the social distribution of resources as a result of the reduction of the protectionist mechanisms introduced after the Second World War, and the weakening of regional economic policy, which is partly a result of the privatisation and liberalisation of the major Swiss public corporations (postal, telecommunications, and rail).

Switzerland has not joined the EU, although, from the point of view of economic policies, its process of integration has intensified throughout the 1990s to the present day. External economic pressure over the past decade does not seem to have strengthened the internal cohesion and approval, but has instead increased internal conflict the political élites and Swiss public opinion; between the economic areas opening to the external markets and the areas that focus on the domestic market; between management and the unions; and between the advocates of a line of traditional independence in foreign policy and those who are, instead, inclined towards change within the context of Swiss integration with the EU, and who have found expression in the federal votes (Brunner and Sciarini, 2002).

These are tensions that the *Schweizerische Volkspartei*, a governmental party at federal level, as well as the main force of opposition to the decisions of the governmental majority with regard to immigration and foreign policy, has partially succeeded in intercepting, and has, thus, established, a new cleavage between the "winners" and "losers" of the process of modernisation, between Alpine and urban Switzerland (Kriesi, 1998a; 2003). Notwithstanding this, on the political agenda of the *Schweizerische Volkspartei*, the centre–periphery theme and that of linguistics are, on the whole, marginal. Historically strong, above all in the rural areas of the protestant Swiss-German cantons, this party has decreasing ties with the agricultural world, from the point of view of its electorate too. Moreover, despite its significant success in the French part of Switzerland, its electoral bases are especially concentrated in the German part, particularly in the cantons of the political and economic "centre" (such as Berne and Zurich) (Sciarini, Hardmeier, and Vatter, 2003; Mazzoleni, 2003b; Selb and Lachat, 2004).

In terms of culture and values, the economic cleavage between rich and poor regions seems to lead to the re-appearance of the ancient division between the Catholic and Protestant cantons, which dates back to the time of the *Sonderbund* civil war (Sciarini, 2002). Established essentially in the cantons with a Catholic tradition, the leading political representative of the religious cleavage in the present-day Swiss party system, the Christian Democrat Party, has, at least partially, defended the interests of the rural regions against the Protestant economic centres, as against the advocates of the centralist trends of the 19th century. Nevertheless, its electoral strength has been declining since the 1970s (21% in the federal elections of 1979; 16% in 1999). Furthermore, in its mobilisation in defence of the peripheries, the Catholic movement has never made direct reference to language, not only due to its own political culture, but also because its presence traverses the various national linguistic boundaries.

On the other hand, in recent years, there has been an increase in the structural and cultural importance of the linguistic cleavage and the decline of the religious cleavage (Trechsel, 1995). Three factors, at least, are responsible for this change: (1) the secularisation and the changing relationship with religion; (2) the diminished importance of the cantonal border compared to the regional one in the definition of the feeling of belonging among the citizens of the French-speaking minority (Kriesi *et al.*, 1996: 54–56); (3) the consolidation of the cultural barriers between the three main linguistic regions by the audio-visual and traditional media, particularly, the increasingly significant role of television in the political communication (Kriesi, 1999a: 21–22; Steiner, 2001: 144–45). However, in spite of the changes that have taken place in recent years, the elements that historically make the emergence of a centre–periphery cleavage in Switzerland exceptional appear to persist. In French-speaking Switzerland, in other words, within the country's main linguistic minority, the conditions for the development of a political force which expresses a centre–periphery cleavage seem to be lacking, despite the contrasts that have, to a greater or lesser extent, emerged with regard to the Swiss-German majority in recent years, and despite the fact that the French speakers appear to attach less importance to national rather than cantonal and regional identity (Kriesi *et al.*, 1996: 55).

However, we still cannot talk about a Swiss-French identity, which is capable of providing claimant support for a political player that would, in any case, have to take the cantonal divisions into account. Moreover, the capacity of the Swiss-French left-wing to articulate a class cleavage to a greater extent than that of the Swiss-Germans, particularly of the Socialist Party (Kriesi, 1998b; Mazzoleni and Wernli, 2002: 120 ff.), "neutralises" the effect between "losers" and "winners" that was revived by the *Schweizerische Volkspartei*. This class cleavage also smothers the development of a virtual centre–periphery cleavage based on the contrast between French and German speakers (see Caramani, 2004).

The complex cultural and particular linguistic and religious cleavages in Switzerland are not superimposed, but intersect, neutralising one another (Lijphart, 1980; Kriesi, 1998a,b). Moreover, while political mobilisation still essentially takes place at canton level, the linguistic boundaries do not coincide with the cantonal borders. It has been established that the economic differences within the linguistic regions are of more concern than those between the various linguistic regions (Joye *et al.*, 1992: 222). On the other hand, the diffusion of the instruments of direct democracy, the weakness of the party structures, and the development of social movements in general, obstruct the construction of an anti-establishment rhetoric which identifies politics as the domination of "self-referencing" parties (Zolo, 1992).

Conclusion

The *Lega dei Ticinesi* is an example of a party that expresses defensive socio-economic claims through populist rhetoric. Its reinterpretation of the geo-economic peripherality of the canton Ticino produces a double challenge against consensus democracy and against European integration.

From the early 1990s up to the present day, the predominant component of the *Lega dei Ticinesi*'s populist rhetoric has been built on the contrast between the canton of Ticino and the canton of Berne, the political capital of Switzerland. However, as I have attempted to show, it is not uniquely a regionalist party: it expresses nationalist and local demands as well. The rhetoric repertory cannot be reduced to a regionalist defence (Ticino *vs.* Berne), whose aim is the defence of the Swiss *Sonderfall*. From this point of view, it has in part been possible for the *Lega* to occupy the political position in Ticino which, in the Swiss-German cantons, is essentially the prerogative of Christoph Blocher's *Schweizerische Volkspartei*.

The *Lega*'s regionalist rhetoric aims at economic protectionism and greater autonomy within Swiss federalism, in order to revive Ticino's image of a discriminated and outcast canton. Its targets are the "political class", the government, and the federal administration. Within the cantonal realm, it defends the principal economic centre against the administrative and political centres, focusing at the same time on anti-fiscal themes and the critique of the "partitocracy", even though this last point seems to be gradually declining in recent years. However, from the point of view of rhetorical content, we can say that the common denominator of the *Lega dei Ticinesi* is a form of "chauvinism of welfare", in other words, a political response to the failed promises of the Swiss "*Sonderfall*", in conjunction with cantonal and national insularity and economic welfare.

As a consequence, the *Lega dei Ticinesi*'s ability to develop a populist rhetoric at different levels at the same or at different times and in relation to the political situation should not be seen solely as the effect of the ephemeral nature of the repertory drawn upon by contemporary populist parties. It has also be seen as a resource that was made available to it by the multi-dimensional nature of the institutional levels involved in Swiss federalism. The *Lega*'s multi-level populism – along with other factors, such as the presence of a charismatic leader and a centralised and flexible party organisation (Mazzoleni, 1999) – is also a resource through which it responds to the challenges of institutional integration.

The question of multi-level opportunities is also crucial for the explanation of the recent electoral decline of the *Lega*. After the mid-1990s, the opportunities at cantonal level were reduced because the cantonal coalition government had partially recovered the claims against Berne. The centre–periphery cleavage partially cuts across the cantonal party system. The local opportunities were declining as the *Lega dei Ticinesi*'s principal leader participated in the Lugano city government coalition after 2000. At the same time, the national opportunities have progressively been reducing, since the Ticino section of *Schweizerische Volkspartei*, which has recently moved towards Blocher's positions, has had an increasing electoral success: in the last national elections, Ticino's *Schweizerische Volkspartei* registered a share of 7.5% of the vote.

However, the necessary social, cultural, political conditions for the emergence and the development of a regionalist party do not appear to be found in any other part of Switzerland. Only the canton Ticino has so many conditions which favour such a development. In this canton, there are nearly identical cantonal and linguistic boundaries, a relative geomorphological insularity, a strong sense of cantonal identity, a tendency towards economic peripherality, and a strong presence of anti-party feelings favoured by the consociational decision-making accommodation. While the institutional and territorial Swiss structure habitually neutralised the centre–periphery cleavages, Ticino has provided many opportunities for a new national-regionalist populist actor.

References

ALMOND, G. and B. POWELL (1966), *Comparative Politics: A Developmental Approach*, Boston: Little, Brown & Co.

ALMOND, G. and S. VERBA (1963), *The Civic Culture: Political Attitudes and Democracy in Five Nations*, Princeton: Princeton University Press.

ALTERMATT, U. (1996), *Das Fanal von Sarajevo: Ethnonationalismus in Europa*, Zürich: Verlag NZZ.

AMESBERGER, H. and B. HALBMAYR (1998), *Rassismen: Ausgewählte Analysen Afrikanisch-Amerikanischer Wissenschafterinnen*, Vienna: Braumüller.

ANDERSON, C. and C. GUILLORY (1997), "Political Institutions and Satisfaction with Democracy: A Cross-National Analysis of Consensus and Majoritarian Systems", *American Political Science Review* 91: 66–81.

ANDERSON, P. (1979), *Lineages in the Absolutist State*, London: Verso.

ATZ, H. (1991), "Verschobene Grenzen: Strukturwandel und ethnische Arbeitsteilung", in HOLZER, A. *et. al.* (eds.), *Nie nirgends daheim: Vom Leben der Arbeiter und Arbeiterinnen in Südtirol*, Bolzano/Bozen: Cierre (Bund der Genossenschaften Südtirols/Lega Provinciale Cooperative).

BADIE, B. and P. BIRNBAUM (1979), *Sociologie de l'Etat*, Paris: Grasset.

BAILER-GALANDA, B. and W. NEUGEBAUER (1997), *Haider und die "Freiheitlichen" in Österreich*, Berlin: Elephanten Press.

BANFIELD, E. (1958), *The Moral Basis of a Backward Society*, Glencoe: The Free Press.

BARTOLINI, S. (1999), "Collusion, Competition, and Democracy, Part I", *Journal of Theoretical Politics* 11, 435–70.

—— (2002), "Institutional Democratization and Political Structuring in the EU. Lessons from the Nation-State Development", in CAVANNA, H. (ed.), *Governance, Globalization, and the European Union. Which Europe for Tomorrow?*, Dublin: Four Courts Press.

BARTOLINI, S. and P. MAIR (1990), *Identity, Competition, and Electoral Availability. The Stabilisation of European Electorates: 1885–1985*, Cambridge: Cambridge University Press.

BATT, J. (2003), "'Fuzzy Statehood' *versus* Hard Borders: The Impact of EU Eastward Enlargement on Romania and Yugoslavia", in KEATING, M. and J. HUGHES (eds.), *The Regional Challenge in Central and Eastern Europe: Territorial Restructuring and European Integration*, Brussels: P.I.E.-Peter Lang.

229

BAUMGÄRTL, M. (ed.) (1995), *Geschichte einer Volkspartei: 50 Jahre CSU, 1945–95*, Munich: Atwerb.

BAUR, S. (2000), *Die Tücken der Nähe: Kommunikation und Kooperation in Mehrheits-Minderheitensituationen. Kontextstudie am Beispiel Südtirol*, Meran: Alpha&Beta Verlag.

BAUR, S., I. VON GUGGENBERG, and D. LARCHEN (1998), *Zwischen Herkunft und Zukunft: Südtirol im Spannungsfeld ethnischer und postnationaler Gesellschaftsstruktur. Ein Forschungsbericht*, Meran: Alpha&Beta Verlag.

BECK, U. (1986), *Risikogesellschaft: Auf dem Weg in eine andere Moderne*, Frankfurt: Suhrkamp.

BENDIX, R. (1977), *Nation-Building and Citizenship: Studies of Our Changing Social Order* (new enlarged edition), Berkeley: University of California Press.

BENZ, A. (1998), "Postparlamentarische Demokratie? Demokratische Legitimation im kooperativen Staat", in GREVEN, M. (ed.), *Demokratie: eine Kultur des Westens?*, Opladen: Leske+Budrich.

—— (2002), "Vertrauensbildung in Mehrebenensystemen", in SCHAMLTZ-BRUNS, R. and R. ZINTL (eds.), *Politisches Vertrauen*, Baden-Baden: Nomos Verlag.

BERGOLD, J. (1997), *Awakening Affinities Between Past Enemies: Reciprocal Perceptions of Italians and Austrians*, Minneapolis: University of Minnesota.

BETTELHEIM, P. and R. BENEDIKTER (1982) (eds.), *Apartheid in Mitteleuropa? Sprache und Sprachenpolitik in Südtirol*, Vienna: Jugend und Volk.

BIORCIO, R. (1991), "La Lega come attore politico: dal federalismo al populismo regionale", in BIORCIO, R., I. DIAMANTI, R. MANNHEIMER, and P. NATALE, *La Lega Lombarda*, Milan: Feltrinelli.

—— (1997), *La Padania Promessa: La storia, le idee e la logica d'Azione della Lega Nord*, Milan: Il Saggiatore.

BETZ, H.-G. (1994), *Radical Right Wing Populism in Western Europe*. Basingstoke: Macmillan.

—— (1998a), "Introduction", in BETZ, H.-G. and S. IMMERFALL (eds.), *The New Politics of the Right: Neo-Populist Parties and Movements in Established Democracies*, Basingstoke: Macmillan.

—— (1998b), "Against Rome: The Lega Nord", in BETZ, H.-G. and S. IMMERFALL (eds.), *The New Politics of the Right: Neo-Populist Parties and Movements in Established Democracies*, Basingstoke: Macmillan.

—— (2001), "Entre succès et échec: l'extrême droite à la fin des années quatre-vingt-dix", in PERRINEAU, P. (ed.), *Les croisés de la société fermée: L'Europe des extrêmes droites*, La Tour d'Aigues: Editions de l'Aube.

—— (2002), "Haider's Revolution or the Future Has Just Begun", in BISCHOF, G., A. PELINKA, and M. GEHLER (eds.), *Austria in the Euro-*

pean Union, Contemporary Austrian Studies (Volume 10), New Brunswick: Transaction.

BETZ, H.-G. and S. IMMERFALL (eds.) (1998), *The New Politics of the Right: Neo-Populist Parties and Movements in Established Democracies*, Basingstoke: Macmillan.

BETZ, H.-G. and C. JOHNSON (forthcoming), "Against the Current – Stemming the Tide: The Nostalgic Ideology of the Contemporary Radical Populuist Right", *The Journal of Political Ideologies*.

BEVAN, R. (1995), *Anti-Party Discourses in Germany*, Vienna: Institut für Höhere Studien.

BIANCHI, R. (1989), *Il Ticino politico contemporaneo: 1921–75*, Locarno: Dadò.

BIORCIO, R. (1997), *La Padania promessa: La storia, le idee e la logica d'azione della Lega Nord*, Milan: Il Saggiatore.

BIRNBAUM, P. (1979), *Le peuple et les gros: Histoire d'un mythe*, Paris: Grasset

BLUMLER, J. and D. KAVANAGH (1999), "The Third Age of Political Communication: Influences and Features", *Political Communication* 16, 209–30.

BOHRER, G. (1983), *Enquête sur les dimensions du populisme à travers l'analyse de la Lega dei Ticinesi*, Université de Lausanne: Mémoire de maîtrise en Science politique.

BOLLIGER, C. and R. ZUERCHER (2003), "Das fakultative Referendum und die Einbindung der katholisch-konservativen Opposition in die schweizerische Regierung". Paper presented at the workhop "Governing under the Constraints of Referendums", Berne: Drei-Länder Tagung.

BRAY, Z. (2004), *Living Boundaries: Frontiers and Identity in the asque Country*, Brussels: P.I.E.-Peter Lang, 273 p.

BRODERO, A. and R. GREMMO (1978), *L'oppressione culturale italiana in Piemonte*, Ivrea: Editrice BS.

BRUBAKER, R. (1992) *Citizenship and Nationhood in France and Germany*, Cambridge: Cambridge University Press.

—— (1996), *Nationalism Reframed: Nationhood and the National Question in the New Europe*, Cambridge: Cambridge University Press.

BRUNNER, M. and P. SCIARINI (2002), "L'opposition ouverture-traditions", in HUG, S. and P. SCIARINI (eds.), *Changements de valeurs et nouveaux clivages politiques en Suisse*, Paris: L'Harmattan.

BRUNNER, M. and L. SGIER (1997), "Crise de confiance dans les institutions politiques suisses? Quelques résultats d'une enquête d'opinion", *Swiss Political Science Review* 1, 105–13.

CACIAGLI, M. (2003), *Regioni d'Europa: Devoluzioni, regionalismi, integrazione europea*, Bologna: Il Mulino.

CANOVAN, M. (1981), *Populism*, New York: Harcourt Brace.

CAPOCCIA, G. (2002), "Anti-System Parties: A Conceptual Reassessment", *Journal of Theoretical Politics* 14, 9–36.

CARAMANI, D. (2002), "L'Italie et l'Union Européenne", *Pouvoirs* 103, 129–42.

—— (2003), "State Administration and Regional Construction in Central Europe: A Historical Perspective", in KEATING, M. and J. HUGHES (eds.), *The Regional Challenge in Central and Eastern Europe: Territorial Restructuring and European Integration*, Brussels: P.I.E.-Peter Lang.

—— (2004), *The Nationalization of Politics: The Formation of National Electorates and Party Systems in Western Europe*, Cambridge: Cambridge University Press.

CARAMANI, D. and C. WAGEMANN (2003), "A Transnational Political Culture? The Alpine Region and its Relationship to European Integration", Edinburgh: ECPR Joint Session.

CARLONI, T. (2003), "Città e territorio: verso un complesso sistema a rete", GHIRINGHELLI, A. (ed.), *Il Ticino nella Svizzera: contributi sul Ticino duecento anni dopo, 1803–2003*, Locarno: Dadò.

CARTOCCI, R. (1994), *Fra Lega e Chiesa: L'Italia in cerca di integrazione*, Bologna: Il Mulino, 1994.

CAVANNA, H. (ed.) (2002), *Governance, Globalization, and the European Union: Which Europe for Tomorrow?*, Dublin: Four Courts Press.

CENTO BULL, A. and M. GILBERT (2001), *The Lega Nord and the Northern Question in Italian Politics*, London: Palgave.

CHAUVEL, L. (1995), "Valeurs régionales et nationales en Europe", *Futuribles* 200, 167–201.

CHIANTERA-STUTTE, P. (2002), *Das Europa der Antieuropäer: Ein Vergleich von Lega Nord und FPÖ*, Florence: EUI Working Papers (2002/9).

CLAUS, T., F. KARLHOFER, G. SEEBER, and C. BOOY (2001), *Jugend und Europa im Spannungsfeld von Demokratie und Extremismus: Forschungsbericht Textband*, Magdeburg: Brochure.

COFFE, H. (2004), *Can Extreme Right Voting be Explained Ideologically?*, Uppsala: ECPR Joint Sessions.

CONNOR, W. (1972), "Nation-Building or Nation-Destroying?", *World Politics* 24, 319–55.

COSTABILE, A. (1991), *Il fronte dell'uomo qualunque e la Lega lombarda*, Roma: Armando.

CORTI, M. (1995), "Italia: quale questione nazionale?", *Quaderni Padani* 2, 15–25.

CREPAZ, M. and H.-G. BETZ (2000), "Postindustrial Cleavages and Electoral Changes in an Advanced Capitalist Democracy: The Austrian Case", in BISCHOF, G., A. PELINKA, and D. STIEFEL (eds.), *The Marshall Plan in Austria*, Contemporary Austrian Studies (Volume 8), New Brunswick: Transaction.

CZADA, R. (2003), "Der Begriff der Verhandlungsdemokratie und die vergleichende Policy-Forschung", in MAYNTZ, R. and W. STREECK (eds.), *Die Reformierbarkeit der Demokratie*, Frankfurt-am-Main: Campus.

DAALDER, H. (1973), "Building Consociational Nations", in EISENSTADT, S. and S. ROKKAN (eds.), *Building States and Nations*, Beverly Hills: Sage (Volume 2).

DAALDER, H. and P. MAIR (eds.) (1983), *Western European Party Systems: Continuity and Change*, London: Sage.

DAHL, R. (1956), *A Preface to Democratic Theory*, Chicago: The University of Chicago Press.

DAY, A. (2000), *Directory of European Union Political Parties*, London: Harper.

DELANNOI, G. and P. TAGUIEFF (eds.) (2001), *Nationalismes en Perspective*, Paris: Berg International.

DIAMANTI, I. (1993a), *La Lega: Geografia, Storia e Sociologia di un Nuovo Soggetto Politico*, Roma: Donzelli.

—— (1993b), "L'Europa secondo la Lega", *Limes* 4, 161–71.

—— (1996), *Il male del Nord: Lega, localismo, secessione*, Roma: Donzelli.

DIANI, M. (1996), "Linking Mobilization Frames and Political Opportunities: Insights From Regional Populism in Italy", *American Sociological Review* 61, 1053–69.

DUPOIRIER, E. and B. ROY (1995), "Le fait régional en 1994", in *Annuaire des Collectivités Locales,* Paris: Librairies Techniques.

EASTON, D. (1965), *A Systems Analysis of Political Life*, New York: Wiley.

ECKSTEIN, H. (1975), "Case Study and Theory in Political Science", in GREENSTEIN, F. and N. POLSBY (eds.), *Handbook of Political Science* (Volume 7), Reading: Addison-Wesley.

ERMACORA, F. (1984), *Südtirol und das Vaterland Österreich*, Vienna: Amalthea.

ERNST, W. (1987), "Zu einer Theorie des Populismus", in PELINKA, A. (ed.), *Populismus in Österreich*, Vienna: Junius.

FAHRENHOLZ, P. (1994), "Die CSU vor einem schwierigen Spagat", *Aus Politik und Zeitgeschichte* B1/94, 17–20.

FALTER, J. (1982) "Bayerns Uhren gehen wirklich anders: Politische Verhaltens- und Einstellungsunterschiede zwischen Bayern und dem Rest der Bundesrepublik", *Zeitschrift für Parlamentsfragen* 4, 504–21.

—— (1988), "Wie gehen sie denn nun wirklich, die bayerischen Uhren?", *Zeitschrift für Parlamentsfragen* 1, 113–14.

FALTER, J. and S. SCHUMANN (1991), "Konsequenzen einer bundesweiten Kandidatur der CSU bei Wahlen: Eine in die unmittelbare Vergangenheit gerichtete Prognose", *Aus Politik und Zeitgeschichte* B 11-12/91, 23–45.

—— (1992), "Die Wahlchancen von CSU und DSU in den neuen Bundesländern", *Aus Politik und Zeitgeschichte* B 19/92, 17–30.

FIX, E. (1999), *Italiens Parteiensystem im Wandel: Von der Ersten zur Zweiten Republik*, Frankfurt: Campus.

FLORA, P. (1999), "Introduction and Interpretation", in ROKKAN, S., *State Formation, Nation-Building, and Mass Politics in Europe: The Theory of Stein Rokkan*, Oxford: Oxford University Press (edited by Flora, P., with S. Kuhnle, and D. Urwin).

FLÜCKIGER, Y. and J.-M. FALTER (2000), *La main-d'oeuvre frontalière et son impact sur les salaires à Genève*, Université de Genève: Observatoire Universitaire de l'Emploi.

FOX, J. (2002), "Ethnic Minorities and the Clash of Civilizations: A Quantitative Analysis of Huntington's Thesis", *British Journal of Political Science* 32, 415–34.

FROIDEVAUX, D. (1997), "Construction de la nation et pluralisme suisses: Idéologie et pratiques", *Swiss Political Science Review* 4, 29–58.

FUCHS, B. and G. HABINGER (eds.) (1996), *Rassismen und Feminismen: Differenzen, Machverhältnisse und Solidarität zwischen Frauen*, Wien: Promedia.

FUKUYAMA, F. (1995), *Trust: The Social Virtues and the Creation of Prosperity*, London: Penguin.

GALLENMÜLLER-ROSCHMANN, J. (1999), "Die drei Sprachgruppen Südtirols im Vergleich", in WAKENHUT, R. (ed.), *Ethnische Identität und Jugend: Eine vergleichende Untersuchung zu den drei Südtiroler Sprachgruppen*, Opladen: Leske+Budrich.

GALLENMÜLLER-ROSCHMANN, J., M. MARTINI, and R. WAKENHUT (eds.) (2000), *Ethnisches und nationales Bewusstsein: Studien zur sozialen Kategorisierung*, Frankfurt: Peter Lang.

GATTERER, C. (1968), *Im Kampf gegen Rom: Bürger, Minderheiten und Autonomien in Italien*, Vienna: Europa Verlag.

GAXIE, D. (1993), *La démocratie représentative*, Paris: Montchrestien.

GEDEN, O. (2004), *Männlichkeitskonstruktionen in der Freiheitlichen Partei Österreichs: Eine qualitativ-empirische Untersuchung*, Opladen: Leske+Budrich.

GHIRINGHELLI, A. (1987), "Appunti sul Ticino: Dalla genesi dei partiti all'affermazione della democrazia consociativa", in *Liberalismo: Premesse, sviluppi e realtà ticinesi*, Lugano: Circolo Liberale di Cultura Carlo Battaglini.

—— (1988), *Il Ticino della transizione, 1889–1922: Verso l'affermazione del multipartitismo e dei prerequisiti della democrazia consociativa*, Locarno: Dadò.

GRUNER, E. (1977), *Die Parteien in der Schweiz*, Bern: Francke.

GIBSON, R. (2002), *The Growth of Anti-Immigrant Parties in Western Europe*, Lewiston: Edwin Mellen Press.

GINGRICH, A. (2002), "A Man for All Seasons: An Anthropological Perspective on Public Representation and Cultural Politics of the Austrian Freedom

Party", in WODAK, R. and A. PELINKA (eds.), *The Haider Phenomenon in Austria*, London: Transaction.

GIOVANNETTI, P. (2000), "Alto Adige: Il partito di raccolta e la democrazia bloccata", *Il Mulino* 2, 285–95.

GOLD, T. (2003), *Lega Nord and Contemporary Politics in Italy*, Basingstoke: Palgrave.

GOMEZ-REINO CACHAFEIRO, M. (2001), *Ethnicity and Nationalism in Italian Politics: Inventing the Padania. Lega Nord and Northern Question*, Aldershot: Ashgate.

GRAMSCI, A. (1951), *La questione meridionale*, Roma: Edizioni Rinascita.

GRANDE, E. (2001), "Parteiensystem und Föderalismus: Institutionnelle Strukturmuster und politische Dynamiken im internationalen Vergleich", *Politische Vierteljahresschrift* 32, 179–212.

GUNTHER, R. *et al.* (eds.) (2002), *Political Parties: Old Concepts and New Challenges*, Oxford: Oxford University Press.

GUIOLO, R. (2000), "I nuovi crociati: La Lega e l'Islam", *Il Mulino* 5, 890–901.

HANNS-SEIDEL-STIFTUNG e.V. (ed.) (1995), *Geschichte einer Volkspartei: 50 Jahre CSU*, Munich: Atwerb.

HARMSEN, R. and M. SPIERING (2004), "Introduction: Euroscepticism and the Evolution of European Political Debate", *European Studies* 20, 13–16.

HARTENSTEIN, W. and R. MÜLLER-HILMER (2002), "Die Bundestagswahl 2002: Neue Themen, neue Allianzen", *Aus Politik und Zeitgeschichte* B 49-50/2002, 18–26.

HARVIE, C. (1994), *The Rise of Regional Europe*, London: Routledge.

HAEUSERMANN, S., A. MACH, and Y. PAPADOPOULOS (2004), "From Corporatism to Partisan Politics: Social Policy Making under Strain in Switzerland", *Swiss Political Science Review* 10, 33–59.

HAUSLEITER, L. (1994), "Krise oder Aufbruch? Die bayerische SPD 1990 bis zur Gegenwart", in OSTERMANN, R. (ed.), *Freiheit für den Freistaat*, Essen: Klartext-Verlag.

HATZENBICHLER, J. *et al.* (1993), *Europa der Regionen*, Graz-Stuttgart: Leopold Stocker Verlag.

HEFTY, G. (1995), "CSU-Geschichte aus der Sicht eines Journalisten: Fünfzig Jahre Lufthoheit über den Stammtischen", in HANNS-SEIDEL-STIFTUNG e.V. (ed.), *Geschichte einer Volkspartei: 50 Jahre CSU*, Munich: Atwerb.

HELMS, L. (1997), "Right-Wing Populist Parties in Austria and Switzerland: A Comparative Analysis of Electoral Support and Conditions of Success", *West European Politics* 20, 37–52.

HENZLER, C. (1995), "Die Christlich-Soziale Union in den ersten Nachkriegsjahren", in HANNS-SEIDEL-STIFTUNG e.V. (ed.), *Geschichte einer Volkspartei: 50 Jahre CSU*, Munich: Atwerb.

HÉRITIER, A. (1999), *Policy-Making and Diversity in Europe: Escaping Deadlock*, Cambridge: Cambridge University Press.

HESSE, J. and T. ELLWEIN (1997), *Das Regierungssystem der Bundesrepublik Deutschland*, (Volume 1), Opladen: Leske+Budrich.

HILMER, R. (2003), "Bundestagswahl 2002: Eine zweite Chance für Rot-Grün", *Zeitschrift für Parlamentswahlen* 34, 187–219.

HILPOLD, P. (2001), *Modernes Minderheitenrecht: Eine rechtsvergleichende Untersuchung des Minderheitenrechtes in Österreich und in Italien unter besonderer Berücksichtigung völkerrechtlicher Aspekte*, Baden-Baden: Nomos.

HIRSCHMAN, A. (1970), *Exit, Voice, and Loyalty: Responses to Decline in Firms, Organizations, and States*, Cambridge, Mass.: Harvard University Press.

HIRTER, H. (2000), *Elections 1999: Composition et orientation politique de l'électorat lors des élections fédérales de 1999*, Berne: Institute of Politics.

HIRTER, H. and W. LINDER (2003), *Analyse der eidgenössischen Abstimmungen vom 24. November 2002*, Berne: GfS Forschungsinstitut (Vox No.79).

HIX, S. and C. LORD (1997), *Political Parties in the European Union*, London: Macmillan.

HLADNIK, M. (1991), "Regionalism in Slovene Rural Prose", *Slovene Studies* XIII/2, 143–53.

HOLTMANN, E. (1994), "Parteien in der lokalen Politik", in ROTH, R. and H. WOLLMANN (eds.), *Kommunalpolitik*, Opladen: Leske+Budrich.

HOLZER, A. (1991), *Die Südtiroler Volkspartei*, Thaur: Kulturverlag.

HOLZER, A. and B. SCHWEGLER (1998), "The Südtiroler Volkspartei: A Hegemonic Ethno-Regionalist party", in DE WINTER, L. and H. TÜRSAN (eds.), *Regionalist Parties in Western Europe*, London: Routledge.

HOOGE, L. and G. MARKS (2001), *Multi-Level Governance and European Integration*, Lanham: Rowman and Littlefield.

HUMMER, W. and A. PELINKA (2002), *Österreich unter "EU-Quarantaene": Die "Massnahmen der 14" gegen die österreichische Bundesregierung aus politikwissenschaftlicher und juristischer Sicht*, Wien: Linde.

HUNTINGTON, S. (1996), *The Clash of Civilizations and the Remaking of World Order*, New York: Simon and Schuster.

IGNAZI, P. (1999), "Les partis d'extrême droite: Les fruits inachevés de la société post-industrielle", Rennes: Sixth Congress of the French political science association.

—— (2003), *Extreme Right Parties in Western Europe*, Oxford: Oxford University Press.

IHL, O., J. CHENE, E. VIAL, and G. WATERLOT (eds.) (2003), *La tentation populiste au cœur de l'Europe*, Paris: La Découverte.

JACHTENFUCHS, M., T. DIEZ, and S. JUNG. (1998), "Which Europe? Conflicting Models of a Legitimate European Political Order", *European Journal of International Relations* 4, 409–45.

JESSE, E. (1996) "Die CSU im vereinigten Deutschland", *Aus Politik und Zeitgeschichte* B 6/96, 29–35.

—— (1997) "Die Parteien im westlichen Deutschland von 1945 bis zur deutschen Einheit 1990", in GABRIEL, O. *et al.* (eds.), *Parteiendemokratie in Deutschland*, Bonn: Bundeszentrale für politische Bildung.

JESSOP, B., K. BONNET, S. BROMLEY, and T. LING (1984), "Autoritarian Populism, Two Nations, and Tatcherism", *New Left Review* 147, 32–60.

JIMÉNEZ BLANCO, J., M. GARCIA FERRANDO, E. LOPEZ ARANGUREN, and M. BELTRÁN VILLALVA (1977), *La conciencia regional en España,* Madrid: Centro de Investigaciones Sociológicas.

JOHANSSON, K. (2002), "European People's Party", in JOHANSSON, K. and P. ZERVAKIS (cds.) (2002), *European Political Parties between Cooperation and Integration,* Baden-Baden: Nomos.

JOHANSSON, K. and P. ZERVAKIS (eds.) (2002), *European Political Parties Between Cooperation and Integration,* Baden-Baden: Nomos.

JOUVE, B. (1998), "D'une mobilisation à l'autre: Dynamique de l'échange politique territorialisé en Rhône-Alpes", in NÉGRIER, E. and B. JOUVE (eds.), *Qui gouverne les régions de l'Europe? Echanges politiques et mobilisations régionales,* Paris: l'Harmattan.

JUDSON, P. (2000), "Austrian Non-Reception of a Reluctant Goldhagen", in ELEY, G. (ed.), *The "Goldhagen Effect": History, Memory, Nazism – Facing the German Past,* Ann Arbor: The University of Michigan Press.

JUNG, G. and G. RIEGER (1995), "Die bayerische Landtagswahl vom 25.September 1994: Noch einmal gelang der CSU ein machiavellisches Lehrstück", *Zeitschrift für Parlamentsfragen* 2, 232–49.

KAPLAN, D. (2000), "Conflict and Compromise among Borderland Identities in Northern Italy", *Tijdschrift voor Economische en Sociale Geografie* 91, 44–60.

KARLHOFER, F., J. MELCHIOR, and H. SICKINGER (eds.) (2001), *Anlassfall Österreich: Die Europäische Union auf dem Weg zu einer Wertegemeinschaft,* Baden-Baden: Nomos.

KATZ, R. (2003), "Cartels, Consensus Democracy, and Representation in the European Union", Edinburgh: ECPR.

KATZ, R. and P. MAIR (1995), "Changing Models of Party Organization and Party Democracy: The Emergence of the Cartel Party", *Party Politics* 1, 5–28.

—— (1996), "Cadre, Catch-All or Cartel?: A Rejoinder", *Party Politics* 2, 527–36.

KATZENSTEIN, P. (1985), *Small States in World Markets. Industrial Policy in Europe*, Ithaca: Cornell University Press.

KAZIN, M. (1995), *The Populist Persuasion: An American History*, New York: Basic Books.

KEATING, M. (1988), *State and Regional Nationalism: Territorial Politics and the European State*, London: Wheatsheaf..

—— (1998), *The New Regionalism in Western Europe: Territorial Restructuring and Political Change*, Aldershot: Edward Elgar.

—— (2001), *Plurinational Democracy: Stateless Nations in a Post-Sovereignty Era*, Oxford: Oxford University Press.

—— (2004), "European Integration and the Nationalities Question", *Politics and Society* 31, 1–22.

KEATING, M. and J. HUGHES (eds.) (2003), *The Regional Challenge in Central and Eastern Europe: Territorial Restructuring and European Integration*, Brussels: P.I.E.-Peter Lang.

KITSCHELT, H. (1986), "Political Opportunity Structures and Political Protest: Anti-Nuclear Movements in Four Democracies", *British Journal of Political Science* 16, 57–85.

—— (1995), *The Radical Right in Western Europe: A Comparative Analysis*, Ann Arbor: University of Michigan Press.

—— (1997), "European Party Sytems: Continuity and change", in RHODES, M. and V. WRIGHT (eds.), *Developments in West European Politics*, London: Macmillan.

—— (2002), "Popular Dissatisaction with Democracy: Populism and Party Systems", in MÉNY, Y. and Y. SUREL, *Democracies and the Populist Challenge*, Basingstoke: Palgrave.

KITSCHELT, H. and A. McCANN (2003), "Die Dynamik der schweizerischen neuen Rechten in komparativer Perspektive: Die Alpenrepubliken", in SCIARINI, P. *et al.* (eds.), *Schweizer Wahlen 1999*, Berne: Haupt.

KNÜSEL, R and J. HOTTINGER (1994), *Regionalist Movement and Parties in Switzerland: A Case Study on the "Lega dei Ticinesi"*, Lausanne: Cahiers de l'IDHEAP.

KOBACH, W. (1997), "Spurn Thy Neighbour: Direct Democracy and Swiss Isolationism", *West European Politics* 3, 185–211.

KOCH, S. (1994), *Parteien in der Region*, Opladen: Leske+Budrich.

KOOLE, R. (1996), "Cadre, Catch-All or Cartel? A Comment on the Notion of Cartel Party", *Party Politics* 2, 509–25.

KLAUSEN, J. and L. TILLY (1997), *European Integration in Social and Historical Perspective*, Lanham: Rowman and Littlefield.

KOHLER-KOCH, B. (1998), *La renaissance de la dimension territoriale en Europe*, EUI Working Papers (RSC 98/38).

KONSTANTINOVIC, Z. (1994), "Verspielte Chancen mitteleuropäischer Literaturausblicke: Über die Zukunft regionaler Kulturen", in PRISCHING, M. (ed.), *Identität und Nachbarschaft: Die Vielfalt der Alpen-Adria-Länder*, Vienna: Böhau.

KRIEGER, W. (1995) "Franz Josef Strauß und die zweite Epoche in der Geschichte der CSU", in HANNS-SEIDEL-STIFTUNG e.V. (ed.), *Geschichte einer Volkspartei: 50 Jahre CSU*, Munich: Atwerb.

KRIESI, H. (1998a), *Le système politique suisse*, Paris: Economica.

—— (1998b), "The Transformation of Cleavage Politics. The 1997 Stein Rokkan Lecture", *European Journal of Political Research* 33, 165–85.

—— (1999a), "Introduction: State Formation and Nation Building in the Swiss Case", in KRIESI, H., K. ARMINGEON, H. SIEGRIST, and A. WIMMER (eds.), *Nation and National Identity: The European Experience in Perspective*, Zurich: Rüegger.

—— (1999b), "Movement of the Left, Movements of the Right: Putting the Mobilization of Two New Types of Social Movements into Political Context", in KITSCHELT, H. *et al.* (eds.), *Continuity and Change in Contemporary Capitalism*, Cambridge: Cambridge University Press.

—— (2002), "Politische Folgen nationaler Identität: Das Beispiel der Eidgenössischen Wahlen von 1999", in C. ROSSHART-PFLUGER, J. JUNG, and F. METZGER (eds.), *Nation und Nationalismus in Europa: Kulturelle Konstruktion von Identitäten*, Frauenfeld: Huber.

—— (2003), "The Transformation of the National Political Space in a Globalizing World", in IBARRA, P. (ed.), *Social Movements and Democracy*, Basingstoke: Palgrave.

KRIESI, H. *et al.* (1996), *Le clivage linguistique: Problèmes de compréhension entre les communautés linguistiques en Suisse*, Berne: UFS.

KYMLICKA, W. (ed.) (1995), *The Rights of Minority Cultures*, Oxford: Oxford University Press.

LADNER, A. (2000), "Participaton politique et réforme des institutions", in SUTER, C. and C. PAHUD (eds.), *Rapport social 2000*, Zurich: Seismo.

LADNER, A. and M. BRÄNDLE (1999), "Does Direct Democracy Matter for Political Parties: An Empirical Test in the Swiss Cantons", *Party Politics* 5, 283–302.

—— (2001), *Die Schweizer Parteien im Wandel: Von Mitgliederparteien zu professionalisierten Wählerorganisationen?*, Zürich: Seismo.

LAFONT, R. (1967), *La révolution régionaliste,* Paris: Gallimard.

LAMPIS, A. (1999), *Autonomia e convivenza: Tutela delle minoranze e regole della convivenza nell'ordinamente giuridico dell'Alto Adige/Südtirol*, Bozen-Bolzano: CEDAM (Arbeitshefte Europäische Akademie Bozen/Quaderni accademia europea Bolzano 17).

LANGER, A. (1988), "Volksgruppen- und Minderheitenpolitik: Südtirol nach dem 'Paketabschluß'", in BAIBOCK, R. *et al.* (eds.), *...und raus bist Du! Ethnische Minderheiten in der Politik*, Vienna: Verlag für Gesellschaftskritik (Österreichische Texte zur Gesellschaftskritik).

LECA, J. (1996), "La démocratie à l'épreuve des pluralismes", *Revue Française de Science Politique* 46, 225–79.

LEERSCH, H.-J. (1992), "Die CSU: Eine neue Form der Bayernpartei?", *Aus Politik und Zeitgeschichte* B 5/1992, 21–28.

LE GALÈS, P. and C. LESQUESNE (eds.) (1997), *Les paradoxes des régions en Europe*, Paris: La Découverte.

LEGGEWIE, C. (1994), "Ethnizität, Nationalismus und multikulturelle Gesellschaft", in BERDING, H. (ed.), *Nationales Bewusstsein und kollektive Identität: Studien zur Entwicklung des kollektiven Bewusstseins in der Neuzeit*, Frankfurt: Suhrkamp.

LEHMBRUCH, G. (1967), *Proporzdemokratie: Politisches System und politische Kultur in der Schweiz und in Österreich*, Tübingen: Mohr.

—— (1996), "Die korporative Verhandlungsdemokratie in Westmitteleuropa", *Swiss Political Science Review* 2, 19–41.

LE ROY LADURIE, E. (2001), *Histoire de France des régions,* Paris: Seuil.

LIJPHART, A. (1968), *The Politics of Accommodation: Pluralism and Democracy in the Netherlands*, Berkeley: University of California Press.

—— (1975), "The Comparable-Cases Strategy in Comparative Research", *Comparative Political Studies* 8, 158–77.

—— (1980), "Language, Religion, Class, and Party Choice: Belgium, Canada, Switzerland and South Africa Compared", in ROSE, R. (ed.), *Electoral Participation: A Comparative Analysis*, Beverly-Hills: Sage.

—— (1999), *Patterns of Democracy: Government Forms and Performance in Thirty-Six Countries*, New Haven: Yale University Press.

LILL, R. (1991), "Die Südtiroler Volkspartei", in VEEN, H.-J. (ed.), *Christlich-demokratische und konservative Parteien in Westeuropa* (Volume 3), Paderborn: Schöningh.

LILLI, W. and R. HARTIG (1995), "Le rôle des aspects culturels et interactionnels dans la définition de l'identité régionale", *Sciences de la Société* 34, 125–35.

LINDER, W. (1994), *Swiss Democracy*, London: Macmillan.

LINZ, J. (1976), "Patterns of Land Tenure, Division of Labor, and Voting Behavior in Europe", *Comparative Politics* 8, 365–430.

LIPSET, S. and S. ROKKAN (1967a), "Cleavage Structures, Party Systems, and Voter Alignments: An Introduction", in LIPSET, S. and S. ROKKAN (eds.), *Party Systems and Voter Alignments. Cross-National Perspectives*, New York: The Free Press.

—— (eds.) (1967b), *Party Systems and Voter Alignments: Cross-National Perspectives*, New York: The Free Press.

LORWIN, V. (1966), "Belgium: Religion, Class, and Language in National Politics", in DAHL, R. (ed.), *Political Oppositions in Western Democracies*, New Haven: Yale University Press.

LOUGHLIN, J. *et al.* (2001), *Subnational Democracy in the European Union: Challenges and Opportunities*, Oxford: Oxford University Press.

LYNCH, P. (1996), *Minority Nationalism and European Integration*, Cardiff: University of Wales Press.

MACH, A. (ed.) (1998), *Globalisation, néo-libéralisme et politiques publiques dans la Suisse des années 1990*, Zürich: Seismo.

MAIER, C. (1994), "Wessen Mitteleuropa? Das Zentrum Europas zwischen Erinnerung und Vergessen", in PRISCHING, M. (ed.), *Identität und Nachbarschaft: Die Vielfalt der Alpen-Adria-Länder*, Vienna: Böhau.

MAIR, P. (2000), "The Limited Impact of Europe on National Party Systems", *West European Politics* 23, 27–51.

—— (2002), "Populist Democracy *vs.* Party Democracy", in MÉNY, Y. and Y. SUREL (eds.), *Democracies and the Populist Challenge*, London: Palgrave.

MANIN, B. (1997), *Principles of Representative Democracy*, Cambridge: Cambridge University Press.

MANNHEIMER, R. *et al.* (1991), *La Lega Lombarda*, Milano: Feltrinelli.

MANOSCHEK, W. (2002), "The Freedom Party of Austria (FPÖ): An Austrian and a European Phenomenon?", in BISCHOF, G., A. PELINKA, and M. GEHLER (eds.), *Austria in the European Union*, Contemporary Austrian Studies (Volume 10), New Brunswick: Transaction.

MARCACCI, M. (2003), "Il cantone e la Confederazione: La difficoltà di essere ticinesi e svizzeri", in GHIRINGHELLI, A. (ed.), *Il Ticino nella Svizzera: Contributi sul Ticino duecento anni dopo. 1803–2003*, Locarno: Dadò.

MARKO, J. (2001), "L'Alto Adige: Un "modello" per la composizione di conflitti etnici in altre aree d'Europa?", in MARKO, J., S. ORTINO, and F. PALERMO (eds.), *L'ordinamento speciale della Provincia autonoma di Bolzano*, Padova: CEDAM (Ius Publicum Europaeum 3).

MARKS, G. and M. STEENBERGEN (2002), "Understanding Political Contestation in the European Union", *Comparative Political Studies* 35, 879–92.

MARKS, G. and C. WILSON (2000), "The Past in the Present: A Cleavage Theory of Party Response to European Integration", *British Journal of Political Science* 30, 433–59.

MAZZOLENI, O. (1995), "Identità e modernizzazione: Una Lega nella Svizzera italiana", in BONOMI, A. and P.-P. POGGOP (eds.), *Ethnos e demos: Dal leghismo al neopopulismo*, Milano: Mimesis.

—— (1999), "La Lega dei Ticinesi: Vers l'intégration?", *Swiss Political Science Review* 3, 79–95.

—— (2001), "Democrazia diretta e democrazia rappresentativa: Il caso ticinese in un confronto intercantonale", *Dati, Statistiche e Società* 3, 81–93.

—— (2003a) "Unité et diversité des 'national-populismes' suisses: L'Union Démocratique du Centre et la Lega dei Ticinesi", in IHL, O. *et al.* (eds.), *La tentation populiste au cœur de l'Europe*, Paris: La Découverte.

—— (2003b), *Nationalisme et populisme en Suisse: La radicalisation de la "nouvelle" UDC*, Lausanne: Presses Polytechniques et universitaires romandes.

MAZZOLENI, G., J. STEWART, and B. HORSFIELD (eds.) (2003), *The Media and Neo-Populism*, Praeger: London.

MAZZOLENI, O. and B. WERNLI (2002), *Cittadini e politica: Interesse, partecipazione, istituzioni e partiti in Svizzera: Ginevra, Ticino e Zurigo a confronto*, Bellinzona: Ufficio di statistica.

MÉNY, Y. and Y. SUREL (2000), *Par le peuple, pour le peuple: Le populisme et les démocraties*, Paris: Fayard.

—— (eds.) (2002), *Democracies and the Populist Challenge*, Basingstoke: Palgrave.

MESSNER, G. (1999), *Jugend in Südtirol: Eine Erhebung an deutschsprachigen Berufs- und Oberschulen Südtirols, durchgeführt im Mai 1998*, Bolzano-Bozen: Conference on "South Tyrolean youth on the path to the multicultural society: Ethnic identities – cohabitation – political attitudes."

MILWARD, A. (1999), *The European Rescue of the Nation-State* (second edition), London: Routledge.

MINÁRIK, M. (1999), *The Evolution of Ethnopolitical Parties: A Comparative Study of Ethno-Political Representation of the German-Speaking Minority in South Tyrol, Italy, and the Hungarian-Speaking Minority in Slovakia*, MA Dissertation, Central European University, Budapest.

MINTZEL, A. (1977), *Geschichte der CSU*, Opladen: Leske+Budrich.

—— (1984), *Die Volkspartei*, Opladen: Leske+Budrich.

—— (1987a), "Gehen Bayerns Uhren wirklich anders?", *Zeitschrift für Parlamentsfragen* 1/1987, 77–93.

—— (1987b), "Politisch-kulturelle Hegemonie und "Gegenkulturen" in Bayern", in LANDSHUTER, W. and E. LIEGEL (eds.), *Beunruhigung in der Provinz: Zehn Jahre Scharfrichterhaus*, Passau: Andreas-Haller-Verlag.

—— (1989), "Die Rolle der CSU-Landesgruppe im politischen Kräftespiel der Bundesrepublik Deutschland", *Politische Studien* 1/1989, 113–34.

—— (1990a), "CSU-Strategie gegen Gewichtsverlust", *Die Neue Gesellschaft-Frankfurter Hefte* 37, 828–31.

—— (1990b), "Political and Socio-Economic Development in the Postwar Era: The Case of Bavaria 1945–89", in ROHE, K. (ed.), *German Parties and Party Systems, 1867-1987*, New York: Berg.

—— (1992), "Die Christlich-Soziale Union in Bayern", in MINTZEL, A. and H. OBERREUTER (eds.), *Parteien in der Bundesrepublik Deutschland*, Bonn: Bundeszentrale für politische Bildung.

—— (1993), "Die CSU in Bayern als Forschungsobjekt: Entwicklung, Stand, Defizite und Perspektiven der CSU-Forschung", in NIEDERMAYER, O. and R. STÖSS (eds.), *Stand und Perspektiven der Parteienforschung in Deutschland*, Opladen: Leske+Budrich.

—— (1995), "Bayern und die CSU", in HANNS-SEIDEL-STIFTUNG e.V. (ed.), *Geschichte einer Volkspartei: 50 Jahre CSU*, Munich: Atwerb.

—— (1999), *Die CSU-Hegemonie in Bayern; Strategie und Erfolg; Gewinner und Verlierer*, Passau: Wissenschaftlicker Verlag Rothe.

MOORE, B. Jr. (1966), *Social Origins of Dictatorship and Democracy: Lord and Peasant in the Making of the Modern World*, Boston: Beacon Press.

MÜLLER, W. (2002), "Evil or the 'Engine of Democracy'? Populism and Party Competition in Austria", in MÉNY, Y. and Y. SUREL (eds.), *Democracies and the Populist Challenge*, Basingstoke: Palgrave.

NEIDHART, L. (1970), *Plebiszit und pluralitäre Demokratie*, Berne: Francke.

NICLAUß, K. (1995), *Das Parteiensystem der Bundesrepublik*, Paderborn: Schöningh.

NORRIS, P. (ed.) (1999), *Critical Citizens*, Oxford: Oxford University Press.

NUSSBAUMER, E. (1971), "Kärntens Eigenart und seine Bedeutung für Osterreich in Vergangenheit und Gegenwart", in JAMBOR, W. (ed.), *Der Anteil der Bundesländer an der Nationswerdung Osterreichs*, Vienna: Kurt Wedl.

OBERREUTER, H. (1995), "Konkurrierende Kooperation: die CSU in der Bundespolitik", in HANNS-SEIDEL-STIFTUNG e.V. (ed.), *Geschichte einer Volkspartei: 50 Jahre CSU*, Munich: Atwerb.

OFFERLÉ, M. (1995), *Sociologie des groupes d'intérêt*, Paris: Montchrestien.

OIP – Observatoire Interrégional du Politique (1997), *Enquête OIP 1997: Le fait régional*, Paris: OIP.

OLSON, M. (1982), *The Rise and Decline of Nations: Economic Growth, Stagflation, and Social Rigidities*, New Haven: Yale University Press.

PALLAVER, G. (2001a), "Die Südtiroler Volkspartei: Erfolgreiches Modell einer ethnoregionalen Partei; Trends und Perspektiven", in INSTITUTE FOR ETHNIC STUDIES (ed.), *Treaties and Documents* (38/39), Ljubliana: Europa.

—— (2001b), "Ist Südtirol ein multikulturelles Land? Probleme und Perspektiven einer mehrsprachigen Gesellschaft", in APPELT, E. (ed.), *Demokratie und das Fremde: Multikulturelle Gesellschaften als demokratische Herausforderung des 21. Jahrhunderts*, Innsbruck: Studienverlag.

—— (2003a), "Südtirols Konkordanzdemokratie: Ethnische Konfliktregelung zwischen juristischem Korsett und gesellschaftlichem Wandel", in CLEMENTI, S. and J. WOELK (ed.), *1992: Ende eines Streits. Zehn Jahre Streitbeilegung im Südtirolkonflikt zwischen Italien und Österreich*, Baden-Baden: Nomos.

—— (2003b), "Die Beziehungen zwischen Südtirol und Nordtirol und die Europaregion Tirol-Südtirol-Trentino", in KARLHOFER, F. and A. PELINKA (ed.), *Politik in Tirol*, Innsbruck: Studienverlag.

—— (2004), "Südtirols Parteiensystem: Versuch einer Typologisierung nach den Landtagswahlen 2003", in FILZMAIER, P., P. PLAIKNER, I. CHERUBINI, and G. PALLAVER (eds.), *Jahrbuch für Politik Tirol und*

Südtirol 2003/La politica in Tirolo e in Sudtirolo 2003, Bolzano/Bozen: Verlagsanstalt Athesia.

PAPADOPOULOS, Y. (1992), *À propos du populisme: Langage simple, phénomène complexe*, Lausanne: Institut de Science Politique.

—— (2002), "Populism, the Democratic Question, and Contemporary Governance", in MÉNY, Y. and Y. SUREL (eds.), *Democracies and the Populist Challenge*, London: Palgrave.

—— (2003), "Cooperative Forms of Governance: Problems of Democratic Accountability in Complex Environments", *European Journal of Political Research* 42, 473–501.

PASQUINO, G. (1995), "La società contro la politica: Un nuovo qualunquismo", *Il Mulino* 44, 801–09.

PARKES, S. (1997), *Understanding Contemporary Germany,* London: Routledge.

PATZELT, W. (1991) "Was ist falsch mit Bayerns SPD? Ergebnisse einer Umfrage unter bayerischen Abgeordneten", *Zeitschrift für Parlamentsfragen* 1/1991, 59–88.

PAULI-BALLEIS, G. (1987), *Polit-PR: Strategische Öffentlichkeitsarbeit politischer Parteien*, Zirndorf: Author.

PELINKA, A. (ed.) (1994), *EU-Referendum: Zur Praxis direkter Demokratie in Österreich*, Vienna: Signum.

—— (1996), *Jaruzelski oder die Politik des kleineren Übels: Zur Vereinbarkeit von Demokratie und Leadership*, Frankfurt: Peter Lang.

—— (1998), *Austria: Out of the Shadow of the Past*, Boulder: Westview.

—— (2002), "Die FPÖ in der vergleichenden Parteienforschung: Zur typologischen Einordnung der Freiheitlichen Partei Österreichs", *Österreichische Zeitschrift für Politikwissenschaft* 31, 281–90.

—— (2004). "Austrian Eurpscepticism: The Shift from the Left to the Right", *European Studies* 20, 207–24.

PELINKA, A. and R. WODAK (eds.) (2002), *Dreck am Stecken: Politik der Ausgrenzung*, Vienna: Czernin.

PERRINEAU, P. (2001), *Les croisés de la société fermée: L'Europe des extrêmes droites*, La Tour d'Aigues: L'Aube.

PFETSCH, B. (1998), "Regieren unter den Bedingungen medialer Allgegenwart", in SARCINELLI, U. (ed.), *Politikvermittlung und Demokratie in der Mediengesellschaft*, Opladen: Westdeutscher Verlag.

PHARR, S. and R. PUTNAM (2000), *Disaffected Democracies*, Princeton: Princeton University Press.

PIEAS, A. (1998), *Die Beziehungen der Südtiroler Volkspartei zu den deutschsprachigen Sozialverbänden*, Ph.D. thesis: Innsbruck.

PIERRE, J. (ed.) (2000), *Debating Governance*, Oxford: Oxford University Press.

PIERRE, J. and B. PETERS (2000), *Governance, Politics, and the State*, London: Macmillan.

PITKIN, H. (1967), *The Concept of Representation*, Berkeley: University of California Press.

PLASSER, F. and P. ULRAM (eds.) (2003), *Wahlverhalten in Bewegung: Analysen zur Nationalratswahl 2002*, Wien: WUV.

POGGESCHI, G. (2001), "Il censimento e la dichiarazione linguistica", in MARKO, J., S. ORTINO, and F. PALERMO (eds.), *L'ordinamento speciale della Provincia autonoma di Bolzano*, Padova: CEDAM (Ius Publicum Europaeum 3).

POGUNTKE, T. (1997), "Parteiorganisationen in der Bundesrepublik Deutschland: Einheit in der Vielfalt?", in GABRIEL, O. *et al.* (eds.), *Parteiendemokratie in Deutschland*, Bonn, Bundeszentrale für politische Bildung.

POLI, G. (1995), *Breve storia/programma della Lega Nord*, Milan: Segreteria Federale.

PREGLAU, M. (2001), *Rechtsextrem oder postmodern? Ein Jahr Regierungspolitik der (Haider-) FPÖ*, Vienna: SWS-Rundschau.

PRZEWORKSI, A. (1985), *Capitalism and Social Democracy*, Cambridge: Cambridge University Press.

PRZEWORSKI, A. and H. TEUNE (1970), *The Logic of Comparative Social Inquiry*, New York: Wiley Interscience.

PUTNAM, R. (1993), *Making Democracy Work: Civic Traditions in Modern Italy*, Princeton: Princeton University Press.

RADUNSKI, P. (1996) "Politisches Kommunikationsmanagement", in BERTELSMANN-STIFTUNG (ed.), *Politik überzeugend vermitteln*, Gütersloh: Verlag Bertelsmann-Stiftung.

REINFELDT, S. (2002), *Nicht-wir und Die-da: Studien zum rechten Populismus*, Vienna: Braumüller.

REITERER, A. (1996), *Kärntner Slowenen: Minderheit oder Elite? Neuere Tendenzen der ethnischen Arbeitsteilung*, Klagenfurt/Celoves: Drava Verlag.

—— (2002), *Postmoderne Ethnizität und globale Hegemonie* (Minderheiten und Minderheitenpolitik in Europa, volume 1), Frankfurt: Peter Lang.

RENZ, T. and G. RIEGER (1999), "Die bayerische Landtagswahl vom 13.September 1998: Laptop, Lederhose und eine Opposition ohne Optionen", *Zeitschrift für Parlamentsfragen* 1/1999, 78–97.

RHODES, R. (1997), *Understanding Governance*, Buckingham: Open University Press.

RIEDELSPERGER, M. (1978), *The Lingering Shadow of Nazism: The Austrian Independent Movement*, New York: Columbia University Press.

RIKER, W. (1982), *Liberalism against Populism*, San Francisco: W.H. Freeman.

ROHE, K. (ed.) (1990), *Elections, Parties, and Political Traditions: Social Foundations of German Parties and Party Systems, 1867–1987*, New York: Berg.

ROKKAN, S. (1974), "Politics Between Economy and Culture: An International Seminar on Albert O. Hirschman's Exit, Voice, and Loyalty", *Social Science Information* 13, 27–38.

—— (1981), "Territories, Nations, Parties: Towards a Geo-economic-Geopolitical Model for the Explanation of Variations within Western Europe", in MERRITT, R. and B. RUSSET (eds.), *From National Development to Global Community: Essays in Honor of Karl W. Deutsch*, London: Allen and Unwin.

—— (1999), *State Formation, Nation-Building, and Mass Politics in Europe: The Theory of Stein Rokkan*, Oxford: Oxford University Press (edited by Flora, P., with S. Kuhnle, and D. Urwin).

ROKKAN, S., D. URWIN, F. AAREBROT, P. MALABA, and T. SANDE (1987), *Centre–Periphery Structures in Europe: An ISSC Workbook in Comparative Analysis*, Frankfurt-New York: Campus.

ROSSI, M. (1984), *Dal più stato al meno stato: Politica economica e finanze pubbliche nel Ticino del dopoguerra*, Lugano: Fondazione Piero Pellegrini.

ROTH, D. and M. JUNG (2002), "Ablösung der Regierung vertagt: Eine Analyse der Bundestagswahl 2002", *Aus Politik und Zeitgeschichte* B 49-50/2002, 3–17.

RUMPLER, H. (2001), "Verlorene Geschichte: Der Kampf um die politische Gestaltung des Alpen-Adria-Raumes", in MORITSCH, A. (ed.), *Alpen-Adria: Zur Geschichte einer Region*, Klagenfurt: Hermagoras.

RUSCONI, G. (1994), "La Lega dei Ticinesi: Gegen die Tessiner 'Partitokratie'", in ALTERMATT, U. *et al.* (eds.), *Rechte und Linke Fundamentalposition: Studien zur Schweizerpolitik, 1965–90*, Basel: Helbing und Lichtenhahn.

RUSSETT, B. (1964), "Inequality and Instability: The Relation of Land Tenure to Politics", *World Politics* 16, 442–54.

SAHLINS, P. (1989), *Boundaries: The Making of France and Spain in the Pyrenees*, Berkeley: University of California Press.

SARTORI, G. (1976): *Parties and Party Systems: A Framework for Analysis*, Cambridge: Cambridge University Press.

—— (1982), *Teoria dei partiti e caso italiano*, Milano: Il Saggiatore.

SCHARPF, F. (1993), "Versuch über Demokratie im verhandelnden Staat", in CZADA, R. and M. SCHMIDT (eds.), *Verhandlungsdemokratie, Interessenvermittlung, Regierbarkeit*, Opladen: Westdeutscher Verlag.

—— (1997), *Games Real Actors Play*, Boulder: Westview.

—— (1999), *Governing in Europe: Effective and Democratic?*, Oxford: Oxford University Press.

SCHARSACH, H.-H. (ed.) (2000), *Haider: Österreich und die rechte Versuchung*, Reinbek: Rowohlt.

SCHEDLER, A. (1996), "Anti-Political-Establishment Parties", *Party Politics* 2, 291–312.

—— (1997), "Introduction: Antipolitics – Closing and Colonizing the Public Sphere", in SCHEDLER, A. (ed.), *The End of Politics?*, Basingstoke: Macmillan.

SCHIEDEL, H. (2001), "Zur Zeit Pilgerstätte der Euro-Rechten", in IDGR: http://www.idgr.de/texte/ rechtsextremismus/medien/zurzeit-pilger.php.

SCHMID, J. (1990), *Die CDU: Organisationsstrukturen, Politiken und Funktionsweisen einer Partei im Föderalismus*, Opladen: Leske+Budrich.

SCHMIDT, M. (1985), "Allerweltsparteien in Westeuropa?", in *Leviathan* 4, 376–97.

—— (1997), *Demokratietheorien* (second edition), Opladen: Leske+Budrich.

SCHMIDTKE, O. (1996), *Politics of Identity: Ethnicity, Territory and the Political Opportunity Structure in Modern Italian Society*, Sinzheim: Pro-Universitate Verlag.

SCHMITTER, P. (2000), *How to Democratize the European Union... and Why Bother?*, Lanham: Rowman and Littlefield.

SCHMITTER, P. and W. STREECK (1999), "The Organization of Business Interests. Studying the Associative Action of Business in Advanced Industrial Societies", Cologne: Max-Planck-Institut für Gesellschaftsforschung (Discussion paper 99/1).

SCHNEIDER, H. (1997), "Parteien in der Landespolitik", in GABRIEL, O. *et al.* (eds.), *Parteiendemokratie in Deutschland*, Bonn: Bundeszentrale für politische Bildung.

SCHOLTEN, I. (1980), "Does Consociationalism Exist?", in ROSE, R. (ed.), *Electoral Participation: A Comparative Analysis*. London: Sage.

SCIARINI, P. (2002), "L'opposition centre–périphérie", in HUG, S. and P. SCIARINI (eds.), *Changement de valeurs et nouveaux clivages politiques en Suisse*, Paris: L'Harmattan.

SCIARINI, P., S. HARDMEIER, and A. VATTER (eds.) (2003), *Schweizer Wahlen 1999* (Swiss Electoral Studies: Volume 5), Berne: Haupt.

SELB, P. und R. LACHAT (2004), *Wahlen 2003: Die Entwicklung des Wahlverhaltens*, Zurich: Institut für Politikwissenschaft.

SETTA, S. (1993), *Profughi di lusso: Industriali e menager di stato dal fascismo all'epurazione mancata*, Milano: Angeli.

SHARPE, L. (ed.) (1993), *The Rise of Meso Government in Europe*, London: Sage.

SMITH, A. (1986), *The Ethnic Origins of Nations*, Oxford: Blackwell.

SNIDERMANN, P. *et al.* (2000), *The Outsider: Prejudice and Politics in Italy*, Princeton, Princeton University Press.

STEINER, J. (1974), *Amicable Agreement* versus *Majority Rule: Conflic Resolution in Switzerland*, Chapel Hill: University of North Carolina Press.

—— (2001), "Switzerland and the European Union: A Puzzle", in KEATING, M. and J. McGARRY (eds.), *Minority Nationalism and the Changing International Order*, Oxford: Oxford University Press.

STEINBERG, J. (1996), *Why Switzerland?* (second edition), Cambridge: Cambridge University Press.

STUHPFARRER, K. (1985), *Umsiedlung Südtirol 1939–40*, Vienna: Löcker.

SULLY, M. (1997), *The Haider Phenomenon*, New York: East European Monographs.

SUTHERLAND, C. (2001a), "Nation, Heimat, Vaterland: The Reinvention of Concepts by the Bavarian CSU", *German Politics* 10, 13–36.

—— (2001b), *Neo-Nationalist Ideology: A Discourse Analysis of the SNP and CSU*, doctoral thesis: University of Edinburgh.

SWANSON, D. and P. MANCINI (1996), "Patterns of Modern Electoral Campaigning and Their Consequences", in SWANSON, D. and P. MANCINI (eds.), *Politics, Media, and Modern Democracy*, London: Praeger.

SZCZERBIAK, A. and P. TAGGART (2000), "Opposing Europe: Party Systems and Opposition to the Union, the Euro, and Europeanisation", Sussex European Institute (Working Paper No.36).

TAGGART, P. (1996), *The New Populism and the New Politics*, Basingstoke: Macmillan.

—— (1998), "A Touchstone of Dissent: Euroscepticism in Contemporary Western European Party Systems", *European Journal of Political Research* 33, 363-88.

—— (2000a), *Populism*, Buckingham: Open University Press.

—— (2000b), "Populism and the Pathology of Representative Politics", in MÉNY, Y. and Y. SUREL (eds.), *Democracies and the Populist Challenge*, Basingstoke: Palgrave.

TAGGART, P. and A. SZCZERBIAK (2002), *Party Politics of Euroscepticism in EU Member and Candidate States*, Turin: ECPR Joint Sessions.

TAGUIEFF, P. (2001), "Populisme, nationalisme, national-populisme: Réflexions critiques sur les approches, les usages et les modèles", in DELANNOI, G. and P. TAGUIEFF (eds.), *Nationalismes en perspective*, Paris: Berg International.

TAMBINI, D. (2001), *Nationalism in Italian Politics: The Stories of the Northern League*, London: Routledge.

TARCHI, M. (1998), "The Lega Nord", in DE WINTER, L. and H. TÜRSAN (eds.), *Regionalist Parties in Western Europe*, London: Routlege.

—— (2003), *L'Italia populista: Dal qualunquismo ai girotondi*, Bologna: Il Mulino.

TARROW, S. (1994), *Power in Movement: Collective Action, Social Movements, and Politics*, Cambridge: Cambridge University Press.

TAYLOR, C. and D. JODICE (1983), *World Handbook of Social and Political Indicators* (third edition), New Haven: Yale University Press.

THORNBERRY, P. (1998), "Images of Autonomy and Individual and Collective Rights in International Instruments on the Right of Minorities", in SUKSI, M. (ed.). *Autonomy: Applications and Implications*, The Hague: Kluwer Law International.

THRÄNHARDT, D. (1987), *Geschichte der Bundesrepublik Deutschland*, Frankfurt: Suhrkamp.

TOMAN-BANKE, M. (1996), *Die Wahlslogans der Bundestagswahlen 1949–94*, Wiesbaden: Deutscher Universitätsverlag.

TONIATTI, R. (2001), "L'evoluzione statutaria dell'autonomia speciale nell'Alto Adige/Südtirol: Dalla garanzia della democrazia consociativa alla 'autodeterminazione territoriale'", in MARKO, J., S. ORTINO, and F. PALERMO (eds.), *L'ordinamento speciale della Provincia autonoma di Bolzano*, Padova: CEDAM (Ius Publicum Europaeum 3).

TÖNNIES, F. (1969), "Gemeinschaft und Gesellschaft", in EISERMANN, G. (ed.), *Soziologisches Lesebuch*, Stuttgart: Ferdinand Enke Verlag.

TOPPI, S. (1998), "L'economia: L'età delle incertezze (1975–90)", in CESCHI, R. (ed.), *Storia del cantone Ticino: Il Novecento*, Bellinzona: Stato del cantone Ticino.

—— (2003), "Conto perdite e recuperi fra Berna e Bellinzona", in GHIRINGHELLI, A. (ed.), *Il Ticino nella Svizzera: Contributi sul Ticino duecento anni dopo, 1803–2003*, Locarno: Dadò.

TORCAL, M., R. GUNTER, and J.R. MONTÉRO (2002), *Anti-Party Sentiments in Southern Europe*, in GUNTHER, R. *et al.* (eds.), *Political Parties: Old Concepts and New Challenges*, Oxford: Oxford University Press.

TRECHSEL, A. (1995), *Clivages en Suisse: Analyse des impacts relatifs des clivages sur l'électorat suisse lors des élections fédérales*, Genève: Université de Genève.

UNION FÜR SÜDTIROL (2002), *Bürgerprogram der Union für Südtirol*, Bolzano: Author.

URWIN, D. (1980), *From Ploughshare to Ballotbox: The Politics of Agrarian Defence in Europe*, Oslo: Universitetsforlaget.

—— (1983), "Harbinger, Fossil or Fleabite? 'Regionalism' and the West European Party Mosaic", in DAALDER, H. and P. MAIR (eds.), *Western European Party Systems: Continuity and Change*, London: Sage.

VAN DER BRUG, J., M. FENNEMA and J. TILLIE (2000), "Anti-immigrant Parties in Europe: Ideological or Protest Vote", *European Journal of Political Research* 37: 71–102.

VATTER, A. (2002), *Kantonale Demokratien im Vergleich: Entstehungsgründe, Interaktionen und Wirkungen politischer Institutionen in den Schweizer Kantonen*, Opladen: Leske +Budrich.

VERDROSS, A. and B. SIMMA (1984), *Universelles Völkerrecht*, Berlin: Duncker und Humblot.

VIAZZO, P.-P. (1990), *Comunità alpine: Ambiente, popolazione, struttura sociale nelle Alpi dal XVI secolo a oggi*, Bologna: Il Mulino.

VITALI, R. (1996), "Politique locale et clientélisme: Analyse du cas tessinois", *Swiss Political Science Review* 3, 47–68.

VON BEYME, K. (1996), "Party Leadership and Change in Party Systems: Towards a Post-Modern Party State?", *Government and Opposition* 31, 135–59.

WAGEMANN, C. (2000), *Das Bild der SPD im "Bayernkurier": Die Berichterstattung seit dem Fall der Mauer*, Wiesbaden: Deutscher Universitätsverlag.

WAKENHUT, R. (ed.) (1999), *Ethnische Identität und Jugend: Eine vergleichende Untersuchung zu den drei Südtiroler Sprachgruppen*, Opladen: Leske+Budrich.

WAKOLBINGER, E. (1995), "Austria: The Danger of Populism", in BAUMGARTL, B. and A. FAVELL (eds.), *New Xenophobia in Europe*, London: Kluwer Law International.

WEBER, E. (1976), *Peasants into Frenchmen: The Modernization of Rural France, 1870–1914*, Stanford: Stanford University Press.

WEILER, J. (1999), "The Transformation of Europe", reprinted in WEILER, J., *The Constitution of Europe*, Cambridge: Cambridge University Press.

WODAK, R. and A. PELINKA (eds.) (2002), *The Haider Phenomenon in Austria*, New Brunswick: Transaction.

WOELK, J. (2002), "Minderheitenschutz durch territoriale Autonomie: 'Reservate' oder nachhaltige Integrationsprozesse?", in JAHRBUCH DES FÖDERALISMUS, *Föderalismus, Subsidiarität und Regionen in Europa* (Europäisches Zentrum für Föderalismusforschung), Baden-Baden: Nomos.

ZELLER, K. (1991), *Volkszählung und Sprachgruppenzugehörigkeit in Südtirol: Völker-, verfassungs- und europarechtliche Aspekte*, Bolzano/Bozen: Athesia.

ZOLO, D. (1992), *Democracy and Complexity: A Realist Approach*, Cambridge: Polity Press.

Quoted Primary Sources

ALTO ADIGE (1999), "Votano tutti SVP, ma si turano il naso", in *Alto Adige*, 23 October 1999.

ASTAT (2002), *Statistisches Jahrbuch für Südtirol/Annuario statistico della Provincia di Bolzano 2002*, Bolzano/Bozen: Grafiche Ponticelli.

—— (2003), *Statistisches Jahrbuch für Südtirol/Annuario statistico della Provincia di Bolzano*, Bolzano/Bozen: Grafiche Ponticelli.

ATZ, Landesinstitut für Statistik Sudrirol, *Handbuch*, 22.

BASSI, P. (2003), "Il Crocifisso torni nei luoghi pubblici", in *La Padania* (18 September 2003).

BICUSEL, Y. (2003), "Früchte der Verharmlosungspolitik", *Schweizerische Volkspartei* Press Services (No.33: 18 August 2003).

BLOCHER, C. (1989), "Sofortmassnahmen im Asylwesen", interpellation at the *Nationalrat* on 15 March 1989, in http://www.parlament.ch/afs/data/d/gesch/1989/d_gesch_19890391_002.htm.

—— (2002), "Chumm Bueb und lueg dis Ländli aa! Von wahren und falschen Eliten", Albisgüetli, in http://www.blocher.ch/de/artikel02/020118albis.pdf.

—— (2003), "Mon discours du 1er août", in http://blocher.ch/fr/artikel/030801 ansprache_fr.pdf.

BOSETTI, G. (2001), "Bossi, sarà lui, non il popolo, a non volere gli immigrati", in *Il Nuovo*, 15 September 2001 (http://www.ilnuovo.it/nuovo/foglia/0,1007,74953,00.html).

BOSSI, U. (1998), "Intervento del Segretario Federale on. Umberto Bossi", *Congresso Federale Straordinario della Lega Nord*, Brescia: 14–25 October 1998 (http://leganord.org/a_2_discorsi_brescia98.htm).

—— (2000a), *Speech at the Party Congress*, Venice: 17 September 2000.

—— (2000b), *Speech in Pontida*, in http://www.prov-varese.leganord.org/doc/bossipontida00.htm.

—— (2001), *Speech in Pontida*, Pontida: 17 June 2001.

—— (2003), *Speech at the Party Congress*, Venice, 21 September 2003.

BOSSI, U. and D. VIMERCATI (1992), *Vento del Nord: La mia lega la mia vita*, Milan: Sperling and Kupfer.

—— (1993), *La rivoluzione: La Lega, storia e idee*, Milano: Sperling and Kupfer.

BRUGGER, S. (1996), *Wahlaufruf der SVP*, Bolzano/Bozen: Südtiroler Volkspartei.

—— (1999), *Für eine starke SVP im neuen Europa: Referat des Parteiobmanns Dr. Siegfried Brugger, 46*, Meran: Ordentliche Landesversammlung der SVP.

—— (2000), *Südtirol geht vor! Referat von Parteiobmann Dr. Siegfried Brugger, 47*, Meran: Ordentliche Landesversammlung der SVP.

—— (2001), *Bericht von Parteiobmann Dr. Siegfried Brugger auf der 48*, Meran: Landesversammlung der SVP.

—— (2002), *Für unser Südtirol! Bericht von Parteiobmann Dr. Siegfried Brugger, 49*, Meran: Landesversammlung der SVP.

BRUNNER, T. (2003), "Rede zum Wahlauftakt", Ennetbühl: 14 August 2003, in http://www.svp-stgallen.ch/Presse/TEXTARCHIV/Wahlen03/030814Rede TBrunner.htm.

COLOMBO, G. (1999), "In difesa dell' Europa", in *La Padania* (31 January 1999).

CSU (1993), *Grundsatzprogramm der CSU in Bayern*, Munich: Atwerb.

DEL VALLE, A. (no date), "La stratégie américaine en Eurasie", in http://utenti.tripod.it/ArchivEurasia/delvalle_sae.html).

—— (no date), "Genèse et actualité de la 'stratégie' pro-islamiste des Etats-Unis", in http://members.es.tripod.de/msrsobrarbe/valle.htm.

—— (no date), "La poussée islamiste dans les Balkans: La responsabilité américaine et occidentale", in http://www.geo-islam.org/content.php3?articleId=23.

ENTI LOCALI PADANI FEDERALI (1998), "Padania, identità, e società multirazziale", in www.leganord.org/documenti/elpf/padania_identità.pdf.

EUROBAROMETER (1991), *Eurobarometer 36.0*, Luxembourg: Office of Publications of the European Communities.

—— (1995), *Eurobarometer 43.1*, Luxembourg: Office of Publications of the European Communities.

FERRARI, G. (2002), "Il Crocifisso non si tocca", in *La Padania* (19 September 2002).

—— (2002), "Crocifissi contro l'Islam: La Lega li vuole ovunque", in *La Repubblica* (18 September 2002).

FEVAL, V. (2003), "L'UDC parle des 'nègres'", in *Le Matin* (27 July 2003).

FREIHEITLICHE PARTEI ÖSTERREICHS (1994), *Freiheitliche Thesen zur politischen Erneuerung Österreichs*, Vienna: Freiheitliches Bildungswerk.

—— (1998), *Das Programm der Freiheitlichen Partei Österreichs*, Vienna.

—— (no date), *Freiheitliche Thesen zur politischen Erneurung Österreichs*, Vienna.

—— (no date), *Österreich zuerst. Volksbegehren: 12 gute Gründe Punkt für Punkt*.

—— (no date), See the text *Vom Parteienstaat zur Bürgerdemokratie: Der Weg zur Dritten Republik*, published by FPÖ's Freiheitliche Akademie.

HAIDER, J. (1993), *Die Freiheit, die ich meine*, Berlin: Ullstein.

—— (1994), *Österreicherklärung zur Nationalratswahl 1994*, Vienna: Freiheitliche Partei Österreichs.

—— (1996), "Wir sind die PLO Österreichs", interview in *Süddeutsche Zeitung* (18 October 1996).

—— (1997), *Befreite Zunkunft jenseits von links und rechts*, Vienna: Ibera & Molden.

—— (2000), "Blair and Me Versus the Forces of Conservatism", *Daily Telegraph*, 22 February 2000.

—— (2003), Interview in *Der Standard*, 29 March 2003.

LEGA NORD (1989), "Anche Tu! Dal 20 febbraio firma per il referendum 'Contro l'invasione di immigrati clandestini'", Milan: Leaflet.

—— (2001), *Elezioni 2001: Ragionamenti per la campagna elettorale*.

—— (2004), "Programma della Lega per le elezioni europee 2004", in http://www.leganord. org/a_1_elezioni_2004.htm.

—— (no date), "Statuto della Lega Nord", in http://www.leganord.org/a_2_en trainl_statuto.htm#16.

—— (no date), *Ragionare sull'immigrazione*.

MIGLIO, G. (1992), *Come cambiare: Le mie riforme*, Milan: Mondadori.

—— (1994), *Io Bossi e la Lega: Diario segreto dei miei quattro anni sul Carroccio*, Milan: Mondadori.

—— (2001), "Oltre lo stato-nazione: L'Europa delle Regioni", www.alpiadria.com.

MEIER, T. (2000), "Irrweg Multikulturelle Gesellschaft", *Schweizerzeit* (3 March 2000).

MÖLZER, A. (1990), *Jörg! Der Eisbrecher*, Klagenfurt: Suxxes.

MORGOGLIONE, C. (2000), "Lodi, la Lega alla guerra santa", in *La Repubblica* (15 October 2000).

NATIONALRAT (1994), *The Nationalrat Election in Austria. Information on 9 October 1994*, Vienna: Austria Documentation/The Federal Press Service.

NICOD, G. (no date), "Ruiniert der Staat die Schweiz?", in http://www.svp.ch/?page_id=411&I=2.

ONETO, G. (1997), *L'invenzione della Padania: La rinascita della comunità più antica d'Europa*, Bergamo: Foedus.

PIAZZO, S. (1999), "No all'impero mondiale", in *La Padania* (29 April 1999).

RUTZ, G. (no date), "Le PS, le PRD et le PDC détruisent notre pays!", in http://www.svp.ch/index.html?page_id=548&l=3.

SAVOINI, G. (2000), "Basta all'invasione islamica", in *La Padania* (15 October 2000).

SÜDTIROLER LANDESREGIERUNG (2003), *Südtiroler Handbuch*, Bolzano/Bozen: Arti Grafiche Tezzele.

SÜDTIROLER VOLKSPARTEI (ed.) (1993), *Das neue Programm der Südtiroler Volkspartei. Beschlossen von der Landesversammlung am 8. Mai 1993*.

—— (2003), "SVP Inside/Organisation/Wirtschaftsausschuß", in www.svpartei.org.

SCHWEIZERISCHE VOLKSPARTEI (1998), *Das Konzept für eine Züricher Ausländerpolitik*, Zurich.

—— (2002), "Wer muss sich hier integrieren?", in *SVP-Hackbrett* (http://www.svp-stadt-luzern.ch/hackbrett-12.htm).

—— (2003), *Wahlplattform 2003 bis 2007*, Berne: Generalsekretariat.

—— (no date), "Das Konzept für eine Zürcher Ausländerpolitik", in http://www.svp-stadt-zuerich.ch/seiten/auslaenderkonzept.asp.

VIMERCATI, D. (1990), *I lombardi alla nuova crociata*, Milan: Mursia.

VON EYSZ, M. (2001, "Der Islam im liberalen Europa: Christlich-abendländische Kultur vor der Selbsauflösung?", *Schweizerzeit* (July 13, 2001).

ZANOLARI, A. (2003a), "Votum von Angelika Zanolari zum Anzug betreffend eine neue Asylpolitik gehalten an der Grossratssitzung vom 09./16.04.2003", in http://www.svp-basel.ch/zanolari54.html).

—— (2003b), "Wollen wir einen Taliban als Regierungsrat?", in http://www.onlinereports.ch/ZanolariStatement.htm.

Notes on the Contributors

Hans-Georg BETZ is a senior research associate at the Canadian Center for German and European Studies at York University in Toronto. He has previously been associate professor at York University and at the John Hopkins University in Washington. He is the author of numerous comparative books and articles in international journals on right-wing populism, including *Radical Right Wing Populism in Western Europe* (Macmillan, 1994) and *The New Politics of the Right* (Macmillan, 1998) co-edited with S. Immerfall. He recently published *La Droite Populiste en Europe* (Autrement, 2004).

Daniele CARAMANI has recently joined the Department of Political Science and International Studies of the University of Birmingham, UK. During the making of this book he was a research professor at the Mannheim Centre for European Social Research. He holds a Ph.D. from the European University Institute (Florence), and has taught at the universities of Geneva and Florence. In 2000–02, he was "Vincent Wright Fellow in Comparative Politics" at the Robert Schuman Centre for Advanced Studies (EUI). He is the author of the book and CD-ROM *Elections in Western Europe since 1815* (Palgrave, 2000) and *The Nationalization of Politics* (Cambridge University Press, 2004) which has been awarded the "Stein Rokkan Prize in Comparative Social Science".

Patricia CHIANTERA-STUTTE teaches history of political thought at the University of Bari. During 2001–02, she was a "Jean Monnet Fellow" at the Robert Schuman Centre for Advanced Studies (European University Institute, Florence). Her recent books include *Julius Evola: Dal Dadaismo alla Rivoluzione Conservatrice* (Aracne, 2001) and *Von der Avantgarde zur Tradition: Die radikalen Futuristen im italienischen Faschismus* (Campus, 2002). Further publications include articles in international journals among which "The Ambiguous Heritage of Mitteleuropa" (*Law and Critique Journal*, 2003), and "Cultures of Populism and the Political Right in Europe" (*CLCWeb Comparative Literature and Culture*, 2003, with Andrea Peto).

Michael KEATING is professor of regional studies at the European University Institute (Florence), and professor of Scottish politics at the University of Aberdeen. Previously, he taught at the Universities of Strathclyde (Scotland) and Western Ontario (Canada). He has published widely in urban and regional politics and minority nationalism. His recent works include *Plurinational Democracy* (Oxford University

Press, 2001), *Culture, Institutions, and Development: A Study of Eight European Regions* (Edward Elgar, 2003), and *The Government of Scotland: Public Policy after Devolution* (Edinburgh University Press, 2005).

Oscar MAZZOLENI is director of the Observatory for Political Research (USTAT) of the Canton Ticino (Switzerland) and lecturer at the Scuola Universitaria della Svizzera Italiana. He has previously been fellow researcher at the University of Turin and has taught at the University of Lausanne. His main research fields are citizens' behaviour and party politics. His last book is *Nationalisme et Populisme en Suisse: La Radicalisation de la "Nouvelle" UDC* (Presses polytechniques et universitaires romandes, 2003). He is the author of numerous articles on party politics and electoral behaviour in Switzerland.

Yves MÉNY is president of the European University Institute (Florence). Previously, he was the founding director of the Robert Schuman Centre for Advanced Studies (EUI) and professor at the Universities of Rennes, Paris 2, and the Institut d'Etudes Politiques (Paris). His main scientific interests are in the fields of comparative politics and policies, French politics, and state administration. His recent publications include *Democracies and the Populist Challenge*, co-edited with Yves Surel (Palgrave, 2002) translated in several languages, *Par le Peuple, Pour le Peuple: Le Populisme et les Démocraties*, co-authored with Yves Surel (Fayard, 2000), and *The Future of European Welfare*, co-edited with Martin Rhodes (Macmillan, 1998).

Günther PALLAVER is associate professor of political science at the University of Innsbruck (Austria). After a career as a journalist, he founded the media research institute Mediawatch in Innsbruck. He has published in the field of Italian and Austrian politics, ethnic minorities and parties, as well as political communication. He recently co-edited the volume *Storia, Istituzioni e Diritto in Carlo Antonio de Martini (1726-1800)* (Università degli Studi di Trento, 2002), *1992 – Fine di un Conflitto: Dieci Anni dalla Chiusura della Questione Sudtirolese* (Il Mulino, 2003), and he is editor of the forthcoming volume *Politische Kommunikation in ethnisch gespaltenen Gesellschaften: Theoretische Ansätze und Fallbeispiele* (2004).

Yannis PAPADOPOULOS is professor of political science at the University of Lausanne and has been, among other appointments, visiting professor at the European University Institute (Florence) and at Sciences Po (Paris), as well as research director with the CNRS in France. He recently co-edited the *Handbook of Swiss Politics* (NZZ Publishing, 2003), and is co-editor (with Arthur Benz) of the forthcoming volume on *Governance and Democracy* (Routledge, 2005). He is the author of several articles in international academic journals.

Anton PELINKA is professor of political science at the University of Innsbruck and director of the Institute for Conflict Research (Vienna). He has taught previously in various German and American universities. He has published in the field of Austrian politics, comparative politics, and democratic theory. Among his most recent publications is *Democracy Indian Style: Subhas Chandra Bose and the Creation of India's Political Culture* (Transaction Press, 2003). On the theme of the present book, he has co-edited (with Ruth Wodak) *The Haider Phenomenon in Austria* (Transaction Press, 2002).

Claudius WAGEMANN is a researcher in the Department of Social and Political Sciences at the European University Institute (Florence), and teaches political science at Rutgers University in Florence. He was previously a researcher at the Max Planck Institute for the Study of Societies (Cologne). His research topics include interest groups, political parties, and research methodology. He has published on the CSU and its communication strategies *Das Bild der SPD im "Bayern-kurier": Die Berichterstattung seit dem Fall der Mauer* (Deutscher Universitäts-Verlag, 2000) and on "Qualitative Comparative Analysis". His current work focuses on the changes of private interest governments in the dairy sector.

Regionalism & Federalism

The contemporary nation-state is undergoing a series of transformations which question its traditional role as a container of social, political and economic systems. New spaces are emerging with the rise of regional production systems, movements for territorial autonomy and the rediscovery of old and the invention of new identities. States have responded by restructuring their systems of territorial government, often setting up an intermediate or regional level. There is no single model, but a range, from administrative deconcentration to federalization. Some states have regionalized in a uniform manner, while others have adopted asymmetrical solutions. In many cases, regions have gone beyond the nation-state, seeking to become actors in broader continental and transnational systems.

The series covers the gamut of issues involved in this territorial restructuring, including the rise of regional production systems, political regionalism, questions of identity, and constitutional change. It includes the emergence of new systems of territorial regulation and collective action within civil society as well as the state. There is no *a priori* definition of what constitutes a region, since these span a range of spatial scales, from metropolitan regions to large federated states, and from administrative units to cultural regions and stateless nations. Disciplines covered include history, sociology, social and political geography, political science and law. Interdisciplinary approaches are particularly welcome. In addition to empirical and comparative studies, books focus on the theory of regionalism and federalism, including normative questions about democracy and accountability in complex systems of government.

*

Series Titles

No.6 – Daniele CARAMANI & Yves MÉNY (eds.), *Challenges to Consensual Politics. Democracy, Identity, and Populist Protest in the Alpine Region*, 2005, 257 p., ISBN 90-5201-250-4

No.5 – Nicola MCEWEN, *Nationalism and the State. Welfare and Identity in Scotland and Quebec* (provisional title, forthcoming), ISBN 90-5201-240-7

No.4 – Carolyn M. DUDEK, *EU Accession and Spanish Regional Development. Winners and Losers* (provisional title, forthcoming), ISBN 90-5201-237-7

No.3 – Stéphane PAQUIN, *Paradiplomatie et relations internationales. Théorie des stratégies internationales des régions face à la mondialisation*, 2004, 189 p., ISBN 90-5201-225-3

No.2 – Wilfried SWENDEN, *Federalism and Second Chambers. Regional Representation in Parliamentary Federations: The Australian Senate and German Bundesrat Compared*, 2004, 423 p., ISBN 90-5201-211-3

No.1 – Michael KEATING & James HUGHES (eds.), *The Regional Challenge in Central and Eastern Europe. Territorial Restructuring and European Integration*, 2003, 208 p., ISBN 90-5201-187-7